Taste of Home's
Favorite Brand Name Recipes
2004

Taste of Home Books

Editor: Heidi Reuter Lloyd
Food Editor: Janaan Cunningham
Associate Food Editor: Diane Werner
Senior Recipe Editor: Sue A. Jurack

Front cover photography by Reiman Publications
Food Photography: Rob Hagen
Senior Food Photography Artist: Stephanie Marchese
Food Photography Artist: Julie Ferron
Photo Studio Manager: Anne Schimmel

Pictured on the front cover *(clockwise from top left):* Bacon Vinaigrette Dressing *(page 30),* Hershey's White Chip Brownies *(page 188)* and Taco Two-Zies *(page 94).*

Pictured on the back cover *(clockwise from top left):* Pizza Meat Loaf *(page 128),* Berry Cobbler Cake *(page 208)* and Savory Chicken Satay *(page 12).*

ISBN: 0-7853-9888-0

Library of Congress Control Number: 2003098109

Manufactured in China.

8 7 6 5 4 3 2 1

Some of the products listed in this publication may be in limited distribution.

Microwave Cooking: Microwave ovens vary in wattage. Use the cooking times as guidelines and check for doneness before adding more time.

Taste of Home's Favorite Brand Name Recipes 2004

343 Family-Favorite Recipes from the Most Trusted Brands

WE PROBABLY SHOULD HAVE put a label on the cover of this book warning that looking through it would make you hungry. It's that kind of book.

Taste of Home's Favorite Brand Name Recipes 2004 is filled with hundreds of delicious recipes and large color photos that will make you want to reach right in and sample a dish or two.

Unfortunately, we can't quite make that happen. But the good news is that the step-by-step directions are so easy, you can start making your first delicious dish from this book in just minutes.

How Recipes Are Chosen

Taste of Home's Favorite Brand Name Recipes 2004 is a unique book that you can doubly trust.

First, all 343 down-home recipes were hand-picked by the experienced home economists at *Taste of Home,* the No. 1 cooking magazine in America. Second, the recipes feature name-brand foods you've used and enjoyed with confidence for years.

This big book is packed with guaranteed-good recipes. We spent considerable time collecting family-pleasing, name-brand favorites so that you don't have to. For example:

• When we wanted something sweet and creamy, we chose a recipe from the folks at Eagle Brand Sweetened Condensed Milk. Check out the tempting photo of Heavenly Chocolate Mousse Pie on page 182 and the recipe on page 202.

• When we wanted a home-style entree that the whole family could dig into, we tapped French's French Fried Onions. Take a look at Chili Meatloaf and Potato Bake on page 174 or Skillet Spaghetti Pizza on page 156, and your mouth will start to water.

Campbell's® Fiesta Taco Salad

• And when we decided we needed some hearty breakfast foods to start the day off right, we turned to Hillshire Farm. The Summer Sausage 'n' Egg Wedges on page 161 will wake up any sleepyhead at your house.

There are hundreds of other recipes that will catch your eye and get your appetite going as well.

What's Inside

We packed over 325 recipes into the 224 pages of this useful book. Many of the recipes include photographs, so you'll be able to see what you're making and how wonderful the finished product will look.

The photos are large; in fact a number are full-page. You'll count more than 150 photographs in all.

This book will take you from the start of a family meal to the finish, giving you plenty of choices for appealing appetizers, delicious desserts and everything in between—soups, salads, entrees, side dishes and breads.

You won't have to worry about running out of clever combinations. You can mix and match to your heart's content. And your family will be happy, too, because every single recipe has been kitchen-tested. Plus, they've been approved by the *Taste of Home* food editors.

Campbell's® Shortcut Beef Stew

Premier White Lemony Cheesecake

How to Find a Recipe

This book is indexed in two helpful ways. The general index, beginning on page 213, lists every recipe by food category, major ingredient and/or cooking style.

For example, if you know you want to serve something using hamburger tonight, turn to "ground beef" in the general index and ponder the many tasty options. You can also look under general categories such as "oven entrees," "skillet dishes" and "grilled and broiled."

The alphabetical index starts on page 221, so once you and your family have discovered a few favorites, it's a snap to find them by name when you're ready to make them again.

We hope you'll enjoy using *Taste of Home's Favorite Brand Name Recipes 2004*. We had a great time putting it together. Now, it's all yours. Happy cooking...and eating!

Appetizers & Snacks

Hawaiian Ribs

(Pictured at left)

1 can (8 ounces) crushed pineapple in juice, undrained
1/3 cup apricot jam
3 tablespoons *French's*® Classic Yellow® Mustard
1 tablespoon red wine vinegar
2 teaspoons grated peeled fresh ginger
1 clove garlic, minced
3 to 4 pounds pork baby back ribs*

*Or, if baby back ribs are not available, substitute 4 pounds pork spareribs, cut in half lengthwise. Cut spareribs into 3- to 4-rib portions. Cook 20 minutes in enough boiling water to cover. Grill ribs 30 to 40 minutes or until no longer pink near bone, brushing with portion of pineapple mixture during last 10 minutes.

1. Combine crushed pineapple with juice, apricot jam, mustard, vinegar, ginger and garlic in blender or food processor. Cover and process until very smooth.

2. Place ribs on oiled grid. Grill over medium heat 40 minutes or until ribs are no longer pink near bone. Brush ribs with portion of pineapple sauce mixture during last 10 minutes of cooking. Cut into individual ribs to serve. Serve remaining sauce for dipping.   *Makes 8 servings (1-1/2 cups sauce)*

Note: Try mixing 2 tablespoons *French's*® Mustard, any flavor, with 3/4 cup peach-apricot sweet 'n' sour sauce to create a delicious luau fruit dip. Serve with assorted cut-up fresh fruit.

Helpful Hint

When purchasing fresh ginger, select firm roots with smooth, tan unwrinkled skin.

Clockwise from top left: *Ginger Wings with Peach Dipping Sauce (p. 10), 7-Layer Ranch Dip (p. 16), Golden Chicken Nuggets (p. 17) and Hawaiian Ribs*

Pizza Fondue

(Pictured at right)

1/2 pound bulk Italian sausage
1 cup chopped onion
2 jars (26 ounces each) meatless pasta sauce
4 ounces thinly sliced ham, finely chopped
1 package (3 ounces) sliced pepperoni, finely chopped
1/4 teaspoon crushed red pepper flakes
1 pound mozzarella cheese, cut into 3/4-inch cubes
1 loaf Italian or French bread, cut into 1-inch cubes

SLOW COOKER DIRECTIONS

Cook sausage and onion in large skillet until sausage is browned. Drain off fat.

Transfer sausage mixture to slow cooker. Stir in pasta sauce, ham, pepperoni and pepper flakes. Cover; cook on LOW 3 to 4 hours.

Serve sauce with cheese cubes, bread cubes and fondue forks.   *Makes 20 to 25 appetizer servings*

Miniature Teriyaki Pork Kabobs

1 pound boneless pork, cut into 4×1×1/2-inch strips
1 small green bell pepper, cut into 1×1/4×1/4-inch strips
1 can (11 ounces) mandarin oranges, drained
1/4 cup teriyaki sauce
1 tablespoon honey
1 tablespoon vinegar
1/8 teaspoon garlic powder

Soak 24 (8-inch) bamboo skewers in water about 10 minutes. Thread 1 pepper strip, then pork strips accordion-style with mandarin oranges on skewers. Place 1 pepper strip on end of each skewer. Arrange skewers on broiler pan.

For sauce, combine teriyaki sauce, honey, vinegar and garlic powder in small bowl; mix well. Brush sauce over kabobs. Broil, 6 inches from heat, about 15 minutes or until pork is done, turning and basting with sauce occasionally.

Makes about 24 appetizers

Favorite recipe from **National Pork Board**

French Bread Florentine

3/4 pound hot or sweet Italian sausage links, removed from casing and crumbled
1/3 cup chopped onion
1 loaf French bread (about 12 inches long), halved lengthwise
1 cup RAGÚ® Pizza Quick® Sauce
1 box (10 ounces) frozen chopped spinach, thawed and squeezed dry
1 cup shredded mozzarella cheese (about 4 ounces)

Preheat oven to 375°F.

In 10-inch nonstick skillet, brown sausage with onion over medium-high heat until sausage is no longer pink.

On baking sheet, arrange bread halves. Evenly spread Ragú Pizza Quick Sauce on bread halves, then top with sausage mixture, then spinach and cheese. Bake 20 minutes or until cheese is melted.

Makes 4 servings

Recipe Tip: These sausage-spinach pizzas are great for parties and after-school snacks. Cut them into 2-inch pieces to fit kid-size mouths.

Orange Iced Tea

2 SUNKIST® oranges
4 cups boiling water
5 tea bags
Ice cubes
Honey or brown sugar to taste

With vegetable peeler, peel each orange in continuous spiral, removing only outer colored layer of peel (eat peeled fruit or save for garnish or other uses). In large pitcher, pour boiling water over tea bags and orange peel. Cover and steep 5 minutes. Remove tea bags; chill tea mixture with peel in covered container. To serve, remove peel and pour over ice cubes in tall glasses. Sweeten to taste with honey. Garnish with orange quarter-cartwheel slices and fresh mint leaves, if desired.

Makes 4 (8-ounce) servings

Sausage Pinwheels

Sausage Pinwheels

(Pictured above)

> **2 cups biscuit mix**
> **1/2 cup milk**
> **1/4 cup butter or margarine, melted**
> **1 pound BOB EVANS® Original Recipe Roll Sausage**

Combine biscuit mix, milk and butter in large bowl until blended. Refrigerate 30 minutes. Divide dough into two portions. Roll out one portion on floured surface to 1/8-inch-thick rectangle, about 10×7 inches. Spread with half the sausage. Roll lengthwise into long roll. Repeat with remaining dough and sausage. Place rolls in freezer until hard enough to cut easily. Preheat oven to 400°F. Cut rolls into thin slices. Place on baking sheets. Bake 15 minutes or until golden brown. Serve hot. Refrigerate leftovers.   *Makes 48 pinwheels*

Notes: This recipe may be doubled. Refreeze after slicing. When ready to serve, thaw slices in refrigerator and bake.

Ginger Wings with Peach Dipping Sauce

(Pictured on page 6)

> **Peach Dipping Sauce (recipe follows)**
> **2 pounds chicken wings**
> **1/4 cup soy sauce**
> **2 cloves garlic, minced**
> **1 teaspoon ground ginger**
> **1/4 teaspoon white pepper**

Preheat oven to 400°F. Line 15×10×1-inch jelly-roll pan with foil.

Prepare Peach Dipping Sauce; set aside.

Cut off and discard wing tips from chicken. Cut each wing in half at joint. Combine soy sauce, garlic, ginger and pepper in large bowl. Add chicken and stir until well coated. Place chicken in single layer in prepared pan. Bake 40 to 50 minutes or until browned, turning over halfway through cooking time. Serve hot with Peach Dipping Sauce.

Makes 6 appetizer servings

Peach Dipping Sauce

> **1/2 cup peach preserves**
> **2 tablespoons light corn syrup**
> **1 teaspoon white vinegar**
> **1/4 teaspoon ground ginger**
> **3/4 teaspoon soy sauce**

Combine preserves, corn syrup, vinegar and ginger in small saucepan. Cook and stir over medium-high heat until mixture simmers. Remove from heat; add soy sauce. Let cool.   *Makes 1/2 cup*

Helpful Hint

There is no need to peel garlic if you are using a garlic press. The garlic passes through the press leaving the skin behind. It's a good idea to clean the garlic press right after using it, before small pieces of garlic dry out and clog the holes. (If you can't wash it right away, let it soak in a bowl of warm water.)

Bite Size Tacos

(Pictured below)

1 pound ground beef
1 package (1.25 ounces) taco seasoning mix
2 cups *French's®* French Fried Onions
1/4 cup chopped fresh cilantro
32 bite-size round tortilla chips
3/4 cup sour cream
1 cup shredded Cheddar cheese

1. Cook beef in nonstick skillet over medium-high heat 5 minutes or until browned; drain. Stir in taco seasoning mix, *3/4 cup water, 1 cup* French Fried Onions and cilantro. Simmer 5 minutes or until flavors are blended, stirring often.

2. Preheat oven to 350°F. Arrange tortilla chips on foil-lined baking sheet. Top with beef mixture, sour cream, remaining onions and cheese.

3. Bake 5 minutes or until cheese is melted and onions are golden.   *Makes 8 appetizer servings*

Crispy Coconut Chicken Fingers

1-1/2 pounds boneless skinless chicken breast halves, cut into 1-inch strips
1/2 teaspoon salt
1/4 teaspoon pepper
1/4 teaspoon garlic powder
1/2 cup flour
1 egg, lightly beaten
1 cup BAKER'S® ANGEL FLAKE® Coconut
1/2 cup plain bread crumbs
1/3 cup butter or margarine, melted
Apricot Dipping Sauce (recipe follows)

SEASON chicken with salt, pepper and garlic powder. Coat with flour. Dip chicken strips in egg; coat with combined coconut and bread crumbs. Place in shallow baking pan. Drizzle with melted butter.

BAKE at 400°F for 15 minutes; turn. Bake 8 to 10 minutes or until chicken is browned and cooked through. Serve with Apricot Dipping Sauce.
Makes about 2 dozen appetizers

Apricot Dipping Sauce: Mix 1 cup apricot preserves and 2 tablespoons Dijon mustard until well blended.

Bite Size Tacos

Savory Chicken Satay

(Pictured at right and on back cover)

1 envelope LIPTON® RECIPE SECRETS®
    Onion Soup Mix
1/4 cup BERTOLLI® Olive Oil
2 tablespoons firmly packed brown sugar
2 tablespoons SKIPPY® Peanut Butter
1 pound boneless, skinless chicken breasts,
    pounded and cut into thin strips
12 to 16 large wooden skewers, soaked in water

1. In large plastic bag, combine soup mix, oil, brown sugar and peanut butter. Add chicken and toss to coat well. Close bag and marinate in refrigerator 30 minutes.

2. Remove chicken from marinade, discarding marinade. On skewers, thread chicken, weaving back and forth.

3. Grill or broil chicken until chicken is thoroughly cooked. Serve with your favorite dipping sauces.
Makes 12 to 16 appetizers

Smoked Turkey Roll-Ups

2 packages (4 ounces each) herb-flavored
    soft spreadable cheese
4 flour (8-inch diameter) tortillas*
2 packages (6 ounces each) smoked turkey
    breast slices
2 green onions, minced
1/4 cup roasted red peppers, drained and finely
    chopped

To keep flour tortillas soft while preparing turkey roll-ups, cover with a slightly damp cloth.

1. Spread one package of cheese evenly over tortillas. Layer turkey slices evenly over cheese, overlapping turkey slices slightly to cover each tortilla. Spread remaining package of cheese evenly over turkey slices. Sprinkle with green onions and red peppers.

2. Roll up each tortilla jelly-roll style. Place roll-ups, seam side down, in resealable plastic bag; refrigerate several hours or overnight.

3. To serve, cut each roll-up crosswise into 1/2-inch slices to form pinwheels. If desired, arrange pinwheels on serving plate and garnish with red pepper slices in center. *Makes 56 appetizer servings*

Favorite recipe from **National Turkey Federation**

Sauerkraut and Swiss Sausage Balls

1 pound BOB EVANS® Original Recipe
    Roll Sausage
2 cups sauerkraut, drained and squeezed dry
2-1/2 cups (10 ounces) shredded Swiss cheese
1-1/2 cups all-purpose flour
10 tablespoons (1 stick plus 2 tablespoons)
    butter or margarine, melted
1 teaspoon Dijon or yellow mustard
1 teaspoon caraway seeds (optional)
    Spicy brown mustard (optional)

Preheat oven to 350°F. Combine sausage and sauerkraut in large bowl; form mixture into approximately 40 (1-inch) balls. Place on ungreased baking sheet; bake 15 minutes. Drain on paper towels; cool slightly.

Increase oven temperature to 400°F. To prepare dough, combine cheese, flour, butter, mustard and caraway seeds, if desired; mix well. Press 2 teaspoons dough firmly around each sausage ball. (Dough handles easiest when warm.) Bake on ungreased baking sheet 15 minutes or until light golden. Serve hot with spicy brown mustard for dipping, if desired. Refrigerate leftovers.
Makes 40 appetizers

Note: Sausage balls may be prepared, covered and refrigerated after wrapping with dough, then baked just before serving. Or, sausage balls can be stored in a resealable plastic bag and frozen up to 1 month.

Helpful Hint

Caraway seeds come from an herb in the parsley family. They have a nutty, mildly anise flavor that is used in breads, cakes, cheese, stews and vegetable dishes; they are most frequently found in Austrian, German and Hungarian cooking. Caraway seeds should be stored in an airtight container in a cool, dry place for up to six months.

Beefy Tortilla Rolls

(Pictured at right)

1/4 cup GREY POUPON® COUNTRY DIJON®
    Mustard
3 ounces cream cheese, softened
2 teaspoons prepared horseradish
2 teaspoons chopped cilantro or parsley
2 (10-inch) flour tortillas
1 cup torn spinach leaves
6 ounces thinly sliced deli roast beef
1 large tomato, cut into 8 slices
    Lettuce leaves

1. Blend mustard, cream cheese, horseradish and cilantro in small bowl. Spread each tortilla with half the mustard mixture. Top each with half the spinach leaves, roast beef and tomato slices. Roll up each tortilla jelly-roll fashion. Wrap each roll in plastic wrap and refrigerate at least 1 hour.*

2. Cut each roll into 10 slices; arrange on lettuce-lined platter. Serve immediately.

Makes 20 appetizers

*Tortilla rolls may be frozen. To serve, thaw at room temperature for 1 hour before slicing.

Glazed Meatballs

1 pound ground beef
1/2 cup fine dry bread crumbs
1/3 cup minced onion
1/4 cup milk
1 egg, beaten
1 tablespoon chopped parsley
1 teaspoon salt
1/2 teaspoon Worcestershire sauce
1/8 teaspoon pepper
2 tablespoons CRISCO® Oil
1/2 cup bottled chili sauce
1 cup (12-ounce jar) SMUCKER'S® Grape Jelly

Combine ground beef, bread crumbs, onion, milk, egg, parsley, salt, Worcestershire sauce and pepper; mix well. Shape into 1-inch meatballs. Cook in hot oil over medium heat for 10 to 15 minutes or until browned. Drain on paper towels.

Combine chili sauce and jelly in medium saucepan; stir well. Add meatballs; simmer 30 minutes, stirring occasionally. Serve in a chafing dish.

Makes about 5 dozen meatballs

Cheddar Cheese Fruit Ball

3/4 cup SUN-MAID® Fruit Bits
1/4 cup apple juice or white grape juice
2 (8-ounce) packages cream cheese, softened
2 tablespoons milk
2 cups finely shredded sharp Cheddar cheese
1/4 cup thinly sliced green onions
3/4 cup chopped walnuts
    Crackers

COMBINE fruit bits and apple juice in a small saucepan or microwave-safe bowl. Bring to a simmer. Stir well and refrigerate 15 minutes.

BEAT cream cheese and milk with electric mixer or food processor until fluffy.

ADD Cheddar cheese and green onions; beat or process until combined.

DRAIN fruit; add to cream cheese mixture, beating at low speed or with on/off pulses just until fruit is combined. Transfer mixture to a sheet of plastic wrap. Bring up edges of the plastic wrap; form the mixture into a 6-inch ball.

CHILL until firm, at least 2 hours or up to 24 hours. Just before serving, unwrap cheese and roll in walnuts. Serve with crackers.

Makes one 6-inch ball, about 12 servings

Mini Tuna Tarts

1 (3-ounce) pouch of STARKIST® Premium
    Albacore or Chunk Light Tuna
2 tablespoons mayonnaise
2 tablespoons sweet pickle relish
1 green onion, including tops, minced
3/4 cup shredded Monterey Jack cheese
    Salt and pepper to taste
1 package (10 count) refrigerated flaky biscuits

Combine tuna, mayonnaise, pickle relish, onion and cheese; mix well. Add salt and pepper. Separate each biscuit into 2 halves. Press each half in bottom of lightly greased muffin pan to form a cup. Spoon scant tablespoon tuna mixture into each muffin cup. Bake in 400°F oven 8 to 10 minutes or until edges of biscuits are just golden. Serve hot or cold.

Makes 20 servings

Beefy Tortilla Rolls

Pizza Snack Cups

Chicken Pesto Pizza

1 loaf (1 pound) frozen bread dough, thawed
8 ounces chicken tenders, cut into 1/2-inch pieces
1/2 red onion, cut into quarters and thinly sliced
1/4 cup prepared pesto
2 large plum tomatoes, seeded and diced
1 cup (4 ounces) shredded pizza cheese blend or mozzarella cheese

1. Preheat oven to 375°F. Roll out bread dough on floured surface to 14×8-inch rectangle. Transfer to baking sheet sprinkled with cornmeal. Cover loosely with plastic wrap and let rise 20 to 30 minutes.

2. Meanwhile, spray large skillet with nonstick cooking spray; heat over medium heat. Add chicken; cook and stir 2 minutes. Add onion and pesto; cook and stir 3 to 4 minutes or until chicken is cooked through. Stir in tomatoes; remove from heat and let cool slightly.

3. Spread chicken mixture evenly over bread dough within 1 inch of edges. Sprinkle with cheese.

4. Bake on bottom rack of oven about 20 minutes or until crust is golden brown. Cut into 2-inch squares.
Makes about 20 appetizers

Pizza Snack Cups

(Pictured above)

1 can (12 ounces) refrigerated biscuits (10 biscuits)
1/2 pound ground beef
1 jar (14 ounces) RAGÚ® Pizza Quick® Sauce
1/2 cup shredded mozzarella cheese (about 2 ounces)

1. Preheat oven to 375°F. In 12-cup muffin pan, evenly press each biscuit in bottom and up side of each cup; chill until ready to fill.

2. In 10-inch skillet, brown ground beef over medium-high heat; drain. Stir in Ragú Pizza Quick Sauce and heat through.

3. Evenly spoon beef mixture into prepared muffin cups. Bake 15 minutes. Sprinkle with cheese and bake an additional 5 minutes or until cheese is melted and biscuits are golden. Let stand 5 minutes. Gently remove pizza cups from muffin pan and serve. *Makes 10 pizza cups*

7-Layer Ranch Dip

(Pictured on page 6)

1 envelope LIPTON® RECIPE SECRETS® Ranch Soup Mix
1 container (16 ounces) sour cream
1 cup shredded lettuce
1 medium tomato, chopped (about 1 cup)
1 can (2.25 ounces) sliced pitted ripe olives, drained
1/4 cup chopped red onion
1 can (4.5 ounces) chopped green chilies, drained
1 cup shredded Cheddar cheese (about 4 ounces)

1. In 2-quart shallow dish, combine soup mix and sour cream.

2. Evenly layer remaining ingredients, ending with cheese. Chill, if desired. Serve with tortilla chips.
Makes 7 cups dip

Campbell's® Mushroom Mozzarella Bruschetta

(Pictured below)

1 loaf (about 1 pound) Italian bread (16 inches long), cut in half lengthwise
1 can (10-3/4 ounces) CAMPBELL'S® Condensed Cream of Mushroom Soup *or* 98% Fat Free Cream of Mushroom Soup
1/4 teaspoon garlic powder
1/4 teaspoon dried Italian seasoning, crushed
1 cup shredded mozzarella cheese (4 ounces)
1 tablespoon grated Parmesan cheese
1 small red pepper, chopped (about 1/2 cup)
2 green onions, chopped (about 1/4 cup)

1. Bake bread on baking sheet at 400°F. for 5 minutes or until lightly toasted.

2. Mix soup, garlic powder and Italian seasoning. Stir in mozzarella cheese, Parmesan cheese, pepper and onions.

3. Spread soup mixture on bread. Bake 5 minutes or until cheese is melted. Cut each bread half into 4 pieces. *Makes 8 servings*

Tip: For convenience, use packaged pre-shredded mozzarella cheese. Half an 8-ounce package will provide the 1 cup needed for this recipe.

Golden Chicken Nuggets

(Pictured on page 6)

1 pound boneless skinless chicken, cut into 1-1/2-inch pieces
1/4 cup *French's®* Sweet & Tangy Honey Mustard
2 cups *French's®* French Fried Onions, finely crushed

1. Preheat oven to 400°F. Toss chicken with mustard in medium bowl.

2. Place French Fried Onions into resealable plastic food storage bag. Toss chicken in onions, a few pieces at a time, pressing gently to adhere.

3. Place nuggets in shallow baking pan. Bake 15 minutes or until chicken is no longer pink in center. Serve with additional honey mustard. *Makes 4 servings*

Campbell's® Mushroom Mozzarella Bruschetta

Steak Nachos

(Pictured at right)

1 (1-pound) beef top round steak, chopped
1/4 cup chopped onion
1 tablespoon vegetable oil
1/2 cup A.1.® Original or A.1.® BOLD & SPICY
    Steak Sauce
5 cups tortilla chips
2 cups KRAFT® Shredded Cheddar Cheese
    (8 ounces)
1 cup chopped fresh tomatoes
1/4 cup diced green chiles or jalapeño pepper
    slices
1/4 cup sliced pitted ripe olives
    BREAKSTONE'S® or KNUDSEN® Sour Cream
    (optional)

1. Cook and stir steak and onion in oil in large skillet over medium-high heat until steak is no longer pink; drain. Stir in steak sauce.

2. Arrange tortilla chips on large heatproof platter or baking sheet. Spoon steak mixture over chips; sprinkle with cheese.

3. Broil 6 inches from heat source 3 to 5 minutes or until cheese melts. Top with tomatoes, chiles and olives. Serve immediately with sour cream on the side, if desired. *Makes 6 appetizer servings*

Cocktail Wraps

16 thin strips Cheddar cheese*
16 HILLSHIRE FARM® Lit'l Smokies, scored
    lengthwise into halves
1 can (8 ounces) refrigerated crescent roll dough
1 egg, beaten *or* 1 tablespoon milk
    Mustard

Or substitute Swiss, taco-flavored or other variety of cheese.

Preheat oven to 400°F.

Place 1 strip cheese inside score of each Lit'l Smokie. Separate dough into 8 triangles; cut each lengthwise into halves to make 16 triangles. Place 1 link on wide end of 1 dough triangle; roll up. Repeat with remaining links and dough triangles. Place links on baking sheet. Brush dough with egg. Bake 10 to 15 minutes.

Serve hot with mustard.

Makes 16 hors d'oeuvres

Pepperidge Farm® Parmesan Cheese Crisps

1/2 package (17-1/4-ounce size) PEPPERIDGE
    FARM® Frozen Puff Pastry Sheets (1 sheet)
1 egg
1 tablespoon water
1/4 cup grated Parmesan cheese
1 tablespoon chopped fresh parsley *or*
    1 teaspoon dried parsley flakes
1/2 teaspoon dried oregano leaves, crushed

1. Thaw pastry sheet at room temperature 30 minutes. Preheat oven to 400°F. Mix egg and water and set aside. Mix cheese, parsley and oregano and set aside.

2. Unfold pastry on lightly floured surface. Roll into 14- by 10-inch rectangle. Cut in half lengthwise. Brush both halves with egg mixture. Top 1 rectangle with cheese mixture. Place remaining rectangle over cheese-topped rectangle, egg-side down. Roll gently with rolling pin to seal.

3. Cut crosswise into 28 (1/2-inch) strips. Twist strips and place 2 inches apart on greased baking sheet, pressing down ends. Brush with egg mixture.

4. Bake 10 minutes or until golden. Serve warm or at room temperature. *Makes 28 appetizers*

Tip: To make ahead, twist strips. Place on baking sheet and brush with egg mixture. Freeze. When frozen, store in plastic bag for up to 1 month. To bake, preheat oven to 400°F. Place frozen strips on greased baking sheet. Bake 15 minutes or until golden.

Helpful Hint

When buying fresh parsley, look for bright green bunches with a fresh aroma and no signs of wilting. To store, wash the parsley well, then shake off the excess water. Wrap in paper towels before placing in a plastic bag. Store in the refrigerator for up to one week.

South-of-the-Border Quiche Squares

(Pictured at right)

1 (8-ounce) package refrigerated crescent dinner
    roll dough
1-1/2 cups shredded Monterey Jack and Colby
    cheese blend (6 ounces)
1/2 cup diced green chiles
1/2 cup chopped onion
4 eggs, beaten
1 cup milk
1/3 cup GREY POUPON® COUNTRY DIJON®
    Mustard
1 tablespoon chopped cilantro or parsley
1/2 teaspoon chili powder
    Chopped tomato and yellow and green bell
    peppers, for garnish

Unroll dough and press perforations together. Press dough on bottom and 1 inch up sides of greased 13×9×2-inch baking pan. Bake crust at 375°F for 5 to 8 minutes or until lightly golden. Remove from oven; sprinkle with half the cheese. Top with chiles, onion and remaining cheese.

Blend eggs, milk, mustard, cilantro or parsley and chili powder in medium bowl. Pour mixture evenly over cheese layer. Bake at 375°F for 25 to 30 minutes or until set. Cool 5 minutes. Garnish with tomato and bell peppers; cut into 2-inch squares. Serve hot.

Makes 24 appetizers

Mexicali Appetizer Meatballs

2/3 cup A.1.® Steak Sauce
2/3 cup thick and chunky salsa
1-1/2 pounds ground beef
1 egg
1/2 cup plain dry bread crumbs

Blend steak sauce and salsa in small bowl. Mix ground beef, egg, bread crumbs and 1/3 cup sauce mixture in separate bowl; shape into 32 (1-1/4-inch) meatballs. Arrange meatballs in single layer in shallow baking pan.

Bake at 425°F for 12 to 15 minutes or until meatballs are cooked through. Serve hot meatballs with remaining sauce mixture as a dip.

Makes 32 (1-1/4-inch) meatballs

Pizza-Stuffed Mushrooms

12 large or 24 medium fresh mushrooms
1/4 cup chopped green bell pepper
1/4 cup chopped pepperoni or cooked, crumbled
    Italian sausage
1 cup (1/2 of 15-ounce can) CONTADINA®
    Pizza Sauce
1/2 cup (2 ounces) shredded mozzarella cheese

1. Wash and dry mushrooms; remove stems.

2. Chop 1/4 cup stems. In small bowl, combine chopped stems, bell pepper, meat and pizza sauce.

3. Spoon mixture into mushroom caps; top with cheese.

4. Broil 6 to 8 inches from heat for 2 to 3 minutes or until cheese is melted and mushrooms are heated through.

Makes 12 large or 24 medium appetizers

Original Ranch® Snack Mix

8 cups KELLOGG'S® CRISPIX®* cereal
2-1/2 cups small pretzels
2-1/2 cups bite-size Cheddar cheese crackers
    (optional)
3 tablespoons vegetable oil
1 packet (1 ounce) HIDDEN VALLEY®
    The Original Ranch® Salad Dressing
    & Seasoning Mix

Kellogg's® and Crispix® are registered trademarks of Kellogg Company.

Combine cereal, pretzels and crackers in a gallon-size Glad® Zipper Storage Bag. Pour oil over mixture. Seal bag and toss to coat. Add salad dressing & seasoning mix; seal bag and toss again until coated. *Makes 10 cups*

South-of-the-Border Quiche Squares

Salads

Campbell's® Fiesta Taco Salad

(Pictured at left)

1 pound ground beef
2 tablespoons chili powder
1 can (10-3/4 ounces) CAMPBELL'S® Condensed
  Tomato Soup
8 cups salad greens torn into bite-size pieces
2 cups tortilla chips
  Chopped tomato
  Sliced green onions
  Shredded Cheddar cheese
  Sliced pitted ripe olives

1. In medium skillet over medium-high heat, cook beef and chili powder until beef is browned, stirring to separate meat. Pour off fat.

2. Add soup. Reduce heat to low and heat through.

3. Arrange salad greens and chips on platter. Spoon meat mixture over salad greens. Top with tomato, onions, cheese and olives.   *Makes 4 servings*

Tip: Save time by using packaged pre-shredded Cheddar cheese and checking the salad bar at your supermarket for pre-cut greens, toppers and trimmings.

Helpful Hint

Chili powder is typically made up of ground dried chilies, cloves, coriander, cumin, garlic and oregano. It should be stored in an airtight container in a cool, dry place for up to six months.

Clockwise from top left: Carrot Raisin Salad with Citrus Dressing (p. 32), Tuna Pasta Salad with Herb Vinaigrette (p. 26), Campbell's® Fiesta Taco Salad and Meditarranean Grilled Chicken Salad (p. 34)

Citrus Pork Tenderloin & Spinach Salad

(Pictured at right)

1 pound pork tenderloin
1/2 cup orange juice
1/4 cup *French's*® Sweet & Tangy Honey Mustard
12 cups baby spinach leaves and/or mixed field greens
1-1/2 cups orange segments (about 3 medium oranges)
1-1/3 cups *French's*® French Fried Onions
1/2 red bell pepper, cut into strips

1. Preheat oven to 425°F. Season pork with salt and pepper. Bake* pork for 30 minutes or until meat reaches internal temperature of 160°F. Cool slightly. Cut into 1/4-inch-thick slices.

2. Combine orange juice and mustard in small bowl. Arrange salad greens on serving plates. Top with pork, oranges and French Fried Onions, dividing evenly. Garnish with bell pepper; serve with mustard dressing. Serve immediately. *Makes 6 servings*

Or grill meat over medium heat for 30 minutes, turning often.

Tip: For extra crispiness, heat *French's*® **French Fried Onions** in microwave for 1 minute.

Blueberry-Peach Salad

1 package (6 ounces) orange-flavored gelatin
1/3 cup sugar
1 teaspoon finely shredded orange peel
2-1/4 cups orange juice, divided
2 cups buttermilk
1 can (8 ounces) crushed pineapple, drained
1 cup chopped pitted halved peeled peaches
1 cup fresh or frozen unsweetened blueberries, thawed
1 carton (8 ounces) dairy sour cream

In medium saucepan combine gelatin and sugar; stir in orange peel and 2 cups orange juice. Cook and stir until gelatin is dissolved; cool. Stir in buttermilk. Refrigerate until partially set. Fold in fruit; spoon into 10 individual molds. Refrigerate 6 hours or until firm. Combine sour cream and remaining 1/4 cup orange juice; refrigerate. Unmold salad; serve with sour cream mixture. *Makes 10 servings*

Favorite recipe from **Wisconsin Milk Marketing Board**

Albacore Salad Tropicale

1 fresh pineapple, halved or 1 can (8-1/4 ounces) crushed pineapple, drain juice and reserve
2 cups cooked elbow, shells or salad macaroni
1 can (8 ounces) water chestnuts, drained and sliced
1/2 cup chopped red bell pepper
1/2 cup sliced green onions, including tops
1 cup Tropicale Dressing (recipe follows)
1 (3-ounce) pouch of STARKIST® Premium Albacore Tuna
4 cups chopped romaine lettuce (optional)
8 cherry tomatoes, halved, for garnish

Hollow out pineapple halves to about 3/4 inch from edge. Core and finely chop pineapple; reserve one cup for salad. Refrigerate remaining pineapple for another use.

Combine macaroni, reserved pineapple, water chestnuts, red pepper and onions. Toss with Tropicale Dressing; refrigerate several hours. Just before serving, add tuna; toss gently. Serve salad from pineapple halves or over lettuce. Garnish with tomatoes. *Makes 4 servings*

Tropicale Dressing

1/4 cup canned pineapple juice or juice reserved from canned crushed pineapple
2 tablespoons lemon juice
1 teaspoon garlic salt
1/2 teaspoon sugar
1/2 teaspoon lemon-pepper seasoning
1/2 teaspoon paprika
1/2 cup olive oil

Whisk together pineapple juice, lemon juice, garlic salt, sugar, lemon-pepper seasoning and paprika. Slowly add oil, whisking continuously, until well blended.

Helpful Hint

For pasta salads, pasta should be rinsed after cooking and draining. Rinsing cools the pasta and washes away excess starch, which causes sticking.

Citrus Pork Tenderloin & Spinach Salad

Turkey, Mandarin and Poppy Seed Salad

(Pictured at right)

1/4 cup orange juice
1-1/2 tablespoons red wine vinegar
1-1/2 teaspoons poppy seeds
1-1/2 teaspoons olive oil
1 teaspoon Dijon-style mustard
1/8 teaspoon ground pepper
5 cups torn stemmed washed red leaf lettuce
2 cups torn stemmed washed spinach
1/2 pound honey roasted turkey breast, cut into 1/2-inch julienne strips
1 can (10-1/2 ounces) mandarin oranges, drained

In small bowl, combine orange juice, vinegar, poppy seeds, oil, mustard and pepper. Set aside. In large bowl, toss together lettuce, spinach, turkey and oranges. Pour dressing over turkey mixture and serve immediately.   *Makes 4 servings*

Favorite recipe from **National Turkey Federation**

Creamy Dijon Coleslaw

1/2 cup GREY POUPON® COUNTRY DIJON® Mustard
1/2 cup prepared ranch, creamy Italian or blue cheese salad dressing
2 tablespoons chopped parsley
1/2 teaspoon celery seed
3 cups shredded green cabbage
2 cups shredded red cabbage
1 cup shredded carrots
1/2 cup chopped onion
1/3 cup chopped red bell pepper

1. Blend mustard, salad dressing, parsley and celery seed in small bowl; set aside.

2. Mix green and red cabbages, carrots, onion and bell pepper in large bowl. Add mustard mixture, tossing to coat well. Refrigerate at least 1 hour before serving.   *Makes about 5 cups*

Tuna Pasta Salad with Herb Vinaigrette

(Pictured on page 22)

4 tablespoons CRISCO® Oil,* divided
3 tablespoons red wine vinegar *or* cider vinegar
1 clove garlic, minced
1 teaspoon dried basil leaves
1/4 teaspoon dried oregano leaves
2-1/2 cups (8 ounces) uncooked small pasta shells or rotini, cooked (without salt or fat) and well drained
1/2 pound fresh green beans, trimmed and cut into 2-inch lengths
1/2 teaspoon salt
1-1/2 cups broccoli flowerets
1 red or green bell pepper, cut into strips
1 can (6-1/2 ounces) chunk white tuna packed in water, drained and flaked

Use your favorite Crisco Oil product.

1. Combine 3 tablespoons oil, vinegar, garlic, basil and oregano in container with tight-fitting lid. Shake well.

2. Place pasta in large bowl. Add remaining one tablespoon oil. Toss to coat.

3. Bring 2 quarts water to a boil in large saucepan. Add beans and salt. Boil 2 minutes. Add broccoli. Bring water back to a boil. Boil 3 minutes. Drain well.

4. Add beans, broccoli, red pepper and tuna to pasta.

5. Shake dressing. Pour over salad. Toss to coat. Season with additional basil and oregano to taste, if desired. Serve in greens-lined bowl, if desired.

TO MICROWAVE
1. Follow steps 1 and 2 above.

2. Place beans, 1/4 cup water and salt in microwave-safe dish. Cover with plastic wrap. Turn back one corner of plastic wrap slightly to vent. Microwave at HIGH 4 minutes, stirring after 2 minutes. Add broccoli. Cover. Vent. Microwave at HIGH 2 minutes. Let stand several minutes. Drain.

3. Follow steps 4 and 5 above.   *Makes 8 servings*

Black Bean Mexicali Salad

(Pictured below)

1 can (15 ounces) black beans, rinsed and
    drained
1 cup fresh or thawed frozen corn
6 ounces roasted red bell peppers, cut into
    thin strips or coarsely chopped
1/2 cup chopped red or yellow onion, divided
1/3 cup mild chipotle or regular salsa
2 tablespoons cider vinegar
2 ounces mozzarella cheese, cut into 1/4-inch
    cubes

1. Place all ingredients except 1 tablespoon onion
and cheese in medium mixing bowl. Toss gently to
blend well. Let stand 15 minutes to absorb flavors.

2. Just before serving, gently fold in all but
2 tablespoons cheese. Sprinkle with remaining
cheese and onion.   *Makes 7 servings*

Note: Serve salad within 30 minutes to take
advantage of flavors at their peak.

Black Bean Mexicali Salad

Greek Isle Rice Salad

1 (6.8-ounce) package RICE-A-RONI®
    Beef Flavor
2 tablespoons margarine or butter
8 ounces thick sliced deli roast beef, cut
    into 1/2-inch pieces
1/2 cup chopped red onion
1/2 cup sliced ripe olives
3 plum tomatoes, seeded and chopped
1/3 cup olive oil
1/4 cup lemon juice
2 cloves garlic, crushed
1/2 teaspoon dried oregano
1/2 teaspoon ground black pepper
1 medium cucumber, thinly sliced
1/2 cup (2 ounces) crumbled feta cheese

1. In large skillet over medium heat, sauté rice-
vermicelli mix with margarine until vermicelli is
golden brown.

2. Slowly stir in 2-1/2 cups water and Special
Seasonings; bring to a boil. Reduce heat to low.
Simmer 15 to 20 minutes or until rice is tender.
Cool completely.

3. In large bowl, combine rice mixture, roast beef,
onion, olives and tomatoes; set aside.

4. In small bowl, combine olive oil, lemon juice,
garlic, oregano and pepper with wire whisk. Toss
rice mixture with dressing. Chill at least 30 minutes.
Garnish with cucumber slices and cheese.

Makes 6 servings

Reuben Salad

1/2 cup Italian salad dressing
1/4 cup *French's*® Bold n' Spicy Brown Mustard
1/2 pound Swiss cheese
1/2 pound pastrami or corned beef
3 cooked medium red potatoes
2 cups sauerkraut, drained
2/3 cup finely chopped dill pickles

1. Combine dressing and mustard in large bowl.

2. Cut cheese, pastrami and potatoes into 1/2-inch
cubes. Add to dressing in bowl with sauerkraut and
pickles; toss to coat. Serve with crusty pumpernickel
bread. Serve on bed of cabbage or lettuce leaves, if
desired.   *Makes 6 servings*

*Smucker's® Three Bean Salad with
Sweet and Sour Apricot Dressing*

Smucker's® Three Bean Salad with Sweet and Sour Apricot Dressing

(Pictured above)

1/2 cup SMUCKER'S® Apricot Preserves
1/4 cup red vinegar
  1 teaspoon celery seeds
  1 (16-ounce) can kidney beans, rinsed and drained
  1 cup cooked fresh or frozen green beans,
     cut into 2-inch pieces
1/4 pound (1 cup) cooked fresh or frozen yellow
     wax beans, cut into 2-inch pieces
  1 small red onion, thinly sliced
    Salt and pepper to taste

Combine SMUCKER'S® Apricot Preserves, vinegar
and celery seeds in medium salad bowl. Add kidney
beans, green and yellow beans and onion. Toss well
to combine. Season with salt and freshly ground
pepper. *Makes 6 servings*

Fiesta Tomato Dressing

  1 large ripe tomato, coarsely chopped
  2 tablespoons *French's®* Bold n' Spicy Brown
     Mustard
  1 tablespoon coarsely chopped fresh basil *or*
     2 teaspoons dried basil leaves
  1 tablespoon olive oil
  1 tablespoon balsamic or red wine vinegar
  1 clove garlic, pressed
1/8 teaspoon salt
1/8 teaspoon black pepper

1. Combine tomato, mustard, basil, oil, vinegar,
garlic, salt and pepper in food processor or blender.
Cover and process until well blended. Cover and
chill in refrigerator until ready to serve.

2. Serve over mixed salad greens, if desired.
Makes 1-1/4 cups dressing

Asian Shrimp & Noodle Salad

 1/3 cup plus 2 tablespoons vegetable oil, divided
 1/4 cup cider vinegar
 2 tablespoons *French's®* Worcestershire Sauce
 2 tablespoons light soy sauce
 2 tablespoons honey
 1 teaspoon grated fresh ginger or 1/4 teaspoon ground ginger
 2 packages (3 ounces each) chicken-flavor ramen noodle soup
 1 pound shrimp, cleaned and deveined with tails left on
 2 cups vegetables such as broccoli, carrots and snow peas, cut into bite-size pieces
1-1/3 cups *French's®* French Fried Onions, divided

1. Combine 1/3 cup oil, vinegar, Worcestershire, soy sauce, honey and ginger until well blended. Prepare ramen noodles according to package directions for soup; drain and rinse noodles. Place in serving bowl.

2. Stir-fry shrimp in 1 tablespoon oil in large skillet over medium-high heat, stirring constantly, until shrimp turn pink. Remove shrimp to bowl with noodles. Stir-fry vegetables in remaining oil in skillet over medium-high heat, stirring constantly, until vegetables are crisp-tender.

3. Add vegetable mixture, dressing and *1 cup* French Fried Onions to bowl with noodles; toss to coat well. Serve immediately topped with remaining onions.

Makes 6 servings

Tip: Purchase cut-up vegetables from the salad bar of your local supermarket to save prep time.

Italian Tortellini Salad

 2 cups broccoli florets
1/2 cup sliced carrot
 8 ounces tortellini, cooked and cooled
 1 cup (6 ounces) CURE 81® ham, cut into strips
 1 cup sliced green bell pepper
 1 cup sliced red bell pepper
1/2 cup sliced red onion
1/2 cup creamy Italian salad dressing

Cook broccoli and carrot in boiling water 2 to 3 minutes or until crisp-tender; drain. Cool. In large bowl, combine broccoli, carrot, cooked tortellini, ham, bell peppers and onion. Toss with dressing.

Makes 4 servings

Refreshing Chicken & Rice Salad

(Pictured at right)

 1 package (4.3 ounces) RICE-A-RONI®
   Long Grain & Wild Rice Pilaf
 1 tablespoon vegetable oil
 2 cups chopped cooked chicken
 2 carrots, sliced lengthwise, cut into slices
 1 cucumber, peeled, seeded, cut into short thin strips
1/2 cup red or green bell pepper, cut into short thin strips
 2 tablespoons sliced green onions
1/3 cup Italian dressing
   Lettuce

1. Prepare Rice-A-Roni® Mix as package directs, substituting oil for margarine. Cool 10 minutes.

2. In large bowl, combine prepared Rice-A-Roni®, chicken, carrots, cucumber, bell pepper, onions and dressing. Chill 4 hours or overnight. Stir before serving.

3. Serve on lettuce-lined platter.

Makes 5 servings

Bacon Vinaigrette Dressing

(Pictured on front cover)

 1 packet (1 ounce) HIDDEN VALLEY®
   The Original Ranch® Salad Dressing & Seasoning Mix
1/4 cup vegetable oil
1/4 cup water
 2 tablespoons cider vinegar
 2 tablespoons crisp-cooked, crumbled bacon*
 1 tablespoon light brown sugar

Bacon pieces can be used.

Whisk together salad dressing & seasoning mix, oil, water, vinegar, bacon and brown sugar. Serve over your favorite salad blend.   *Makes about 3/4 cup*

Serving Suggestion: For a tasty spinach salad, toss dressing with torn spinach, sliced fresh mushrooms, quartered cherry tomatoes and croutons.

Refreshing Chicken & Rice Salad

Rice and Bean Salad

(Pictured at right)

1 can (14-1/2 ounces) chicken broth
2 cups uncooked instant brown rice
1 tablespoon olive oil
1 medium onion, chopped
3 cloves garlic, minced
2 medium carrots, cut into 1-inch julienne strips
1 medium zucchini, halved lengthwise and diagonally sliced
1 can (14-1/2 ounces) Italian-style stewed tomatoes
1 can (16 ounces) kidney beans, rinsed and drained
1/2 cup (2 ounces) grated Parmesan cheese
1/2 cup Italian salad dressing
1/4 cup fresh basil leaves, finely chopped

1. Bring chicken broth to a boil in medium saucepan over high heat; add rice and cover. Reduce heat and cook 10 minutes or until chicken broth is absorbed. Remove from heat; set aside.

2. Heat oil in large skillet over medium-high heat. Add onion and garlic; cook and stir 2 to 3 minutes or until onion is tender. Add carrots and zucchini; cook and stir 3 to 4 minutes or until vegetables are crisp-tender. Remove from heat. Add tomatoes, beans and rice; stir to combine.

3. Place rice mixture in large bowl. Cover with plastic wrap and refrigerate overnight.

4. Add Parmesan cheese, salad dressing and basil to rice mixture; toss lightly. Season to taste with black pepper. *Makes 6 servings*

Serving Suggestion: Serve with flaky breadsticks or croissants and juicy chunks of watermelon.

Helpful Hint

Fresh basil is sold in bunches at farmer's markets and in small plastic packages in the produce section of many supermarkets. To store, place the basil, stems down, in a glass of water with a plastic bag over the leaves; refrigerate for up to five days, changing the water occasionally.

Carrot Raisin Salad with Citrus Dressing

(Pictured on page 22)

3/4 cup sour cream
1/4 cup milk
1 tablespoon honey
1 tablespoon orange juice concentrate
1 tablespoon lime juice
Grated peel of 1 medium orange
1/4 teaspoon salt
8 medium carrots, peeled and coarsely shredded (about 2 cups)
1/4 cup raisins
1/3 cup chopped cashews

1. Combine sour cream, milk, honey, orange juice concentrate, lime juice, orange peel and salt in small bowl. Blend well and set aside.

2. Combine carrots and raisins in large bowl. Pour dressing over; toss to coat. Cover and refrigerate 30 minutes. Toss again before serving. Top with cashews. *Makes 8 servings*

Easy Antipasto Salad

1 can (14.5 ounces) CONTADINA® Stewed Tomatoes, drained
1/2 cup thinly sliced cucumber
1/2 cup thinly sliced onion
2 jars (6 ounces each) marinated artichoke hearts, drained, cut in half
1 ounce thinly sliced salami (optional)
1/2 cup sliced pitted ripe olives, drained
1/2 cup thinly sliced green bell pepper
1/2 cup Italian dressing
Lettuce leaves (optional)

1. Layer tomatoes, cucumber, onion, artichoke hearts, salami, olives and bell pepper in 1-quart casserole dish.

2. Pour dressing over salad; cover. Chill before serving. Serve over lettuce leaves, if desired. *Makes 6 servings*

Shell Salad with Peas and Bacon

1 package (16 ounces) BARILLA® Medium Shells
1 package (10 ounces) frozen peas
8 ounces (12 slices) bacon, cooked and
   crumbled
1/2 cup chopped red onion
1 cup mayonnaise
1 cup sour cream
1/2 cup (2 ounces) grated Parmesan cheese
1-1/2 teaspoons salt
1/2 teaspoon pepper
1/2 teaspoon garlic powder

1. Cook pasta shells according to package directions; drain.

2. Combine pasta shells, peas, bacon and onion in serving bowl.

3. Combine mayonnaise, sour cream, cheese, salt, pepper and garlic powder in medium bowl; add to pasta mixture. Stir gently to combine. Cover and refrigerate at least one hour before serving.

Makes 10 servings

Albacore and White Bean Salad with Orange Dressing

2 cans (15 ounces each) Great Northern beans,
   rinsed and drained
3 hard-cooked eggs, chopped
1/3 cup chopped green onions, including tops
1/3 cup chopped red onion
3/4 teaspoon salt
1/3 cup bottled Italian dressing
1 tablespoon frozen orange juice concentrate,
   thawed
2 teaspoons grated orange peel
1/2 to 1 teaspoon crushed red pepper
1 (3-ounce) pouch of STARKIST® Premium
   Albacore Tuna
2 chopped plum tomatoes, drained
   Quartered orange slices and chives, for garnish

In large bowl, combine beans, eggs, green onions, red onion and salt. In glass measuring cup, blend dressing, orange juice concentrate, orange peel and crushed red pepper. Add to salad in bowl. Chill several hours or overnight. Just before serving, gently toss in tuna and tomatoes. Garnish with orange slices and chives. *Makes 6 servings*

Mediterranean Grilled Chicken Salad

(Pictured on page 22)

2/3 cup LAWRY'S® Herb & Garlic Marinade
   With Lemon Juice, divided
4 boneless, skinless chicken breasts
2 tablespoons BERTOLLI® Olive Oil
4 to 5 cups torn romaine lettuce
1 large Roma tomato, diced
1/4 cup shredded Parmesan cheese (optional)
   Croutons (garnish)

In large resealable plastic bag, combine 1/3 cup Herb & Garlic Marinade with chicken; seal bag. Marinate in refrigerator for 30 minutes. Remove chicken from bag, discarding used marinade. Grill chicken until no longer pink and juices run clear when cut, about 6 to 8 minutes per side. Let chicken cool slightly then slice into strips. In small bowl, whisk together remaining Marinade with olive oil. In large salad bowl, gently toss together remaining ingredients, except croutons, with Marinade mixture. Arrange salad on 4 plates and top with chicken and croutons. Serve immediately.

Makes 4 servings

Easy Greek Salad

(Pictured at right)

6 leaves romaine lettuce, torn into 1-1/2-inch
   pieces
1 cucumber, peeled and sliced
1 tomato, chopped
1/2 cup sliced red onion
1 ounce feta cheese, crumbled (about 1/3 cup)
2 tablespoons extra-virgin olive oil
2 tablespoons lemon juice
1 teaspoon dried oregano leaves
1/2 teaspoon salt

1. Combine lettuce, cucumber, tomato, onion and cheese in large serving bowl.

2. Whisk together oil, lemon juice, oregano and salt in small bowl. Pour over lettuce mixture; toss until coated. Serve immediately. *Makes 6 servings*

Easy Greek Salad

Thai-Style Warm Noodle Salad

Thai-Style Warm Noodle Salad

(Pictured above)

>   8 ounces uncooked angel hair pasta
> 1/2 cup chunky peanut butter
> 1/4 cup soy sauce
> 1/4 to 1/2 teaspoon crushed red pepper flakes
>   2 green onions, thinly sliced
>   1 carrot, shredded

Cook pasta according to package directions.

Meanwhile, blend peanut butter, soy sauce and red pepper flakes in serving bowl until smooth.

Drain pasta, reserving 5 tablespoons water. Mix hot pasta water with peanut butter mixture until smooth; toss pasta with sauce. Stir in green onions and carrot. Serve warm or at room temperature.

Makes 4 servings

Notes: This salad is as versatile as it is easy to make. It can be prepared a day ahead and served warm or cold—perfect for potlucks, picnics and even lunch boxes. You can also make it into a heartier meal by adding leftover chicken or beef.

Smoked Turkey and Strawberry Spinach Salad

DRESSING
> 1/2 cup SMUCKER'S® Strawberry Jelly
>   2 tablespoons red vinegar
> 1/2 teaspoon grated lemon peel

SALAD
>   4 cups torn spinach
>   2 cups cubed cooked smoked turkey or chicken
> 1-1/3 cups sliced or halved fresh strawberries
>   1 (11-ounce) can mandarin oranges, chilled, drained
>   2 thin slices red onion, separated into rings

In small saucepan, combine jelly, vinegar and lemon peel. Cook over medium-high heat until jelly is melted, stirring frequently. Cool 10 minutes.

Meanwhile, arrange spinach, turkey, strawberries, oranges and onion rings on 4 individual salad plates. Serve with dressing.   *Makes 4 servings*

Waldorf Sweet Potato Salad

SALAD
> 1/3 cup walnuts
>   3 cups grated peeled sweet potato
>   1 red apple, unpeeled, cored and coarsely chopped
> 1/2 cup chopped celery
> 1/2 cup red seedless grapes, cut in half
> 1/3 cup crumbled blue cheese (optional)
>   Red leaf lettuce leaves (optional)

DRESSING
>   3 tablespoons apple juice
>   2 tablespoons vegetable oil
>   1 tablespoon plus 1 teaspoon white wine vinegar
>   1 teaspoon sugar
> 1/2 teaspoon salt

Toast walnuts in oven or toaster oven at 350°F until golden, about 10 minutes. Cool. Place all salad ingredients, except lettuce, in large bowl.

To make dressing, whisk together all dressing ingredients until blended. Pour over salad and toss well. If desired, serve on red leaf lettuce leaves.

Makes 6 servings

Favorite recipe from **North Carolina SweetPotato Commission**

Parsley, Ham and Pasta Salad

(Pictured below)

2 cups uncooked elbow macaroni
2 cups (12 ounces) CURE 81® ham, cut into strips
1 cup sliced celery
1/2 cup sliced green onions
1 cup mayonnaise or salad dressing
1 cup packed parsley, finely chopped
1/4 cup grated Parmesan cheese
1/4 cup white wine vinegar
1 clove garlic, minced

Cook macaroni according to package directions. In large bowl, combine ham, macaroni, celery and green onions.

In small bowl, combine mayonnaise, parsley, cheese, vinegar and garlic; toss with pasta. Cover and refrigerate 1 to 2 hours to blend flavors. *Makes 6 to 8 servings*

Oven-Broiled Italian Style Salad

1/4 cup FILIPPO BERIO® Olive Oil
1 clove garlic, crushed
2 medium red onions, thinly sliced into rounds
3 large beefsteak tomatoes, thinly sliced into rounds
1 (8-ounce) package thinly sliced part-skim mozzarella cheese
1 tablespoon balsamic vinegar
3 tablespoons shredded fresh basil *or*
    1 tablespoon dried basil leaves
Salt and freshly ground black pepper

In small bowl, combine olive oil and garlic. Brush 2 tablespoons mixture over onion slices. In large nonstick skillet, cook onions over medium heat 5 minutes or until beginning to brown, turning halfway through cooking time. In large, shallow, heatproof serving dish, arrange slightly overlapping slices of onion, tomatoes and mozzarella. Whisk vinegar into remaining 2 tablespoons olive oil mixture; drizzle over onion mixture. Broil, 4 to 5 inches from heat, 4 to 5 minutes or until cheese just begins to melt. Sprinkle with basil. Season to taste with salt and pepper. *Makes 4 servings*

Parsley, Ham and Pasta Salad

Kielbasa Tomato Salad

(Pictured at right)

1 pound BOB EVANS® Kielbasa Sausage
1 pound tomatoes, cut into wedges
1 large red onion, chopped
1 red bell pepper, chopped
1 yellow bell pepper, chopped
3 green onions with tops, cut into 1/2-inch
    pieces
1/2 cup chopped fresh parsley
1/3 cup balsamic vinegar
2 teaspoons salt
1 teaspoon chopped fresh rosemary
1 teaspoon chopped fresh thyme
1 teaspoon black pepper
1/2 cup olive oil
    Fresh rosemary sprig (optional)

Cut kielbasa into 1/2-inch rounds; place in medium skillet. Cook over medium heat until browned, turning occasionally. Remove sausage to large glass bowl. Add tomatoes, red onion, bell peppers and green onions to sausage; toss lightly. Combine all remaining ingredients except oil and rosemary sprig in small bowl. Whisk in oil gradually until well blended. Pour over sausage mixture; cover and refrigerate 2 hours or until chilled. Garnish with rosemary sprig, if desired. Serve cold. Refrigerate leftovers. *Makes 8 side-dish servings*

Sweet Mustard Dressing

1/4 cup FILIPPO BERIO® Olive Oil
2 tablespoons honey
2 tablespoons white wine vinegar
4-1/2 teaspoons Dijon mustard
1 tablespoon balsamic vinegar
    Salt and freshly ground black pepper

In small screw-topped jar, combine olive oil, honey, white wine vinegar, mustard and balsamic vinegar. Shake vigorously until well blended. Season to taste with salt and pepper. Store dressing in refrigerator up to 1 week. Shake well before using.
Makes about 1/2 cup

Hidden Valley® Chopstick Chicken Salad

1 packet (1 ounce) HIDDEN VALLEY®
    The Original Ranch® Salad Dressing
    & Seasoning Mix
1 cup milk
1 cup mayonnaise
2 tablespoons soy sauce
8 cups torn lettuce
2 cups shredded cooked chicken
1 cup chopped green onions
1 cup chopped water chestnuts
1 cup toasted sliced almonds (optional)

In a bowl, combine salad dressing & seasoning mix with milk and mayonnaise. Mix well. Cover and refrigerate. Chill 30 minutes to thicken. Stir in soy sauce. Toss with lettuce, chicken, onions and water chestnuts; top with almonds, if desired.
Makes 4 to 6 servings

Citrus Shrimp and Spinach Salad

1/3 cup GREY POUPON® COUNTRY DIJON®
    Mustard
1/4 cup honey
1/4 cup orange juice
1 tablespoon balsamic vinegar
3 cups torn romaine lettuce leaves
3 cups torn spinach leaves
1 small red onion, thinly sliced
1 medium cucumber, thinly sliced
2 large oranges, peeled, sectioned and chopped
1 pound small shrimp, peeled, deveined and
    steamed
1/3 cup PLANTERS® Pecan Pieces, toasted

1. Mix mustard, honey, orange juice and vinegar; refrigerate until serving time.

2. Layer lettuce leaves, spinach, onion slices, cucumber slices, orange pieces and shrimp on large serving platter. Sprinkle with pecans and drizzle with prepared salad dressing to serve.
Makes 6 servings

Apricot-Pineapple Mold

1/2 cup SMUCKER'S® Apricot Preserves
1/2 cup SMUCKER'S® Pineapple Topping
2 tablespoons vinegar
2-1/2 cups water
1 teaspoon whole cloves
1 (4-inch) stick cinnamon
2 (3-ounce) packages orange-flavor gelatin
1/2 cup sour cream

In saucepan, combine preserves, pineapple topping, vinegar and water. Tie cloves and cinnamon in small square of cheesecloth; place in saucepan. Simmer mixture over low heat for 10 minutes. Remove spice bag.

Dissolve 1 package of gelatin in 2 cups of preserve mixture; stir until dissolved. Pour into a 6-cup mold and refrigerate until almost firm.

Meanwhile, dissolve remaining package of gelatin in remaining preserve mixture; stir until dissolved. Refrigerate until partially set. Beat with an electric mixer until fluffy. Fold in sour cream. Pour over first layer in mold. Refrigerate until firm, about 8 hours or overnight. Unmold to serve.

Makes 8 to 10 servings

Mandarin Chicken Salad

(Pictured at right)

1 can (15-1/2 ounces) DEL MONTE® Pineapple Chunks in Heavy Syrup, undrained
3 tablespoons vegetable oil
3 tablespoons cider vinegar
1 tablespoon soy sauce
4 cups shredded cabbage or iceberg lettuce
1 can (14-1/2 ounces) DEL MONTE Diced Tomatoes with Garlic and Onion, drained
2 cups cubed cooked chicken
1/3 cup packed cilantro, chopped, *or* 1/2 cup sliced green onions

1. Drain pineapple, reserving 1/4 cup syrup. In small bowl, combine reserved syrup, oil, vinegar and soy sauce; stir briskly with fork.

2. Toss cabbage with pineapple, tomatoes, chicken and cilantro in large bowl. Add dressing as desired; gently toss.

3. Sprinkle with crumbled dry noodles (from Oriental noodle soup mix), toasted slivered almonds or toasted sesame seeds, if desired.

Makes 4 servings

Neon Turkey Pasta Salad

2 cups cubed cooked BUTTERBALL® Breast of Young Turkey
2 cups tri-colored rotini pasta, cooked and drained
1 small zucchini, sliced
2 small tomatoes, cut into wedges
1/2 cup chunked yellow bell pepper
1/2 cup chunked red bell pepper
1/2 cup chunked green bell pepper
1/2 cup crumbled feta cheese
1 can (2-1/4 ounces) sliced ripe olives, drained
1/3 cup fresh basil leaves, cut into strips
1 cup prepared Italian salad dressing

Combine turkey, pasta, vegetables, cheese, olives and basil in large bowl. Toss with salad dressing. Chill at least 2 hours before serving.

Makes 6 servings

Coleslaw With Peanuts

1 package (8 ounces) pre-shredded coleslaw mix (6 cups)
3/4 cup chopped green onions, including tops
1-3/4 cups chopped celery, including leaves
1/3 cup chopped cocktail peanuts
1/2 cup Italian salad dressing
3/4 teaspoon LAWRY'S® Seasoned Salt
1/2 teaspoon LAWRY'S® Seasoned Pepper

In large bowl, toss cabbage, onions, celery and peanuts together lightly. Pour dressing over salad and add Seasoned Salt and Seasoned Pepper; toss. Chill thoroughly before serving.

Makes 6 to 8 servings

Mandarin Chicken Salad

Grilled Bratwurst German Potato Salad

(Pictured at right)

4 medium baking potatoes
1 package BOB EVANS® Bratwurst
    (approximately 5 links)
1 cup red wine vinegar
1/2 cup vegetable oil
1 small yellow onion, chopped
2 tablespoons chopped fresh chives
2 teaspoons Dijon mustard
1 clove garlic, minced
1/2 teaspoon salt
1/4 teaspoon freshly cracked black pepper
4 to 5 dashes hot pepper sauce
1 small cucumber, thinly sliced

Prepare grill for medium coals. Cook unpeeled potatoes in 4 quarts boiling water just until tender. Drain, peel and cut into 1/8-inch slices. Place in large bowl. Precook sausage 10 minutes in 2 quarts gently boiling water. Meanwhile, combine vinegar, oil, onion, chives, mustard, garlic, salt, black pepper and hot pepper sauce in small bowl; mix well. Remove bratwurst from water; grill until well browned. Cut bratwurst diagonally into 1/2-inch slices and add to bowl with potatoes. Pour vinegar mixture over potatoes and bratwurst. Add cucumber; toss gently to mix. Serve warm or cold. Refrigerate leftovers. *Makes 6 to 8 servings*

Ham Salad Bread Bowls

3/4 pound thick sliced deli ham
2/3 cup shredded Swiss cheese
1/2 cup HIDDEN VALLEY® The Original Ranch®
    Dressing
1/4 cup chopped green onions
1/4 cup finely chopped sweet gherkin or dill
    pickles
4 whole Kaiser rolls (4-inch diameter)

Finely dice ham to make about 2-1/3 cups; combine with cheese, dressing, onions and pickles in a medium mixing bowl. Cut a thin slice off the top of each roll. Scoop out center to within 1/4 inch from edge, forming a bowl. Stuff ham salad gently into bread bowls. *Makes 4 servings (or 3 cups salad)*

Couscous Chicken Salad

1 tablespoon plus 1/4 cup olive oil, divided
1 yellow or orange bell pepper, chopped
1 small zucchini, chopped
1 green onion, finely chopped
1 pound chicken tenders, cut into bite-size
    pieces
2 cans (about 14-1/2 ounces each) chicken broth
1 package (10 ounces) couscous
1 can (15 ounces) chickpeas or garbanzo beans,
    rinsed and drained
1 large tomato, seeded and chopped
1/2 cup chopped fresh cilantro
1/3 cup lemon juice
1 teaspoon ground cumin
1/4 teaspoon garlic salt
3 dashes hot pepper sauce

Heat 1 tablespoon oil in large skillet over high heat. Add bell pepper, zucchini and onion; stir-fry 2 minutes or until crisp-tender. Remove from skillet and set aside in large bowl.

Add chicken and chicken broth to skillet. Bring broth to a boil over high heat; reduce heat to medium and simmer 4 to 5 minutes or until chicken is no longer pink. Remove chicken from broth with slotted spoon. Place in bowl with vegetables; cool.

Add couscous to broth. Remove skillet from heat. Cover and let stand 5 minutes or until all liquid is absorbed. Cool.

Combine chicken mixture, couscous, chickpeas, tomato and cilantro in large bowl.

Whisk together lemon juice, remaining 1/4 cup oil, cumin, garlic salt and pepper sauce in small bowl. Pour over couscous mixture. Serve warm or chill 1 hour before serving. *Makes 6 servings*

Helpful Hint

Chicken tenders are the lean, tender strips that are found on the underside of the breast. They are skinless and boneless and have virtually no waste. Boneless chicken breasts or thighs can be substituted in most recipes that call for tenders.

*Grilled Bratwurst
German Potato Salad*

Side Dishes

Macaroni & Cheese with Bacon

(Pictured at left)

    8 ounces uncooked rotini pasta (about 3 cups)
    2 tablespoons butter or margarine
    2 tablespoons all-purpose flour
  1/4 teaspoon salt
  1/4 teaspoon ground mustard
  1/8 teaspoon pepper
1-1/2 cups milk
    8 ounces (2 cups) shredded sharp cheddar cheese
  1/2 pound sliced bacon, cooked and crumbled*
    2 medium tomatoes, sliced

*Can substitute 1 cup of cubed cooked ham for the bacon.

Preheat oven to 350°F. Lightly grease 1-1/2-quart shallow baking dish.

Cook pasta according to package directions; drain and return to saucepan.

Melt butter in another saucepan over medium-low heat. Whisk in flour, salt, mustard and pepper until smooth; cook and stir 1 minute. Whisk in milk. Bring to a boil over medium heat, stirring frequently. Reduce heat; simmer 2 minutes or until thickened. Remove from heat. Add cheese; stir until melted.

Add cheese mixture and bacon to pasta; stir until well blended. Transfer to prepared baking dish. Bake, uncovered, 20 minutes. Arrange tomato slices on top. Bake 5 to 8 minutes more or until bubbly.   *Makes 4 servings*

Helpful Hint

To make separating bacon slices easier, roll the package of bacon into a tube and secure it with a rubber band before refrigerating.

Clockwise from top left: Corn Bread Stuffing with Sausage and Apple (p. 46), Macaroni & Cheese with Bacon, Mexican Rice (p. 64) and Green Beans wth Toasted Pecans (p. 52)

Roasted Butternut Squash

(Pictured at right)

1 pound butternut squash, peeled and cut into
    1-inch cubes (about 4 cups)
2 medium onions, coarsely chopped
8 ounces carrots, peeled and cut into 1/2-inch
    slices (about 2 cups)
1 tablespoon brown sugar
1/4 teaspoon salt
    Pepper to taste
1 tablespoon butter or margarine, melted

Preheat oven to 400°F. Line large baking sheet with
foil and coat with nonstick cooking spray. Arrange
vegetables in single layer on foil; coat lightly with
cooking spray. Sprinkle vegetables with brown
sugar, salt and pepper.

Bake, uncovered, 30 minutes. Stir gently; bake
10 to 15 minutes longer or until vegetables are
tender. Drizzle with butter and toss to coat.

Makes 5 (1-cup) servings

Balsamic Onions with Honey

3 large red onions (about 3 pounds)
1 tablespoon plus 1/4 cup water
6 tablespoons honey
1/4 cup balsamic or red wine vinegar
3 tablespoons butter or margarine, melted
1 teaspoon paprika
1 teaspoon ground coriander
1/2 teaspoon salt
1/8 teaspoon ground red pepper

Peel onions and cut crosswise into halves. Place
cut-side down in shallow baking dish just large
enough to hold onions in single layer. Sprinkle with
1 tablespoon water; cover with foil. Bake at 350°F
30 minutes. Combine honey, vinegar, remaining
1/4 cup water, butter, paprika, coriander, salt and
red pepper in small bowl. Remove onions from oven
and turn cut side up. Spoon half of honey mixture
over onions. Bake, uncovered, 15 minutes more.
Baste with remaining honey mixture; bake
15 minutes more or until tender. Serve with
poultry or pork. *Makes 6 servings*

Favorite recipe from **National Honey Board**

Apple Buttered Sweet Potatoes

1 pound sweet potatoes, cooked, peeled and
    sliced
1 cup (11-ounce jar) SMUCKER'S® Cider Apple
    Butter
1/3 cup SMUCKER'S® Pineapple Topping
2 tablespoons butter or margarine, melted
1/2 teaspoon salt
1/4 teaspoon ground cinnamon
1/4 teaspoon paprika

Arrange sliced sweet potatoes in ungreased shallow
baking dish. Combine apple butter and remaining
ingredients; mix well. Drizzle mixture over sweet
potatoes.

Bake at 350°F for 20 to 30 minutes or until heated
through. *Makes 6 servings*

Crumb-Topped Snowball

1 large head cauliflower (about 1-1/4 pounds)
1/4 cup butter or margarine
1 cup soft bread crumbs (about 2 slices)
2 green onions, thinly sliced
2 eggs, hard-cooked and finely chopped
2 tablespoons lemon juice

Remove and discard leaves and stem from
cauliflower. Cut around core with sharp knife,
being careful not to separate florets from head;
discard core. Rinse.

Pour 1 inch of water into large saucepan. Place
cauliflower in water, stem side down; cover. Bring
to a boil over high heat; reduce heat to low. Simmer
10 to 12 minutes or until crisp-tender; drain. Place
cauliflower in greased 8-inch square baking dish.

Preheat oven to 375°F. Melt butter over medium heat
in small skillet. Stir in bread crumbs and onions; cook
until crumbs are lightly browned. Stir in eggs and
lemon juice. Press crumb mixture evenly over top of
cauliflower. Place any extra crumb mixture in baking
dish. Bake at 375°F 10 minutes or until crumb mixture
is crispy and lightly browned. Serve immediately.

Makes 6 side-dish servings

Brown Rice & Vegetable Stuffed Squash

(Pictured below)

2 large acorn or golden acorn squash (about 1-1/2 pounds each)
1 cup uncooked quick-cooking brown rice
2 cups fresh broccoli florets, chopped
1/2 teaspoon salt
1/2 teaspoon pepper
1/4 cup chopped almonds, toasted
3/4 cup shredded sharp cheddar or Gouda cheese

1. Cut squash in half widthwise; discard seeds. Trim off stem ends to allow squash to stand. Place squash halves cut sides down on microwavable plate; microwave at HIGH 12 to 15 minutes or until almost tender. Place squash halves cut sides up in greased 13×9-inch baking pan. Cover and let stand 3 minutes or until ready to fill. Preheat oven to 375°F.

2. Meanwhile, cook rice according to package directions adding broccoli, salt and pepper during last 5 minutes of cooking. Stir in almonds.

3. Spoon rice mixture into squash, overflowing into dish if necessary; sprinkle with cheese. Bake, uncovered, 20 to 25 minutes or until squash is tender and cheese is melted.   *Makes 4 servings*

Brown Rice & Vegetable Stuffed Squash

Pepperidge Farm® Scalloped Apple Bake

1/4 cup margarine *or* butter, melted
1/4 cup sugar
2 teaspoons grated orange peel
1 teaspoon ground cinnamon
1-1/2 cups PEPPERIDGE FARM® Corn Bread Stuffing
1/2 cup coarsely chopped pecans
1 can (16 ounces) whole berry cranberry sauce
1/3 cup orange juice *or* water
4 large cooking apples, cored and thinly sliced (about 6 cups)

1. Lightly mix margarine, sugar, orange peel, cinnamon, stuffing and pecans and set aside.

2. Mix cranberry sauce, juice and apples. Add *half* the stuffing mixture. Mix lightly. Spoon into 8-inch square baking dish. Sprinkle remaining stuffing mixture over apple mixture.

3. Bake at 375°F. for 40 minutes or until apples are tender.   *Makes 6 servings*

Tip: To melt margarine, remove wrapper and place in microwave-safe cup. Cover and microwave on HIGH 45 seconds.

Creamy Spinach Italiano

1 cup ricotta cheese
3/4 cup half-and-half or milk
2 packages (10 ounces each) frozen chopped spinach, thawed and squeezed dry
1-1/3 cups *French's*® French Fried Onions, divided
1/2 cup chopped roasted red pepper
1/4 cup chopped fresh basil
1/4 cup grated Parmesan cheese
1 teaspoon garlic powder
1/4 teaspoon salt

1. Preheat oven to 350°F. Whisk together ricotta cheese and half-and-half in large bowl until well combined. Stir in spinach, *2/3 cup* French Fried Onions, red pepper, basil, Parmesan, garlic powder and salt. Pour mixture into greased deep-dish 9-inch pie plate.

2. Bake for 25 minutes or until heated through; stir. Sprinkle with remaining *2/3 cup* onions. Bake for 5 minutes or until onions are golden.

Makes 4 servings

*Velveeta® Twice Baked
Ranch Potatoes*

Velveeta® Twice Baked Ranch Potatoes

(Pictured above)

4 baking potatoes
1/2 cup KRAFT® Ranch Dressing
1/4 cup BREAKSTONE'S® or KNUDSEN®
    Sour Cream
1 tablespoon OSCAR MAYER® Real Bacon Bits
1/4 pound (4 ounces) VELVEETA® Pasteurized
    Prepared Cheese Product, cut up

1. Bake potatoes at 400°F for 1 hour. Slice off tops of potatoes; scoop out centers, leaving 1/8-inch shell.

2. Mash potatoes. Add dressing, sour cream and bacon bits; beat until fluffy. Stir VELVEETA into potato mixture. Spoon into shells.

3. Bake at 350°F for 20 minutes.

Makes 4 servings

How to Bake Potatoes: Russet potatoes are best for baking. Scrub potatoes well, blot dry and rub the skin with a little oil and salt. Prick the skin of the potatoes with a fork so steam can escape. Stand them on end in a muffin tin. Bake at 400°F for 60 minutes or until tender.

Helpful Hint

Russet potatoes are ideal for baking, as they have a low moisture and high starch content. (Russets are also called Idaho potatoes, whether or not they were grown in Idaho.) Try to purchase potatoes that are about the same size, so they will cook evenly and be ready at the same time.

Old-Fashioned Onion Rings

(Pictured at right)

1/2 cup buttermilk
1/2 cup prepared Ranch dressing
  2 large onions, sliced 1/2 inch thick and separated into rings
    WESSON® Vegetable or Canola Oil
  2 cups self-rising flour
  2 teaspoons garlic salt
  2 teaspoons lemon pepper
1/2 teaspoon cayenne pepper
  2 eggs, slightly beaten with 2 tablespoons water

In large bowl, combine buttermilk and Ranch dressing; blend well. Add onions and toss until well coated. Cover; refrigerate at least 1 hour or overnight. Fill large deep-fry pot or electric skillet to no more than half its depth with Wesson® Oil. Heat oil between 325°F to 350°F. In large bowl, combine flour, garlic salt, lemon pepper and cayenne pepper; blend well. Working in small batches, place onion rings in flour mixture; coat well. Remove; dip into egg mixture. Return rings to flour mixture; coat well. Lightly shake off excess flour; fry until golden brown. Drain on paper towels. Sprinkle with additional garlic salt, if desired.

Makes 4 servings

Potato-Zucchini Pancakes

  1 medium baking potato, unpeeled and shredded
1/2 small zucchini, shredded
  1 green onion, thinly sliced
  1 egg white
  2 tablespoons all-purpose flour
  1 tablespoon vegetable oil

Combine potato, zucchini, onion, egg white and flour in medium bowl until well blended. Add salt and pepper to taste.

Heat oil in large skillet over medium heat. Drop potato mixture into skillet by 1/3 cupfuls. Flatten pancakes with spatula; cook about 5 minutes per side or until browned. *Makes 2 servings*

Tip: Save time by shredding both the potato and zucchini in a food processor fitted with a shredding disc. There's no need to wash the bowl in between because all the ingredients are mixed together before cooking.

Sautéed Garlic Potatoes

2 pounds boiling potatoes, peeled and cut into 1-inch pieces
3 tablespoons FILIPPO BERIO® Olive Oil
6 cloves garlic, skins on
1 tablespoon lemon juice
1 tablespoon chopped fresh chives
1 tablespoon chopped fresh parsley
  Salt and freshly ground black pepper

Place potatoes in large colander; rinse under cold running water. Drain well; pat dry. In large nonstick skillet, heat olive oil over medium heat until hot. Add potatoes in a single layer. Cook, stirring and turning frequently, 10 minutes or until golden brown. Add garlic. Cover; reduce heat to low and cook very gently, shaking pan and stirring mixture occasionally, 15 to 20 minutes or until potatoes are tender when pierced with fork. Remove garlic; discard skins. In small bowl, crush garlic; stir in lemon juice. Add to potatoes; mix well. Cook 1 to 2 minutes or until heated through. Transfer to serving dish; sprinkle with chives and parsley. Season to taste with salt and pepper.

Makes 4 servings

Italian Broccoli with Tomatoes

  4 cups fresh broccoli florets
1/2 cup water
  2 medium tomatoes, cut into wedges
1/2 teaspoon Italian seasoning
1/2 teaspoon dried parsley flakes
1/4 teaspoon salt (optional)
1/8 teaspoon pepper
1/2 cup shredded mozzarella cheese

MICROWAVE DIRECTIONS
Place broccoli and water in 2-quart microwavable dish; cover. Cover and microwave at HIGH (100% power) 5 to 8 minutes or until crisp-tender. Drain. Stir in tomatoes, Italian seasoning, parsley, salt and pepper. Microwave, uncovered, at HIGH 2 to 4 minutes or until tomatoes are heated through. Sprinkle with cheese. Microwave 1 minute or until cheese is melted. *Makes 6 servings*

BBQ Corn Wheels

(Pictured at right)

4 ears corn on the cob, husked and cleaned
3 red, green or yellow bell peppers, cut into
   large chunks
3/4 cup barbecue sauce
1/2 cup honey
1/4 cup *French's®* Worcestershire Sauce
   Vegetable cooking spray

1. Cut corn into 1/2-inch slices. Alternately thread corn and pepper chunks onto four metal skewers. (Pierce tip of skewer through center of corn wheel to thread.) Combine barbecue sauce, honey and Worcestershire.

2. Coat kabobs with vegetable cooking spray. Grill kabobs on greased rack over medium heat for 5 minutes. Cook 5 minutes more until corn is tender, turning and basting with barbecue sauce mixture. Serve any extra sauce on the side with grilled hamburgers, steaks or chicken.

Makes 4 servings

Taco Potatoes

2 pounds russet or red potatoes, cut into small
   chunks
1/3 cup vegetable oil
1 package (1.0 ounce) LAWRY'S® Taco Spices
   & Seasonings

In large Ziploc® bag, place potatoes, oil and Taco Spices & Seasonings. Seal bag and shake to coat. Spray 13×9×2-inch baking dish with nonstick cooking spray. Add seasoned potatoes and bake in 400°F oven for 45 minutes, stirring after 20 minutes.

Makes 4 to 6 side dish servings

Meal Idea: Serve with your favorite burgers or sandwiches.

Variation: Cheesy Chili Potatoes: Top with 1 cup shredded cheddar cheese during last 10 minutes of baking time.

Hint: May substitute 1 package (1.48 ounces) LAWRY'S® Spices & Seasonings for Chili.

Green Beans with Toasted Pecans

(Pictured on page 44)

3 tablespoons I CAN'T BELIEVE IT'S NOT
   BUTTER!® Spread, melted
1 teaspoon sugar
1/4 teaspoon garlic powder
   Pinch ground red pepper
   Salt to taste
1/3 cup chopped pecans
1 pound green beans

In small bowl, blend I Can't Believe It's Not Butter!® Spread, sugar, garlic powder, pepper and salt.

In 12-inch nonstick skillet, heat 2 teaspoons garlic mixture over medium-high heat and cook pecans, stirring frequently, 2 minutes or until pecans are golden. Remove pecans and set aside.

In same skillet, heat remaining garlic mixture and stir in green beans. Cook, covered, over medium heat, stirring occasionally, 6 minutes or until green beans are tender. Stir in pecans.

Makes 4 servings

Vegetable-Barley Pilaf

3/4 cup chopped onion
3/4 cup chopped celery
3/4 cup sliced fresh mushrooms
1 cup water
3/4 cup sliced yellow summer squash
1/2 cup quick-cooking barley
1/2 cup sliced carrot
1/4 cup minced fresh parsley
2 teaspoons chopped fresh basil *or* 1/2 teaspoon
   dried basil
1/2 teaspoon chicken bouillon granules
1/8 teaspoon pepper

Coat large skillet with nonstick cooking spray. Add onion, celery and mushrooms; cook and stir over medium heat until vegetables are tender.

Stir in water, squash, barley, carrot, parsley, basil, bouillon and pepper. Bring to a boil over high heat. Reduce heat to medium-low. Cover and simmer 10 to 12 minutes or until barley and vegetables are tender.

Makes 4 servings

Harvard Beets

Broccoli Casserole with Crumb Topping

2 slices day-old white bread, coarsely crumbled (about 1-1/4 cups)
1/2 cup shredded mozzarella cheese (about 2 ounces)
2 tablespoons chopped fresh parsley (optional)
2 tablespoons BERTOLLI® Olive Oil
1 clove garlic, finely chopped
6 cups broccoli florets and/or cauliflowerets
1 envelope LIPTON® RECIPE SECRETS® Onion Soup Mix
1 cup water
1 large tomato, chopped

1. In small bowl, combine bread crumbs, cheese, parsley, 1 tablespoon oil and garlic; set aside.

2. In 12-inch skillet, heat remaining 1 tablespoon oil over medium heat and cook broccoli, stirring frequently, 2 minutes.

3. Stir in onion soup mix blended with water. Bring to a boil over high heat. Reduce heat to low and simmer uncovered, stirring occasionally, 8 minutes or until broccoli is almost tender. Add tomato and simmer 2 minutes.

4. Spoon vegetable mixture into 1-1/2-quart casserole; top with bread crumb mixture. Broil 1-1/2 minutes or until crumbs are golden and cheese is melted.

Makes 6 servings

Harvard Beets

(Pictured above)

2 teaspoons cornstarch
1/4 teaspoon salt (optional)
1/4 teaspoon grated orange peel
    Dash pepper
    Dash ground allspice
1 can (16 ounces) sliced beets, drained, reserving 1/3 cup liquid
2 tablespoons cider vinegar
1 tablespoon orange juice

MICROWAVE DIRECTIONS
Combine cornstarch, salt, if desired, orange peel, pepper and allspice in 1-quart microwavable dish. Blend in reserved beet liquid, vinegar and orange juice.

Microwave, uncovered, at HIGH (100% power) 1-3/4 to 2-1/2 minutes or until thickened, stirring every minute. Add beets. Microwave at HIGH 2 to 4 minutes or until beets are thoroughly heated.

Makes 4 servings

Creamed Corn

1 package (22 ounces) frozen whole kernel corn, defrosted and drained
1 cup heavy cream
1 cup milk
1/2 teaspoon LAWRY'S® Seasoned Salt
3 tablespoons sugar
    Dash white pepper
1/3 cup butter, melted
1/2 cup flour

In large saucepan, combine corn, cream, milk, Seasoned Salt, sugar and white pepper; mix thoroughly. Heat over medium just until warm. In small bowl, whisk together butter and flour. Slowly add to corn mixture, stirring constantly. Bring just to a boil; quickly reduce heat to low and cook for 7 to 10 minutes, until slightly thickened.

Makes 4 to 6 servings

Eggplant and Feta Skillet

(Pictured below)

1/4 cup olive oil
1 medium eggplant, cut into 1-inch pieces
1 medium zucchini, cut into 1/2-inch slices
1 package (16 ounces) frozen bell peppers and
    onions blend, thawed and drained
2 teaspoons minced garlic
2 cans (14-1/2 ounces each) Italian-style diced
    tomatoes, drained
1 can (2-1/4 ounces) sliced ripe olives, drained
1-1/2 cups seasoned croutons
3/4 cup feta cheese with basil and tomato,
    crumbled

1. Heat oil in large skillet over high heat until hot.

2. Add eggplant, zucchini, peppers and onions and
garlic; cook and stir 6 minutes. Add tomatoes;
simmer 3 minutes. Stir in olives.

3. Sprinkle with croutons and feta cheese.
Makes 6 servings

Curried Vegetables

1 package (7.2 ounces) RICE-A-RONI®
    Herb & Butter
1/3 cup raisins
2 tablespoons margarine or butter
1 medium onion, chopped
2 cloves garlic, minced
1 tablespoon all-purpose flour
2 teaspoons curry powder
1 package (16 ounces) frozen mixed carrot,
    broccoli and red pepper vegetable medley
1 cup water
1/2 teaspoon salt (optional)
1/4 cup slivered almonds, toasted (optional)

1. Prepare Rice-A-Roni® Mix as package directs,
adding raisins with contents of seasoning packet.

2. In 3-quart saucepan, melt margarine over medium
heat. Add onion and garlic; sauté 3 to 4 minutes. Add
flour and curry powder; cook and stir 30 seconds.

3. Add frozen vegetables, water and salt. Cover;
bring to a boil over high heat. Cover; reduce heat.
Continue cooking 10 minutes, stirring occasionally.
Serve rice topped with vegetable mixture; sprinkle
with almonds. *Makes 4 servings*

Eggplant and Feta Skillet

Zippy Oven Fries

(Pictured at right)

1 pound russet potatoes, sliced into
    1/4-inch wedges
3 tablespoons melted butter or vegetable oil
2 tablespoons *Frank's® RedHot®* Original
    Cayenne Pepper Sauce, at room temperature
2 cups *French's®* French Fried Onions, finely
    crushed
1/2 cup grated Parmesan cheese
    Zestup Ketchup (recipe follows)

1. Preheat oven to 400°F. Place potatoes, butter
and *Frank's RedHot* Sauce in large resealable
plastic bag. Seal bag and toss potatoes to coat.

2. Combine French Fried Onions and cheese on
sheet of waxed paper. Coat potatoes in crumb
mixture, pressing firmly.

3. Arrange potatoes in single layer in shallow baking
pan coated with nonstick cooking spray. Bake,
uncovered, 25 minutes or until potatoes are tender
and golden brown. Splash on more *Frank's RedHot*
Sauce or serve with Zestup Ketchup.

Makes 4 servings

Zestup Ketchup: Combine 1 cup ketchup with
1 to 2 tablespoons *Frank's RedHot* Sauce.

Almond Broccoli Stir-Fry

1 bunch (about 1 pound) broccoli
3/4 cup BLUE DIAMOND® Chopped Natural
    Almonds
3 tablespoons vegetable oil
3 cloves garlic, thinly sliced
2 tablespoons soy sauce
1 tablespoon sugar
1 teaspoon grated fresh ginger *or* 1/4 teaspoon
    ground ginger
1 teaspoon lemon juice

Cut broccoli into florets. Trim and peel stalks; cut
on diagonal into thin slices and reserve. In large
skillet or wok, cook and stir almonds in oil 1 minute.
Add broccoli and stir-fry until barely tender, about
2 minutes. Add garlic and stir-fry until just tender,
about 1 minute. Stir in soy sauce, sugar and ginger.
Continue stir-frying until sugar dissolves, about
1 minute. Stir in lemon juice. *Makes 4 servings*

Elegant Ranch Spinach

2 packages (10 ounces each) frozen chopped
    spinach
1/4 pound fresh mushrooms, sliced
1/4 cup butter or margarine
2 cups prepared HIDDEN VALLEY®
    The Original Ranch® Dressing
1/2 cup grated Parmesan cheese
1 can (14 ounces) quartered artichoke hearts,
    drained

Preheat oven to 350°F. Cook spinach according to
package directions; drain thoroughly, squeezing out
excess liquid. In skillet, sauté mushrooms in butter
until softened, about 5 minutes. In large bowl, whisk
together salad dressing and cheese; stir in spinach,
mushrooms and artichoke hearts. Pour mixture into
lightly buttered 2-quart casserole. Cover and bake
until heated through, 20 to 30 minutes.

Makes 6 servings

Corn Bread Stuffing with Sausage and Apple

(Pictured on page 44)

1/3 cup chopped pecans
1 pound bulk pork sausage
1 large Jonathan apple, coarsely chopped
1-1/3 cups chicken broth
1/4 cup apple juice
1 package (6 ounces) seasoned corn bread
    stuffing mix

Preheat oven to 300°F. Place pecans in shallow
baking pan. Bake 6 to 8 minutes or until lightly
browned, stirring frequently.

Crumble sausage into large skillet; cook and stir
over high heat 10 minutes or until meat is no
longer pink. Drain off drippings.

Place apple in large saucepan. Stir in broth, apple
juice and contents of seasoning packet from stuffing
mix. Bring to a boil over high heat. Remove from
heat; stir in stuffing mix. Cover and let stand 3 to
5 minutes or until stuffing is moist and tender.
Stir in sausage. Transfer stuffing to serving bowl;
sprinkle with pecans. *Makes 4 servings*

Golden Apples and Yams

2 large yams or sweet potatoes
2 Washington Golden Delicious apples,
 cored and sliced crosswise into rings
1/4 cup firmly packed brown sugar
1 teaspoon cornstarch
1/8 teaspoon ground cloves
1/2 cup orange juice
2 tablespoons chopped pecans or walnuts

Heat oven to 400°F. Bake yams 50 minutes or until soft but still hold their shape. (This can also be done in microwave.) Let yams cool enough to handle. *Reduce oven to 350°F.*

Peel and slice yams crosswise. In shallow 1-quart baking dish, alternate apple rings and yam slices, overlapping edges slightly. In small saucepan, combine sugar, cornstarch and cloves; stir in orange juice and mix well. Heat orange juice mixture over medium heat, stirring, until thickened; pour over apples and yams. Sprinkle with nuts; bake 20 minutes or until apples and yams are tender.

Makes 6 servings

Favorite recipe from **Washington Apple Commission**

Bow Tie Zucchini

1/4 cup vegetable oil
1 cup chopped onion
2 garlic cloves, minced
5 small zucchini, cut into thin strips
2/3 cup heavy whipping cream
1 package (16 ounces) bow tie pasta, cooked
 and drained
3 tablespoons grated Parmesan cheese
 Salt and pepper

Preheat oven to 350°F.

Heat oil in large skillet over medium-high heat. Add onion and garlic; cook and stir until onion is tender. Add zucchini; cook and stir until tender.

Add cream; cook and stir until thickened. Add pasta and cheese to skillet. Season with salt and pepper to taste. Transfer mixture to 2-quart casserole. Cover and bake 15 minutes or until heated through.

Makes 8 servings

Stuffed Tomatoes

(Pictured at right)

3 large ripe red tomatoes, cored
 Salt
2 tablespoons olive oil, divided
1 pound BOB EVANS® Italian Roll Sausage
1 cup chopped green bell pepper
1/2 medium onion, finely chopped
2 cloves garlic, minced
1/2 cup hot milk
1 cup dried bread crumbs
1 egg, beaten
4 tablespoons chopped fresh parsley, divided
1 teaspoon dried basil leaves
1 teaspoon dried oregano leaves
 Black pepper to taste
1 cup (4 ounces) shredded mozzarella cheese
1/4 cup grated Parmesan cheese

With core side up, cut each tomato in half horizontally; remove seeds. Sprinkle interior of tomatoes lightly with salt to help remove moisture. Place tomato halves, cut sides down, on paper towels to drain about 15 minutes.

Preheat oven to 350°F. Grease baking dish with 1 tablespoon olive oil. Heat remaining tablespoon olive oil in large skillet over medium heat. Add tomato halves and cook 4 minutes on each side. Remove tomatoes from skillet and place, cut sides up, in prepared baking dish. Crumble sausage into same skillet. Add bell pepper, onion and garlic; cook until sausage is browned and onion is tender. Transfer sausage mixture to bowl with slotted spoon. Stir in milk and bread crumbs; let cool slightly. Add egg, 2 tablespoons parsley, basil and oregano. Season with salt and pepper to taste. Divide mixture evenly among tomato halves; bake 10 minutes. Remove from oven; sprinkle with mozzarella cheese. Top with Parmesan cheese. Place tomatoes under broiler until cheese is melted and golden brown. Garnish with remaining 2 tablespoons parsley and serve hot. Refrigerate leftovers.   *Makes 6 side-dish servings*

Helpful Hint

Firm, underripe tomatoes can be placed, stem sides down, in a warm, sunny spot for a few days. They will soften and improve in flavor.

Mediterranean-Style Roasted Vegetables

(Pictured at right)

- 1-1/2 pounds red potatoes
- 2 tablespoons olive oil, divided
- 1 red bell pepper
- 1 yellow or orange bell pepper
- 1 small red onion
- 2 garlic cloves, minced
- 1/2 teaspoon salt
- 1/4 teaspoon black pepper
- 1 tablespoon balsamic vinegar
- 1/4 cup minced fresh basil leaves

1. Preheat oven to 425°F. Spray large shallow roasting pan with nonstick cooking spray. Cut potatoes into 1-1/2-inch chunks; place in pan. Drizzle with 1 tablespoon oil; toss to coat. Bake 10 minutes.

2. Cut bell peppers into 1-1/2-inch chunks. Cut onion into 1/2-inch wedges. Add bell peppers and onion to pan. Drizzle with remaining 1 tablespoon oil; sprinkle with garlic, salt and black pepper. Toss well to coat. Return to oven; bake 18 to 20 minutes or until vegetables are browned and tender, stirring once.

3. Transfer to large serving bowl. Drizzle with vinegar; toss to coat. Add basil; toss again. Serve warm or at room temperature with additional pepper, if desired. *Makes 6 servings*

Campbell's® Ham & Cheese Hash Browns

- 1 tablespoon margarine *or* butter
- 1/2 cup chopped cooked ham
- 1 medium onion, sliced (about 1/2 cup)
- 1/4 cup diced green *or* sweet red pepper
- 1 can (10-3/4 ounces) CAMPBELL'S® Condensed Cheddar Cheese Soup *or* Condensed Broccoli Cheese Soup
- 1/2 cup milk
- 1 teaspoon prepared mustard
- 4 cups frozen diced potatoes (hash browns)

1. In medium skillet over medium heat, heat margarine. Add ham, onion and pepper and cook until vegetables are tender-crisp.

2. Add soup, milk, mustard and potatoes. Heat to a boil. Reduce heat to low. Cover and cook 10 minutes or until potatoes are tender, stirring often. *Makes 6 servings*

Tip: These creamy hash browns make a delicious dinner side dish with ham, beef or chicken!

Vegetable Stew Medley

- 2 tablespoons CRISCO® Oil*
- 4 medium onions, thinly sliced and separated into rings
- 3 medium green bell peppers, cut into strips
- 2 cloves garlic, minced
- 4 medium zucchini, cut into 1/2-inch pieces
- 1 medium eggplant, cut into 1/2-inch pieces (about 1 pound)
- 1 can (14-1/2 ounces) no-salt-added whole tomatoes, drained and chopped, *or* 4 or 5 fresh tomatoes, peeled and quartered
- 1 teaspoon dried dill weed
- 3/4 teaspoon dried basil leaves
- 1/2 teaspoon dried oregano leaves
- 1/2 teaspoon black pepper
- 1/4 teaspoon salt
- 1 package (9 ounces) frozen peas
- 1/4 cup lemon juice
- 2 tablespoons chopped fresh parsley *or* 2 teaspoons dried parsley

Use your favorite Crisco Oil product.

1. Heat oil in Dutch oven (non-reactive or non-cast iron) on medium heat. Add onions, bell peppers and garlic. Cook and stir until tender.

2. Add zucchini and eggplant. Cook 5 minutes, stirring occasionally. Stir in tomatoes, dill weed, basil, oregano, black pepper and salt. Reduce heat to low. Cover. Simmer 20 minutes, stirring occasionally.

3. Stir in peas. Simmer 3 to 5 minutes or until peas are thawed and heated, stirring occasionally. Stir in lemon juice. Serve hot or chilled sprinkled with parsley. *Makes 12 servings*

Mediterranean-Style Roasted Vegetables

Oniony Corn Spoonbread

1 can (14-3/4 ounces) cream-style corn
1 can (11 ounces) Mexican-style corn
1 cup sour cream
1 package (6-1/2 to 8-1/2 ounces) corn
    muffin mix
1/2 cup diced red and green bell pepper
2 tablespoons butter or margarine, melted
1 large egg
1-1/3 cups *French's*® French Fried Onions, divided
1/2 cup (2 ounces) shredded Cheddar cheese
    Garnish: red bell pepper and chopped parsley
    (optional)

1. Preheat oven to 350°F. Combine corn, sour cream, corn muffin mix, bell peppers, butter, egg and *2/3 cup* French Fried Onions. Pour mixture into greased shallow 2-quart baking dish.

2. Bake 40 minutes or until set. Top with cheese and remaining onions; bake 5 minutes or until onions are golden. Garnish with bell pepper and parsley, if desired. *Makes 8 servings*

Variation: For added Cheddar flavor, substitute *French's*® **Cheddar French Fried Onions** for the original flavor.

Easy Fried Rice

(Pictured at right)

1/4 cup BERTOLLI® Olive Oil
4 cups cooked rice
2 cloves garlic, finely chopped
1 envelope LIPTON® RECIPE SECRETS®
    Onion Mushroom Soup Mix
1/2 cup water
1 tablespoon soy sauce
1 cup frozen peas and carrots, partially thawed
2 eggs, lightly beaten

1. In 12-inch nonstick skillet, heat oil over medium-high heat and cook rice, stirring constantly, 2 minutes or until rice is heated through. Stir in garlic.

2. Stir in soup mix blended with water and soy sauce and cook 1 minute. Stir in peas and carrots and cook 2 minutes or until heated through.

3. Make a well in center of rice and quickly stir in eggs until cooked. *Makes 4 servings*

Savory Apple Roast

2 baking apples
2 sweet potatoes
2 Vidalia onions
1 tablespoon olive oil
2 teaspoons chopped garlic
1 tablespoon balsamic vinegar

Preheat oven to 450°F. Line roasting pan with aluminum foil. Core and cut apples into quarters. Cut sweet potatoes into 6 to 8 large pieces. Cut onions into small wedges. Combine apples, vegetables, oil and garlic; toss to coat. Bake in prepared pan 40 to 45 minutes or until sweet potatoes are tender. Sprinkle with balsamic vinegar before serving. Serve hot or cold.
Makes 6 servings

Favorite recipe from **New York Apple Association, Inc.**

Brussels Sprouts with Lemon-Dill Glaze

1 pound brussels sprouts *
2 teaspoons cornstarch
1/2 teaspoon dill weed
1/2 cup chicken broth
3 tablespoons lemon juice
1/2 teaspoon grated lemon peel

*Or, substitute 1 package (10 ounces) frozen brussels sprouts for fresh brussels sprouts. Cook according to package directions; drain.

Trim brussels sprouts. Cut an X in stem ends. Bring 1 cup water to a boil in large saucepan over high heat. Add brussels sprouts; return to a boil. Reduce heat to medium-low. Simmer, covered, 10 minutes or until just tender. Drain well; return to pan. Set aside.

Meanwhile, combine cornstarch and dill weed in small saucepan. Blend in broth and lemon juice until smooth. Stir in lemon peel. Cook and stir over medium heat 5 minutes or until mixture boils and thickens. Cook and stir 1 minute more.

Pour glaze over brussels sprouts; toss gently to coat. Serve hot. *Makes 4 servings*

Glazed Maple Acorn Squash

(Pictured at right)

> 1 large acorn squash
> 1/4 cup water
> 2 tablespoons maple syrup
> 1 tablespoon butter or margarine, melted
> 1/4 teaspoon ground cinnamon

Preheat oven to 375°F.

Cut stem and blossom ends from squash. Cut squash widthwise into four equal slices. Discard seeds and membrane. Place water in 13×9-inch baking dish. Arrange squash in dish; cover with foil. Bake 30 minutes or until tender.

Combine syrup, butter and cinnamon in small bowl; mix well. Uncover squash; carefully pour off water. Brush squash with syrup mixture, letting excess pool in center of squash.

Return to oven; bake 10 minutes or until syrup mixture is bubbly. *Makes 4 servings*

Mexican Rice

(Pictured on page 44)

> 2 tablespoons butter or margarine
> 1 cup long-grain white rice*
> 1/2 cup chopped onion
> 2 cloves garlic, finely chopped
> 1 jar (16 ounces) ORTEGA® Salsa
>   Thick & Chunky
> 1-1/4 cups water*
> 3/4 cup (1 large) peeled, shredded carrot
> 1/2 cup frozen peas, thawed (optional)

For a quick-cook Mexican Rice, use 4 cups instant rice instead of 1 cup long-grain white rice, and 2-1/2 cups water instead of 1-1/4 cups water. After salsa mixture comes to a boil, cook for a length of time recommended on instant rice package.

MELT butter in large saucepan over medium heat. Add rice, onion and garlic; cook, stirring occasionally, for 3 to 4 minutes or until rice is golden. Stir in salsa, water, carrot and peas. Bring to a boil. Reduce heat to low; cook, covered, for 25 to 30 minutes or until liquid is absorbed and rice is tender.

Makes 8 servings

Tip: Serve this traditional side dish to complete any Mexican meal.

Sweet Potato Gratin

> 3 pounds sweet potatoes (about 5 large)
> 1/2 cup butter or margarine, divided
> 2 tablespoons plus 1/4 cup brown sugar, divided
> 2 eggs
> 2/3 cup orange juice
> 2 teaspoons ground cinnamon, divided
> 1/2 teaspoon salt
> 1/4 teaspoon ground nutmeg
> 1/3 cup all-purpose flour
> 1/4 cup old-fashioned oats
> 1/3 cup chopped pecans or walnuts

Preheat oven to 350°F. Bake sweet potatoes about 1 hour or until tender. Or, pierce sweet potatoes several times with fork and place on microwavable plate. Microwave, uncovered, at HIGH (100%) 16 to 18 minutes, rotating and turning potatoes after 9 minutes. Let stand 5 minutes.

Cut hot sweet potatoes lengthwise into halves. Scoop out hot pulp from skins into large mixing bowl.

Beat 1/4 cup butter and 2 tablespoons brown sugar into sweet potatoes with electric mixer at medium speed until butter is melted. Add eggs, orange juice, 1-1/2 teaspoons cinnamon, salt and nutmeg. Beat until smooth. Pour mixture into greased 1-1/2-quart baking dish or gratin dish; smooth top.

For topping, combine flour, oats, remaining 1/4 cup brown sugar and 1/2 teaspoon cinnamon in medium bowl. Cut in remaining 1/4 cup butter until mixture resembles coarse crumbs. Stir in pecans. Sprinkle topping over sweet potatoes.*

Bake, uncovered, 25 to 30 minutes or until heated through. *Makes 6 to 8 servings*

At this point, Sweet Potato Gratin may be covered and refrigerated up to 1 day. Let stand at room temperature 1 hour before baking.

Helpful Hint

Sweet potatoes should be handled gently since their skins are very thin. Store them in a cool, dry, dark place. They will keep for up to two weeks at room temperature or up to one month at about 55°F.

Glazed Maple Acorn Squash

Soups

Tuna Minestrone with Parmesan Cheese

(Pictured at left)

2 cans (14-1/2 ounces *each*) chicken broth *plus* water
    to equal 4 cups
1 can (14-1/2 ounces) ready-cut Italian-style tomatoes,
    undrained
1 can (15-1/4 ounces) kidney beans, drained
1/4 cup tomato paste
1 teaspoon Italian herb seasoning
1/2 teaspoon salt
1/8 teaspoon ground red pepper
1/2 cup uncooked small shell pasta
2 cups Italian-style frozen vegetables (zucchini, carrots,
    cauliflower, Italian green beans, lima beans)
1 (7-ounce) pouch of STARKIST® Premium Albacore Tuna
3 cups fresh romaine lettuce, cut crosswise into 1-inch
    strips
Freshly grated Parmesan cheese

In 4-quart saucepan, combine chicken broth mixture, tomatoes with liquid, kidney beans, tomato paste, herb seasoning, salt and red pepper; bring to a boil over high heat. Add pasta and frozen vegetables; simmer 8 minutes. Remove from heat; add tuna and romaine. Serve with cheese.

Makes 6 to 8 servings

Helpful Hint

Romaine lettuce has elongated heads with dark green outer leaves and lighter, more tender hearts. The leaves are crisp and sturdy, making them a good choice for soups.

Clockwise from top left: Albacore Corn Chowder (p. 72), Chili Corn Soup (p. 76), Thai Noodle Soup (p. 70) and Tuna Minestrone with Parmesan Cheese

Aztec Corn Soup

(Pictured at right)

2 packages (10 ounces each) frozen
　　whole kernel corn
3-1/2 cups chicken broth
1/4 teaspoon salt
1 large tomato, peeled and seeded
1/4 cup coarsely chopped onion
1/2 teaspoon dried oregano leaves
2 tablespoons butter or margarine
1/2 cup heavy whipping cream
　　Green pepper strips (optional)

Combine corn, broth and salt in 3-quart saucepan. Bring to a boil over high heat. Reduce heat to low. Cover and simmer 4 to 5 minutes until corn is tender. Remove 1/2 cup corn from saucepan with slotted spoon; set aside. Process remaining soup until smooth, half at a time, in blender. Return soup to saucepan.

Process tomato, onion and oregano in blender until smooth. Heat butter over medium heat until hot; add tomato mixture. Cook and stir 4 to 5 minutes or until thickened.

Add tomato mixture to corn mixture in saucepan; bring to a boil over high heat. Reduce heat to low; simmer uncovered, 5 minutes.

Remove soup from heat; gradually stir in cream. Heat over very low heat 30 seconds or just until hot. Do not boil. Ladle into bowls. Garnish with reserved corn and green pepper.　　*Makes 4 to 6 servings*

Curried Carrot Soup

2 tablespoons vegetable oil
1 cup chopped onion (1 large)
1-1/2 teaspoons curry powder
3-1/2 cups low-sodium chicken broth
1 pound carrots, peeled and sliced (4 cups)
2 stalks celery, sliced (1 cup)
1 bay leaf
1/2 teaspoon ground cumin
1/2 teaspoon TABASCO® brand Pepper Sauce
1 tablespoon cornstarch
2 cups plain yogurt

Heat oil in large saucepan over medium-high heat. Add onion and curry powder; cook 3 to 5 minutes or until onion is translucent.

Reduce heat to low. Add chicken broth, carrots, celery, bay leaf, cumin and TABASCO® Sauce; mix well. Heat to boiling; reduce heat and simmer 25 minutes or until vegetables are tender. Remove bay leaf.

Spoon mixture in several batches into blender or food processor; blend until smooth. Add cornstarch to yogurt in small bowl and stir until well blended.

Gradually add yogurt to soup mixture, stirring after each addition. Serve with additional TABASCO® Sauce, if desired.　　*Makes 6 servings*

Pork and Cabbage Soup

1/2 pound pork loin, cut into 1/2-inch cubes
1 medium onion, chopped
2 strips bacon, finely chopped
2 cups canned chicken broth
2 cups canned beef broth
1 can (28 ounces) tomatoes, cut-up, drained
2 medium carrots, sliced
3/4 teaspoon dried marjoram
1 bay leaf
1/8 teaspoon black pepper
1/4 medium cabbage, chopped
2 tablespoons chopped fresh parsley, plus
　　additional parsley for garnish

Cook and stir pork, onion and bacon in 5-quart Dutch oven over medium heat until meat loses its pink color and onion is slightly tender. Remove from heat. Drain fat.

Stir in chicken and beef broth. Add tomatoes to pork mixture. Add carrots, marjoram, bay leaf and pepper. Bring to a boil over high heat. Reduce heat to medium-low; simmer, uncovered, about 30 minutes. Discard bay leaf. Skim off fat.

Stir cabbage into soup. Bring to a boil over high heat. Reduce heat to medium-low; simmer, uncovered, about 15 minutes or until cabbage is tender.

Remove soup from heat; stir in 2 tablespoons parsley. Ladle into bowls. Garnish each serving with additional parsley.　　*Makes 6 servings*

Quick Tuscan Bean, Tomato and Spinach Soup

(Pictured at right)

2 cans (14-1/2 ounces each) diced tomatoes
    with onions, undrained
1 can (14-1/2 ounces) chicken broth
2 teaspoons sugar
2 teaspoons dried basil leaves
3/4 teaspoon Worcestershire sauce
1 can (15 ounces) small white beans, rinsed and
    drained
3 ounces fresh baby spinach leaves or chopped
    spinach leaves, stems removed
2 teaspoons olive oil

Combine tomatoes with juice, chicken broth, sugar, basil and Worcestershire sauce in Dutch oven or large saucepan; bring to a boil over high heat. Reduce heat and simmer, uncovered, 10 minutes.

Stir in beans and spinach; cook 5 minutes longer or until spinach is tender.

Remove from heat; stir in oil just before serving.
Makes 4 (1-1/2-cup) servings

Thai Noodle Soup

(Pictured on page 66)

1 package (3 ounces) ramen noodles
3/4 pound chicken tenders
2 cans (about 14 ounces each) chicken broth
1/4 cup shredded carrot
1/4 cup frozen snow peas
2 tablespoons thinly sliced green onion tops
1/2 teaspoon minced garlic
1/4 teaspoon ground ginger
3 tablespoons chopped fresh cilantro
1/2 lime, cut into 4 wedges

Break noodles into pieces. Cook noodles according to package directions, discarding flavor packet. Drain and set aside.

Cut chicken tenders into 1/2-inch pieces. Combine broth and chicken tenders in large saucepan or Dutch oven; bring to a boil over medium heat. Cook 2 minutes.

Add carrot, snow peas, green onion tops, garlic and ginger. Reduce heat to low; simmer 3 minutes. Add cooked noodles and cilantro; heat through. Serve soup with lime wedges. *Makes 4 servings*

Grandma's Chicken Soup

8 chicken thighs, skinned, fat trimmed
2 carrots, cut into 1/4-inch slices
2 ribs celery, cut into 1/4-inch slices
2 medium turnips, peeled and cubed
1 large onion, chopped
8 cups water
1-1/2 teaspoons salt
1/4 teaspoon pepper
1/4 teaspoon poultry seasoning
1/8 teaspoon dried thyme leaves
1 cup wide egg noodles, uncooked

In large saucepan or Dutch oven, layer chicken, carrots, celery, turnips and onion. Add water, salt, pepper, poultry seasoning and thyme. Cook, covered, over medium heat until liquid boils. Reduce heat; cover and simmer about 45 minutes or until chicken and vegetables are fork-tender. Remove chicken; cool. Separate meat from bones; discard bones. Cut chicken into bite-size pieces. Heat soup mixture to boiling; stir in noodles. Cook, uncovered, about 5 to 7 minutes or until noodles are done. Stir in chicken. *Makes 8 servings*

Favorite recipe from **Delmarva Poultry Industry, Inc.**

Dutch Potage

2 medium potatoes, peeled and diced
1 medium onion, chopped
1-1/2 cups thinly sliced carrots
1 quart water
1/4 teaspoon black pepper
1/2 cup prepared HIDDEN VALLEY®
    The Original Ranch® Dressing
Salt, to taste

In large saucepan, combine vegetables, water and pepper. Bring to boil; cover and cook over medium heat until vegetables are tender, about 15 minutes. Drain vegetables, reserving liquid. In blender, purée vegetables with 1 cup reserved liquid until smooth. Return purée and remaining liquid to pan; add salad dressing and salt. Cook until heated through. Serve hot. Spoon additional salad dressing into center of each serving. *Makes 4 to 6 servings*

*Quick Tuscan Bean, Tomato and
Spinach Soup*

Velveeta® Cheesy Broccoli Soup

Velveeta® Cheesy Broccoli Soup

(Pictured above)

1/4 cup chopped onion
1 tablespoon butter or margarine
1-1/2 cups milk
3/4 pound (12 ounces) VELVEETA® Pasteurized
    Prepared Cheese Product, cut up
1 package (10 ounces) frozen chopped broccoli,
    thawed, drained
Dash pepper

1. Cook and stir onion in butter in large saucepan on medium-high heat until tender.

2. Add remaining ingredients; stir on low heat until VELVEETA is melted and soup is thoroughly heated.
Makes 4 (3/4-cup) servings

Use Your Microwave: Microwave onion and butter in 2-quart microwaveable casserole or bowl on HIGH 30 seconds to 1 minute or until onion is tender. Add remaining ingredients; mix well. Microwave 6 to 8 minutes or until VELVEETA is melted and soup is thoroughly heated, stirring every 3 minutes.

Albacore Corn Chowder

(Pictured on page 66)

2 tablespoons butter or margarine
1/2 cup sliced celery
1/2 cup chopped onion
3/4 cup chopped carrot
2 to 3 tablespoons flour
1 teaspoon dried thyme or Italian seasoning
1 can (17 ounces) cream-style corn
2 cups milk
1 (7-ounce) pouch of STARKIST® Premium
    Albacore Tuna
1 cup water
1 teaspoon chicken flavor instant bouillon

In medium saucepan, melt butter over medium heat; sauté celery, onion and carrot about 3 minutes. Add flour and thyme; blend well. Cook 3 more minutes. Add corn, milk, tuna, water and bouillon, stirring to blend. Cover and simmer (do not boil) 5 minutes to heat through, stirring occasionally.
Makes 4 servings

Seafood Gumbo

1/2 cup chopped onion
1/2 cup chopped green bell pepper
1/2 cup (about 2 ounces) sliced fresh mushrooms
1 clove garlic, minced
2 tablespoons butter or margarine
1 can (28 ounces) whole tomatoes, undrained
2 cups chicken broth
1/2 to 3/4 teaspoon ground red pepper
1/2 teaspoon dried thyme leaves
1/2 teaspoon dried basil leaves
1 package (10 ounces) frozen cut okra, thawed
3/4 pound white fish, cut into 1-inch pieces
1/2 pound peeled, deveined shrimp
3 cups hot cooked rice

Cook onion, green pepper, mushrooms and garlic in butter in large saucepan or Dutch oven over medium-high heat until crisp-tender. Stir in tomatoes and juice, broth, red pepper, thyme and basil. Bring to a boil. Reduce heat; simmer, uncovered, 10 to 15 minutes. Stir in okra, fish and shrimp; simmer until fish flakes with fork, 5 to 8 minutes. Serve rice on top of gumbo.
Makes 6 servings

Favorite recipe from **USA Rice Federation**

Chicken and Wild Rice Soup

(Pictured below)

3 cans (14-1/2 ounces each) chicken broth
1 pound boneless skinless chicken breasts or
    thighs, cut into bite-size pieces
1 package (6 ounces) converted long grain
    and wild rice mix with seasoning packet
2 cups water
1 cup sliced celery
1 cup diced carrots
1/2 cup chopped onion
1 tablespoon dried parsley flakes
1/2 teaspoon pepper

SLOW COOKER DIRECTIONS
Combine all ingredients in slow cooker; mix well.
Cover; cook on LOW 6 to 7 hours or on HIGH 4 to
5 hours.   *Makes 9 (1-1/2 cups) servings*

Note: Make sure the rice mix you use contains
converted rice, not quick-cooking or instant.

Zesty Black-Eyed Pea Soup

4 strips bacon, chopped
1 cup chopped onion
2 cloves garlic, minced
2 cans (15-1/2 ounces *each*) black-eyed peas,
    undrained
1 can (14-1/2 ounces) chicken broth
3 tablespoons *Frank's® RedHot®* Original
    Cayenne Pepper Sauce
1 teaspoon dried thyme leaves

1. Cook and stir bacon in large saucepan over
medium-high heat 5 minutes or until crisp. Transfer
to dish. Add onion and garlic to saucepan; cook and
stir 3 minutes or until tender.

2. Stir in remaining ingredients. Add *1/2 cup water.*
Heat to boiling. Reduce heat to medium-low. Cook
15 minutes, stirring occasionally. Sprinkle reserved
bacon on top of soup before serving. Serve with hot
cooked rice tossed with minced parsley, if desired.
           Makes 6 (1-cup) servings

Chicken and Wild Rice Soup

Hearty Vegetable Pasta Soup
(Pictured at right)

- 1 tablespoon vegetable oil
- 1 small onion, chopped
- 3 cups canned chicken broth
- 1 can (14-1/2 ounces) tomatoes, cut-up, undrained
- 1 medium potato, unpeeled and cubed
- 2 carrots, sliced
- 1 rib celery, sliced
- 1 teaspoon dried basil leaves, crushed
- 1/2 teaspoon salt
- 1/8 teaspoon black pepper
- 1/3 cup uncooked tiny bow-tie pasta
- 2 ounces fresh spinach, washed and stemmed

Heat oil in Dutch oven over medium-high heat. Cook and stir onion until crisp-tender and translucent. Add broth, tomatoes, potato, carrots, celery, basil, salt and pepper to Dutch oven. Bring to a boil over high heat. Reduce heat to medium-low; simmer, uncovered, 20 minutes or until carrots and potato are very tender and flavors are blended, stirring occasionally.

Add pasta to soup; simmer, uncovered, 8 minutes or until pasta is tender.

Meanwhile, coarsely chop spinach leaves. Stir spinach into soup. Simmer, uncovered, 2 minutes or until spinach is wilted. Serve immediately.
Makes 6 servings

Creamy Tomato Bisque

- 1/2 cup chopped onion
- 1/2 cup chopped celery
- 1 large garlic clove, crushed
- 3 tablespoons butter
- 1/4 cup all-purpose flour
- 3/4 teaspoon basil leaves
- 1/2 teaspoon marjoram leaves
- 1/2 teaspoon salt
- 1/8 teaspoon white pepper
- 1 can (28 ounces) CONTADINA® Recipe Ready Crushed Tomatoes
- 1 can (10.5 ounces) chicken broth
- 3/4 cup water
- 1 cup milk, divided

1. Sauté onion, celery and garlic in butter in medium saucepan. Stir in flour and seasonings.

2. Stir in tomatoes, chicken broth and water. Heat to boiling.

3. Reduce heat and boil gently, uncovered, 30 minutes.

4. Pour half of tomato mixture and half of milk into blender container. Process until blended. Repeat with remaining soup and milk. Serve warm or cold.
Makes 6-1/2 cups

Microwave Directions: Combine onion, celery, garlic and butter in 2-quart microwave-safe casserole. Cover loosely. Microwave on HIGH (100%) power for 5 minutes. Mix in flour and seasonings. Stir in tomatoes and juice, chicken broth and water. Cover again and microwave on HIGH (100%) power for 15 minutes, stirring halfway through cooking time. Process in blender as above.

Lentil and Brown Rice Soup

- 1 envelope LIPTON® RECIPE SECRETS® Onion Recipe Soup Mix*
- 4 cups water
- 3/4 cup lentils, rinsed and drained
- 1/2 cup uncooked brown or regular rice
- 1 can (14-1/2 ounces) whole peeled tomatoes, undrained and coarsely chopped
- 1 medium carrot, coarsely chopped
- 1 large stalk celery, coarsely chopped
- 1/2 teaspoon dried basil leaves
- 1/2 teaspoon dried oregano leaves
- 1/4 teaspoon dried thyme leaves (optional)
- 1 tablespoon finely chopped fresh parsley
- 1 tablespoon apple cider vinegar
- 1/4 teaspoon pepper

Also terrific with LIPTON® RECIPE SECRETS® Beefy Onion or Beefy Mushroom Recipe Soup Mix.

In large saucepan or stockpot, combine onion recipe soup mix, water, lentils, uncooked rice, tomatoes with liquid, carrot, celery, basil, oregano and thyme. Bring to a boil, then simmer covered, stirring occasionally, 45 minutes or until lentils and rice are tender. Stir in remaining ingredients.
Makes about 3 (2-cup) servings

Hearty Vegetable Pasta Soup

Sausage & Zucchini Soup

(Pictured at right)

1 pound BOB EVANS® Italian Roll Sausage
1 medium onion, diced
1 (28-ounce) can stewed tomatoes
2 (14-ounce) cans beef broth
2 medium zucchini, diced or sliced
    (about 2 cups)
2 small carrots, diced
2 stalks celery, diced
4 large mushrooms, sliced
    Grated Parmesan cheese for garnish

Crumble and cook sausage and onion in large saucepan over medium heat until sausage is browned. Drain off any drippings. Add remaining ingredients except cheese; simmer, uncovered, over low heat about 40 minutes or until vegetables are tender. Garnish with cheese. Refrigerate leftovers.

Makes 8 servings

1-2-3 Steak Soup

1 pound boneless beef sirloin steak, cut into
    1-inch cubes
1 tablespoon vegetable oil
1/2 pound sliced mushrooms (about 2-1/2 cups)
2 cups *French's*® French Fried Onions, divided
1 package (16 ounces) frozen vegetables for
    stew (potatoes, carrots, celery and pearl
    onions)
2 cans (14-1/2 ounces each) beef broth
1 can (8 ounces) tomato sauce
1 tablespoon *French's*® Worcestershire Sauce
    Garnish: chopped parsley (optional)

1. Cook beef in hot oil in large saucepan over medium heat until browned, stirring frequently. Remove beef from pan; set aside.

2. Sauté mushrooms and *2/3 cup* French Fried Onions in drippings in same pan over medium heat until golden, stirring occasionally. Stir in vegetables, broth, tomato sauce and Worcestershire. Return beef to pan.

3. Heat to a boil over high heat; reduce heat to low. Cover and simmer 20 minutes or until vegetables are tender, stirring occasionally. Spoon soup into serving bowls; top with remaining onions. Garnish with chopped parsley, if desired.

Makes 8 servings

Chili Corn Soup

(Pictured on page 66)

2 tablespoons vegetable oil
2 medium potatoes, diced
1 medium onion, diced
1 tablespoon chili powder
1 (16-ounce) can red kidney beans, drained
    and rinsed
1 (15-1/4-ounce) can corn, drained
1 (13-3/4-ounce) can chicken broth
1-1/2 teaspoons TABASCO® brand Pepper Sauce
1 teaspoon salt

Heat oil in 4-quart saucepan over medium heat. Add potatoes and onion; cook about 5 minutes, stirring occasionally. Add chili powder; cook 1 minute, stirring frequently.

Stir in beans, corn, chicken broth, TABASCO® Sauce and salt. Heat to boiling over high heat. Reduce heat to low; cover and simmer 15 to 20 minutes or until potatoes are tender, stirring occasionally.

Makes 6 servings

Dilled Vichyssoise

1 cup chopped leeks
1 large potato, peeled and cubed
1/4 cup finely chopped green onions
2 cloves garlic, minced
2 teaspoons sugar
3 cups chicken broth
1 cup water
3/4 cup 2% milk
2 tablespoons fresh dill, chopped finely

Place leeks, potato, green onions, garlic and sugar in large saucepan. Add chicken broth and water; simmer over medium heat 15 to 20 minutes or until potatoes are very tender. Remove from heat; purée soup in food processor or blender in batches. Stir in milk and dill. Cover and refrigerate at least 3 hours before serving. *Makes 6 servings*

Favorite recipe from **The Sugar Association, Inc.**

Italian Bow Tie Vegetable Soup

3 cans (14-1/2 ounces each) chicken broth
1 can (14-1/2 ounces) Italian-style or regular
    stewed tomatoes
1/2 teaspoon Italian seasoning
1-1/2 cups (4 ounces) uncooked bow tie pasta
    (farfalle)
1 package (about 1 pound) small frozen
    precooked meatballs
1 medium zucchini, cut into 1/4-inch slices
1/2 cup diced red or green bell pepper
1-1/2 cups *French's*® French Fried Onions

1. Combine broth, tomatoes and Italian seasoning in
large saucepan. Bring to a boil.

2. Stir in pasta, meatballs, zucchini and bell pepper.
Simmer for 12 minutes or until pasta is cooked
al dente and meatballs are heated through, stirring
occasionally. Spoon soup into serving bowls; top
with French Fried Onions.   *Makes 6 servings*

Potato-Bacon Soup

(Pictured at right)

2 cans (about 14 ounces each) chicken broth
3 russet potatoes (1-3/4 to 2 pounds), peeled
    and cut into 1/2-inch cubes
1 medium onion, finely chopped
1 teaspoon dried thyme
4 to 6 strips bacon (4 to 6 ounces), chopped
1/2 cup (2 ounces) shredded Cheddar cheese

1. Combine broth, potatoes, onion and thyme in
Dutch oven; bring to a boil over high heat. Reduce
heat to medium-high and boil 10 minutes or until
potatoes are tender.

2. While potatoes are cooking, place bacon in
microwavable container. Cover with paper towels
and cook on HIGH (100%) 6 to 7 minutes or until
bacon is crisp, stirring after 3 minutes.

3. Immediately transfer bacon to broth mixture;
simmer 3 to 5 minutes. Season to taste with salt and
pepper. Ladle into bowls and sprinkle with cheese.
          Makes 4 servings

Tip: Instead of using a knife to chop the bacon, try
snipping it with a pair of kitchen scissors while it is
partially frozen—you'll find this method quicker and
easier.

Milan Chickpea Soup

1 can (6 ounces) CONTADINA® Tomato Paste
4 cups water or chicken broth
2 cans (15 ounces each) chickpeas or garbanzo
    beans, undrained
1/2 pound mild Italian sausage, casing removed,
    sliced 1/2 inch thick
1 cup sliced fresh mushrooms
1 cup chopped onion
1-1/2 teaspoons salt
1/4 teaspoon ground black pepper
1/4 teaspoon marjoram
2 teaspoons grated Parmesan cheese

1. Combine tomato paste and water in large
saucepan; stir until well blended.

2. Add chickpeas and liquid, sausage, mushrooms,
onion salt, pepper and marjoram; stir.

3. Cover. Bring to a boil. Reduce heat to low; simmer
30 minutes or until sausage is no longer pink in
center. Sprinkle with Parmesan cheese just before
serving.   *Makes about 10 cups*

Tortilla Soup

1/2 pound lean ground pork
1/2 cup chopped onion
4 cups canned crushed tomatoes
2 cups chicken broth
1 (8-ounce) jar salsa, medium or hot
1 teaspoon ground cumin
1 teaspoon chili powder
1/2 teaspoon salt
1/2 teaspoon garlic powder
1/2 teaspoon ground black pepper
4 corn tortillas, cut into thin strips

Brown pork and onion over medium-high heat in
large saucepan, stirring occasionally. Add remaining
ingredients except tortilla strips. Cover and simmer
20 minutes. Stir tortilla strips into soup and simmer
5 to 10 minutes more, until tortilla strips are
softened. Serve hot.   *Makes 6 servings*

Favorite recipe from **National Pork Board**

Potato-Bacon Soup

Creamy Turkey Soup

(Pictured at right)

2 cans (10-1/2 ounces each) cream of chicken
    soup
2 cups chopped cooked turkey breast meat
1 package (8 ounces) sliced mushrooms
1 medium yellow onion, chopped
1 teaspoon rubbed sage *or* 1/2 teaspoon dried
    poultry seasoning
1 cup frozen peas, thawed
1/2 cup milk
1 jar (about 4 ounces) diced pimiento

SLOW COOKER DIRECTIONS
Combine soup, turkey, mushrooms, onion and sage
in slow cooker. Cover; cook on LOW 8 hours or on
HIGH 4 hours.

If cooking on LOW, turn to HIGH; stir in peas, milk
and pimiento. Cook an additional 10 minutes or until
heated through.   *Makes 5 to 6 servings*

Cheesy Potato Soup

4 baking potatoes (about 1-1/2 pounds)
1 medium onion, sliced
2 tablespoons butter
2 tablespoons all-purpose flour
1 teaspoon beef bouillon granules
1 can (12 ounces) evaporated milk
4 ounces Wisconsin Brick cheese, cut into
    1-inch cubes
1 teaspoon chopped fresh parsley
3/4 teaspoon salt
3/4 teaspoon black pepper
3/4 teaspoon Worcestershire sauce

MICROWAVE DIRECTIONS
Microwave potatoes on HIGH until tender; cool.
Place onion and butter in large microwavable bowl.
Cook on HIGH until onion is tender, about 2 minutes.
Stir in flour until blended. Add bouillon and 2 cups
water; mix well. Cook on HIGH 2 minutes or until
hot. Scoop out potatoes, leaving pieces in chunks;
discard skins. Add potatoes, evaporated milk,
cheese and seasonings to onion mixture. Microwave
on HIGH 2-1/2 to 4 minutes or until cheese is melted
and soup is heated through.   *Makes 6 servings*

Favorite recipe from **Wisconsin Milk Marketing
Board**

Mexican Pork and Bean Soup

1/2 pound lean ground pork
1 small onion, diced
1 clove garlic, minced
1 (15-ounce) can pinto beans, drained
1 (14-1/2-ounce) can chicken broth
1 (14-1/2-ounce) can Mexican-style chopped
    tomatoes
1 teaspoon chili powder
1 teaspoon ground cumin
1/2 teaspoon dried oregano leaves
1/2 teaspoon salt
1/4 teaspoon cayenne pepper

In large heavy saucepan, crumble and brown ground
pork. Stir in onion and garlic; cook and stir until
onion is soft, about 3 minutes. Stir in all remaining
ingredients. Bring to a boil, lower heat and simmer
about 10 minutes.   *Makes 6 (1-cup) servings*

Favorite recipe from **National Pork Board**

Spicy Peanut Soup

1 tablespoon vegetable oil
1 large onion, chopped
1 medium sweet potato, diced
2 cloves garlic, minced
8 cups chicken broth
1 cup MAHATMA® or CAROLINA® Rice
1 teaspoon dried crushed thyme leaves
1/2 teaspoon ground cumin
3 (16-ounce) cans garbanzo beans, drained
    and rinsed
1-1/2 cups thick and chunky salsa
1 cup diced unpeeled zucchini
2/3 cup creamy peanut butter

In large saucepan, heat vegetable oil and sauté
onion, sweet potato and garlic, stirring occasionally,
until onion is softened (about 5 minutes). Add
chicken broth, rice, thyme and cumin. Bring to a
boil; reduce heat to simmer. Simmer 20 minutes.
Stir in beans, salsa and zucchini; cook 10 minutes.
Add peanut butter; stir until completely blended.
Remove from heat.   *Makes 8 servings*

Sweet Potato and Ham Soup

(Pictured below)

1 tablespoon butter or margarine
1 small leek, sliced
1 clove garlic, minced
1/2 pound ham, cut into 1/2-inch cubes
2 medium sweet potatoes, peeled and cut into 3/4-inch cubes
4 cups chicken broth
1/2 teaspoon dried thyme
2 ounces fresh spinach, rinsed, stemmed and coarsely chopped

Melt butter in large saucepan over medium heat. Add leek and garlic. Cook and stir until leek is tender.

Add ham, sweet potatoes, broth and thyme to saucepan. Bring to a boil over high heat. Reduce heat to medium-low; cook 10 minutes or until sweet potatoes are tender.

Stir spinach into soup. Simmer, uncovered, 2 minutes more or until spinach is wilted. Serve immediately.

Makes 6 servings

Sweet Potato and Ham Soup

Cuban Chicken Bean Soup

8 chicken thighs, skinned, fat trimmed
8 cups water
2 cloves garlic, minced
2 teaspoons salt
2 bay leaves
1 cup chopped green bell pepper
1 cup chopped onion
2 cans (16 ounces each) black beans, drained, rinsed
2 tablespoons lime juice
1-1/4 teaspoons ground cumin
1 teaspoon sugar
1/2 teaspoon dried oregano leaves
1/2 teaspoon hot pepper sauce
1-1/4 cups cooked rice
1/4 cup sliced green onions

In large saucepan or Dutch oven, place chicken; add water, garlic, salt and bay leaves. Cook over medium-high heat until mixture boils; cover, reduce heat to low and cook about 35 minutes or until chicken is fork-tender. Remove chicken; set aside. Chill broth until fat solidifies and can be skimmed from surface. Separate meat from bones; cut into bite-size pieces and set aside. To skimmed broth in same pan, add green pepper and onion, cook over medium heat 10 minutes or until vegetables are crisp-tender. Add chicken, black beans, lime juice, cumin, sugar and oregano. Cook over medium heat 10 minutes. Remove bay leaves. Stir in hot pepper sauce. Place 2 tablespoons cooked rice in individual bowls; ladle soup over rice. Sprinkle with green onions. *Makes 10 (1-cup) servings*

Favorite recipe from **Delmarva Poultry Industry, Inc.**

Helpful Hint

Select firm, heavy limes that have a natural sheen to their skin, and avoid those that appear to be dried out or that are light for their size. Small brown patches on the skin, called scald, are not indicative of poor quality. One medium lime will yield about 1-1/2 tablespoons juice and 1-1/2 teaspoons grated peel.

Spicy Gazpacho

Spicy Gazpacho

(Pictured above)

1-1/2 cups tomato juice
1-1/2 pounds fresh tomatoes, seeded and chopped
1 medium cucumber, peeled, seeded and chopped
1/4 cup minced green bell pepper
1/4 cup minced onion
2 tablespoons BERTOLLI® Olive Oil
2 tablespoons white wine vinegar
1-1/2 teaspoons LAWRY'S® Garlic Salt
1/4 teaspoon oregano
LAWRY'S® Seasoned Pepper

In large bowl, combine all ingredients, except Seasoned Pepper; stir gently yet thoroughly. Chill before serving. Add a sprinkle of Seasoned Pepper to each serving. Serve in chilled individual glass bowls.   *Makes 5 to 6 servings*

Variation: For spicier version, stir in 1/4 teaspoon hot pepper sauce before chilling.

Chicken Tortilla Soup

1 clove garlic, minced
1 jar (16 ounces) mild chunky-style salsa
1 can (14-1/2 ounces) chicken broth
2 tablespoons *Frank's® RedHot®* Original Cayenne Pepper Sauce
1 package (10 ounces) fully cooked carved chicken breasts
1 can (8-3/4 ounces) whole kernel corn, undrained
1 tablespoon chopped fresh cilantro (optional)
1 cup crushed tortilla chips
1/2 cup (2 ounces) shredded Monterey Jack cheese

1. Heat *1 teaspoon oil* in large saucepan over medium-high heat. Cook garlic 1 minute or until tender. Add salsa, broth, *3/4 cup water* and **Frank's RedHot** Sauce. Stir in chicken, corn and cilantro. Heat to boiling. Reduce heat to medium-low. Cook, covered, 5 minutes.

2. Stir in tortilla chips and cheese. Serve hot.
          Makes 4 servings

Nita Lou's Cream of Broccoli Soup

(Pictured at right)

1/3 cup plus 1 tablespoon WESSON® Vegetable Oil
3 cups coarsely chopped broccoli florets and stems
1 cup diced carrots
1-1/2 cups fresh chopped leeks
3 tablespoons all-purpose flour
1-1/2 teaspoons minced fresh garlic
2 (12-ounce) cans evaporated milk
1-1/2 cups homemade chicken stock or canned chicken broth
1/2 teaspoon garlic salt
1/4 teaspoon ground nutmeg
1/8 teaspoon pepper
3 tablespoons chopped fresh parsley
Salt to taste

In a large saucepan, heat *3 tablespoons* Wesson® Oil. Add broccoli and carrots; sauté until tender. Remove vegetables; set aside. Add *remaining* oil, leeks, flour and garlic; sauté until leeks are limp and flour is lightly browned, about 2 minutes, stirring constantly. Whisk in the evaporated milk and stock. Continue to cook, whisking constantly until the flour has dissolved and the mixture is smooth. *Do not bring mixture to a boil.* Reduce heat to LOW. Add cooked vegetables along with any juices, garlic salt, nutmeg and pepper. Simmer 5 minutes longer, being careful not to bring soup to a boil. Remove the pan from the heat; stir in parsley. Let soup stand 5 minutes before serving. Add salt to taste.   *Makes 6 servings*

Picante Black Bean Soup

4 slices bacon
1 large onion, chopped
1 clove garlic, minced
2 cans (15 ounces each) black beans, undrained
1 can (about 14 ounces) beef broth
1-1/4 cups water
3/4 cup picante sauce
1/2 to 1 teaspoon salt
1/2 teaspoon dried oregano leaves
Sour cream
Crackers and additional picante sauce for serving

1. Using scissors, cut through several slices of bacon at once, cutting into 1/2×1/2-inch pieces.

2. Cook and stir bacon in large saucepan over medium-high heat until crisp. Remove with slotted spoon; drain on paper towels. Set bacon aside.

3. Add onion and garlic to drippings in saucepan; cook and stir 3 minutes.

4. Add beans with liquid, broth, water, 3/4 cup picante sauce, salt to taste and oregano. Reduce heat to low. Simmer, covered, 20 minutes.

5. Ladle into soup bowls; dollop with sour cream. Sprinkle with bacon. Serve with crackers and additional picante sauce.   *Makes 6 to 8 servings*

Hearty Corn, Chile and Potato Soup

2 tablespoons butter
2 stalks celery, sliced
1 medium onion, coarsely chopped
2-1/2 cups water
2 cups diced potatoes
1 can (14-3/4 ounces) cream-style corn
1 can (11 ounces) whole kernel corn, undrained
1 can (4 ounces) ORTEGA® Diced Green Chiles
2 MAGGI® Chicken Bouillon Cubes
1 teaspoon paprika
1 bay leaf
1 can (12 ounces) NESTLÉ® CARNATION® Evaporated Milk
2 tablespoons flour
Salt and ground pepper to taste

MELT butter in large saucepan over medium-high heat. Add celery and onion; cook for 1 to 2 minutes or until onion is tender. Add water, potatoes, corn, chiles, bouillon, paprika and bay leaf. Bring to a boil. Reduce heat to low; cover.

COOK, stirring occasionally, for 15 minutes or until potatoes are tender. Stir a small amount of evaporated milk into flour in small bowl to make a smooth paste; gradually stir in remaining milk. Stir milk mixture into soup. Cook, stirring constantly, until soup comes just to a boil and thickens slightly. Season with salt and pepper.

Makes 8 to 10 servings

Nita Lou's Cream of Broccoli Soup

Taco Soup

(Pictured at right)

1 pound BOB EVANS® Original Recipe or
   Zesty Hot Roll Sausage
1-1/2 tablespoons olive oil
1/2 small Spanish onion, diced
1 jalapeño pepper, seeded and diced
1-1/2 cups beef broth
1 cup peeled, seeded, diced fresh or
   canned tomatoes
1 cup vegetable juice
1/2 tablespoon ground cumin
1/2 tablespoon chili powder
1/4 teaspoon salt
1/3 cup shredded Cheddar cheese
12 tortilla chips, broken into pieces

Crumble and cook sausage in olive oil in Dutch oven until no longer pink but not yet browned. Add onion and pepper; cook until onion is tender. Add remaining ingredients except cheese and chips; bring to a boil over high heat. Reduce heat to low and simmer, uncovered, 15 minutes. Ladle soup into bowls; garnish with cheese and chips. Refrigerate leftovers.   *Makes 6 servings*

Corn, Bacon & Rice Chowder

1 package (7.2 ounces) RICE-A-RONI® Rice Pilaf
2 tablespoons margarine or butter
1 can (13-3/4 ounces) reduced-sodium or
   regular chicken broth
1-1/2 cups frozen corn *or* 1 can (16 or 17 ounces)
   whole kernel corn, drained
1 cup milk
1 cup water
1/2 cup sliced green onions
2 slices crisply cooked bacon, crumbled

1. In 3-quart saucepan, sauté rice-pasta mix in margarine over medium heat, stirring frequently until pasta is lightly browned.

2. Stir in chicken broth and Special Seasonings; bring to a boil over high heat.

3. Cover; reduce heat. Simmer 8 minutes.

4. Stir in corn, milk, water and onions. Simmer, uncovered, 10 to 12 minutes, stirring occasionally. Stir in bacon before serving.   *Makes 4 servings*

Potato and Albacore Chowder

2 tablespoons butter or margarine
1/4 cup chopped onion
1/4 cup chopped celery
1 cup chopped or grated cooked potato
1 can (10-3/4 ounces) cream of potato soup
2/3 cup milk or half & half
2/3 cup chicken broth
1 (3-ounce) pouch of STARKIST® Premium
   Albacore Tuna
Freshly ground black pepper
Shredded Cheddar cheese
Snipped chives

In medium saucepan, melt butter over medium heat. Sauté onion and celery until onion is tender. Add potato; continue cooking 2 to 3 minutes. Add soup, milk, chicken broth and tuna; heat thoroughly over low heat. Top each serving with pepper, cheese and chives.   *Makes 2 servings*

Tip: Recipe is easily doubled.

Butternut Squash-Apple Soup

3 packages (12 ounces each) frozen cooked
   winter squash, thawed and drained *or* about
   4-1/2 cups mashed cooked butternut squash
2 cans (about 14-1/2 ounces each) chicken broth
   (3 to 4 cups)
1 medium Golden Delicious apple, peeled and
   chopped
2 tablespoons minced onion
1 tablespoon packed light brown sugar
1 teaspoon minced fresh sage *or* 1/2 teaspoon
   ground sage
1/4 teaspoon ground ginger
1/2 cup heavy whipping cream or half-and-half

SLOW COOKER DIRECTIONS
1. Combine all ingredients except cream in slow cooker. Cover; cook on HIGH about 3 hours or on LOW about 6 hours.

2. Purée soup in blender or food processor. Stir in cream just before serving.   *Makes 6 to 8 servings*

Minestrone

(Pictured at right)

   3 slices bacon, diced
 1/2 cup chopped onion
   1 large clove garlic, minced
   2 cans (10-1/2 ounces each) beef broth
1-1/2 cups water
   2 cans (15-1/2 ounces each) Great Northern
      white beans, undrained
   1 can (6 ounces) CONTADINA® Tomato Paste
   1 teaspoon Italian herb seasoning
 1/4 teaspoon ground black pepper
   2 medium zucchini, sliced
   1 package (10 ounces) frozen mixed vegetables
 1/2 cup elbow macaroni, uncooked
 1/2 cup (2 ounces) grated Parmesan cheese
      (optional)

1. Sauté bacon in large saucepan until crisp. Add onion and garlic; sauté until onion is tender.

2. Add broth, water, beans and liquid, tomato paste, Italian seasoning and pepper.

3. Reduce heat to low; simmer, uncovered, for 10 minutes. Add zucchini, mixed vegetables and macaroni. Return to a boil over high heat, stirring to break up vegetables.

4. Reduce heat to low; simmer for 8 to 10 minutes or until vegetables and macaroni are tender. Sprinkle with Parmesan cheese just before serving, if desired. *Makes 8 cups*

Hoppin' John Soup

4 strips uncooked bacon, chopped
1 large onion, chopped
2 cloves garlic, minced
2 cans (15 ounces each) black-eye peas,
   undrained
1 can (14-1/2 ounces) reduced-sodium
   chicken broth
3 to 4 tablespoons *Frank's® RedHot®*
   Original Cayenne Pepper Sauce
1 teaspoon dried thyme leaves
1 bay leaf
2 cups cooked long-grain rice (3/4 cup
   uncooked rice)
2 tablespoons minced fresh parsley

1. Cook bacon, onion and garlic in large saucepan over medium-high heat 5 minutes or until vegetables are tender.

2. Add peas with liquid, broth, *1/2 cup water*, *Frank's RedHot* Sauce, thyme and bay leaf. Bring to a boil. Reduce heat to low; cook, covered, 15 minutes, stirring occasionally. Remove and discard bay leaf.

3. Combine rice and parsley in medium bowl. Spoon rice evenly into 6 serving bowls. Ladle soup over rice. *Makes 6 servings*

Note: For an attractive presentation, pack rice mixture into small ramekin dishes. Unmold into soup bowls. Ladle soup around rice.

Chunk Beef and Vegetable Soup

    1 tablespoon corn oil
1-1/4 pounds beef shank cross cuts
    2 quarts water
    1 cup diced celery
  1/2 cup chopped onion
    1 package (10 ounces) frozen mixed vegetables
    1 cup salt-free canned tomatoes, chopped
    1 can (6 ounces) salt-free tomato paste
    1 tablespoon sugar
2-1/2 teaspoons MRS. DASH® All-Purpose
      Original Blend
    2 teaspoons vinegar
  1/4 cup cold water
    3 tablespoons cornstarch

Heat oil in 3-quart saucepan or Dutch oven. Add beef and brown over medium heat. Add 2 quarts water, celery and onion. Bring to a boil; reduce heat and simmer for 2 hours. Remove shanks to cool. Stir mixed vegetables, tomatoes, tomato paste, sugar, All-Purpose Original Blend and vinegar into broth mixture. Simmer for 1 hour. Remove meat from shanks and cut into small chunks: return to vegetable mixture. Combine 1/4 cup water and cornstarch in small bowl; mix well until smooth. Stir into vegetable mixture and heat until slightly thickened. *Makes 8 servings*

Sandwiches

Campbell's® Southwestern Chicken & Pepper Wraps

(Pictured at left)

2 tablespoons vegetable oil
1 pound skinless, boneless chicken breasts, cut into strips
1 medium red pepper, cut into 2-inch long strips
    (about 1-1/2 cups)
1 medium green pepper, cut into 2-inch long strips
    (about 1-1/2 cups)
1 small onion, sliced (about 1/4 cup)
1 can (10-3/4 ounces) CAMPBELL'S® Condensed Golden
    Mushroom Soup
1 cup water
1 cup black beans, rinsed and drained (optional)
1 cup *uncooked* instant rice
8 flour tortillas (8-inch)

1. In medium skillet over medium-high heat, heat **half** the oil. Add chicken and cook 10 minutes or until no longer pink and juices evaporate, stirring often.

2. Reduce heat to medium. Add remaining oil. Add peppers and onion and cook until tender-crisp, stirring often.

3. Add soup, water and beans. Heat to a boil. Stir in rice. Cover and remove from heat. Let stand 5 minutes.

4. Spoon **3/4 cup** chicken mixture down center of each tortilla. Fold tortilla around filling.   *Makes 4 servings*

Helpful Hint

Most recipes suggest rinsing canned beans before using them—this removes excess salt.

Clockwise from top left: Campbell's® Southwestern Chicken & Pepper Wrap, Chile Rellenos Monte Cristo (p. 95), Croque Monsieur (p. 97) and Hearty BBQ Beef Sandwich (p. 100)

America's Favorite Cheddar Beef Burgers

1 pound ground beef
1/3 cup A.1.® Steak Sauce, divided
1 medium onion, cut into strips
1 medium green or red bell pepper, cut into strips
1 tablespoon margarine or butter
4 ounces Cheddar cheese, sliced
4 hamburger rolls
4 tomato slices

Mix ground beef and 3 tablespoons steak sauce; shape mixture into 4 burgers. Set aside.

Cook and stir onion and pepper in margarine or butter in medium skillet until tender. Stir in remaining steak sauce; keep warm.

Grill burgers over medium heat for 4 minutes on each side or until done. When almost done, top with cheese; grill until cheese melts. Spoon 2 tablespoons onion mixture onto each roll bottom; top each with burger, tomato slice, some of remaining onion mixture and roll top. Serve immediately. *Makes 4 servings*

Croque Monsieur

(Pictured on page 90)

8 slices firm white sandwich bread
2 tablespoons butter, softened
8 slices SARGENTO® Deli Style Sliced Swiss Cheese
2 tablespoons honey mustard
4 slices CURE 81® ham
4 slices cooked turkey breast

1. Spread one side of each slice of bread with butter; place butter side down on waxed paper. Top 4 slices of bread with 4 slices of cheese. Spread mustard over cheese; top with ham, turkey and remaining cheese. Close sandwiches with remaining bread, butter side out.

2. Heat a large skillet or griddle over medium heat until hot. Cook sandwiches in batches in skillet or on the griddle until golden brown, about 3 minutes per side. *Makes 4 servings*

Super Hero Sandwich

(Pictured at right)

1 (1-pound) loaf frozen bread dough, thawed
3/4 cup mayonnaise or salad dressing
2 tablespoons Dijon mustard
2 teaspoons sugar
2 drops hot pepper sauce
1-1/2 cups shredded Cheddar cheese
12 to 16 fresh spinach leaves
8 ounces thinly sliced CURE 81® ham
12 cucumber slices

Roll bread dough into a rope about 20 inches long; place on greased baking sheet. Form dough into ring; pinch ends together to seal. Place greased custard cup or empty metal can in center of ring. Cover dough; let rise in warm place 1 hour or until doubled in size. Cut several diagonal slashes in top of dough with sharp knife, if desired. Heat oven to 375°F. Bake for 20 minutes or until golden brown.

Combine mayonnaise, mustard, sugar and hot pepper sauce; mix well. Stir in cheese. Slice bread ring in half horizontally. Spread each half with cheese mixture. Arrange spinach, ham and cucumber slices on bottom half of bread ring; cover with top. Secure with wooden picks. Cut into wedges to serve. *Makes 8 servings*

Buffalo Chicken Sandwich

2 tablespoons butter or margarine
Juice of one lemon (3 to 4 tablespoons)
4 to 8 dashes hot pepper sauce to taste
1 package (about 1 pound) PERDUE® FIT 'N EASY® Skinless & Boneless Chicken Breasts
1 loaf (10 ounces) frozen garlic bread
4 tablespoons prepared blue cheese dressing

Prepare outdoor grill for cooking or preheat broiler. In small saucepan over low heat, melt butter with lemon juice and hot sauce. Coat chicken with seasoned butter; grill or broil 5 to 6 inches from heat source 6 to 8 minutes per side, until cooked through. Meanwhile, warm bread following package directions. Cut bread into 4 sandwich-sized slices. Place chicken on bottom layer of bread. Top chicken with 1 tablespoon blue cheese dressing and remaining bread. *Makes 4 servings*

Super Hero Sandwich

Quick Greek Pitas

(Pictured at right)

1 pound ground beef
1 package (10 ounces) frozen chopped spinach,
    thawed and well drained
4 green onions, chopped
1 can (2-1/4 ounces) sliced ripe olives, drained
1 teaspoon dried oregano, divided
1/4 teaspoon pepper
1 large tomato, diced
1 cup plain yogurt
1/2 cup mayonnaise
6 (6-inch) pita breads, split and warmed
    Lettuce leaves
1 cup (4 ounces) crumbled feta cheese

1. Cook and stir ground beef in large skillet over medium-high heat until crumbly and no longer pink. Drain off drippings. Add spinach, green onions, olives, 1/2 teaspoon oregano and pepper; cook and stir 2 minutes. Stir in tomato.

2. Combine yogurt, mayonnaise and remaining 1/2 teaspoon oregano in small bowl. Split open pita breads; line each with lettuce leaf. Stir cheese into beef mixture and divide among pita pockets. Serve with yogurt sauce. *Makes 6 servings*

Taco Two-Zies

(Pictured on front cover)

1 pound ground beef
2 packages (1 ounce each) LAWRY'S®
    Taco Spices & Seasonings, divided
3/4 cup water
1 can (1 pound 14 ounces) refried beans,
    warmed
10 small flour tortillas (fajita size), warmed to
    soften
10 jumbo size taco shells, heated according to
    package directions

TACO TOPPINGS
    Shredded lettuce, shredded cheddar cheese
    and chopped tomatoes

In large skillet, brown ground beef over medium high heat until crumbly; drain fat. Stir in 1 package Taco Spices & Seasonings and water. Bring to a boil; reduce heat to low and cook, uncovered, 10 minutes, stirring occasionally. In medium bowl, mix together beans and remaining package

Taco Spices & Seasonings. Spread about 1/3 cup seasoned beans all the way to edges of each flour tortilla. Place a taco shell on center of each bean-covered tortilla; fold edges up around shell, lightly pressing to 'stick' tortilla to shell. Fill each taco with about 3 tablespoons taco meat. Top with your choice of taco toppings. *Makes 10 tacos*

Variations: May use lean ground turkey, chicken or pork in place of ground beef. May use LAWRY'S® Chicken Taco Spices & Seasonings or Lawry's® Hot Taco Spices & Seasonings instead of Taco Spices & Seasonings.

Eggplant Italiano Open-Faced Sandwiches

1 medium eggplant (about 1-1/2 pounds),
    peeled, cut into 8 slices
2 eggs, lightly beaten
1 cup CONTADINA® Italian Bread Crumbs
1/2 cup olive or vegetable oil, divided
4 sandwich-size English muffins, split, toasted
1 can (14.5 ounces) CONTADINA Recipe Ready
    Diced Tomatoes with Italian Herbs, drained,
    divided
1/2 cup (2 ounces) shredded mozzarella cheese,
    divided

1. Dip eggplant slices into eggs in a shallow dish; coat with bread crumbs.

2. Heat 2 tablespoons oil in large skillet over medium heat. Add eggplant slices, a few at a time, to skillet.

3. Cook 2 to 3 minutes on each side or until golden brown. Remove from oil with slotted spoon. Drain on paper towels. Repeat with remaining oil and eggplant.

4. Place muffin halves on large, ungreased baking sheet; top with eggplant, tomatoes and cheese.

5. Bake in preheated 350°F oven 5 to 7 minutes or until cheese is melted. *Makes 8 servings*

Quick Greek Pita

Provolone Tuna Melt

Huevos Rancheros Sandwich

1/2 cup drained, canned cooked black beans
4 BAYS® English Muffins, split
1/2 cup (2 ounces) shredded Cheddar cheese, divided
2 teaspoons butter or margarine, divided
4 eggs
1/4 cup prepared medium salsa, divided
Lettuce leaves (optional)

MICROWAVE DIRECTIONS

Place beans in small bowl and mash with fork. Spread beans on bottom half of each muffin with spoon. Sprinkle 2 teaspoons cheese on top of bean layer. Cover and set aside. Lightly grease four microwave-safe custard cups. Break one egg into each cup and pierce yolks with toothpick. Cover with plastic wrap; microwave on MEDIUM (50%) power, 4 to 5 minutes, rotating cups halfway through cooking time. Let stand, covered, to complete cooking. Carefully remove eggs from custard cups. Place egg on top of bean/cheese layer; top with additional 2 teaspoons cheese, then salsa and remaining cheese. Place top half of muffin on sandwich. Microwave on HIGH (100%) power 15 to 30 seconds to melt cheese and heat sandwich. Add lettuce, if desired. Serve immediately.

Makes 4 servings

Provolone Tuna Melt

(Pictured above)

1 can (12 ounces) white tuna in water, drained
1/4 cup diced drained bottled roasted red bell peppers
1/4 cup chopped pitted kalamata or ripe olives
3 tablespoons creamy Caesar salad dressing or mayonnaise
1 tablespoon chopped fresh basil or parsley
4 large slices Vienna or sourdough bread, lightly toasted
8 slices SARGENTO® Deli Style Sliced Provolone Cheese

1. Combine tuna, bell peppers, olives, dressing and basil; mix well. Spread mixture evenly over toast; top with cheese, overlapping as necessary to cover filling and edges of toast.

2. Place on foil-lined baking sheet; broil 4 to 5 inches from heat source until cheese melts and sandwiches are hot, 2 to 3 minutes. *Makes 4 servings*

Reuben Roll-Ups

8 (7-inch) flour tortillas
3/4 cup *French's®* Bold n' Spicy Brown Mustard
1 pound sliced corned beef
2 cups (8 ounces) shredded Swiss cheese
1/2 cup sauerkraut

Spread each tortilla with about 1-1/2 tablespoons mustard. Layer corned beef, cheese and sauerkraut on tortillas, dividing evenly. Roll up tortillas jelly-roll style. Secure with toothpicks.*

Place tortillas on oiled barbecue grill grid. Grill over medium-low coals about 10 minutes or until tortillas are toasted and cheese begins to melt, turning often. Remove toothpicks before serving.

Makes 4 servings

*Soak toothpicks in water 20 minutes to prevent burning.

Mexican Pita Pile Ups

4 whole-grain pita breads
1 cup diced cooked chicken breast
1 tablespoon lime juice
1 teaspoon ground cumin
1/4 cup chopped green chilies
1 cup chopped seeded tomato
1/4 cup minced fresh cilantro or parsley
1 can (2-1/4 ounces) sliced ripe olives, drained
1 cup shredded sharp cheddar cheese

Place pita breads on work surface. Top each with 1/4 cup chicken, then sprinkle each pita with lime juice, cumin, chilies, tomato, cilantro, olives and cheese.

Place each pita in resealable plastic bag. Seal and refrigerate until ready to serve.

To serve, place pita on microwavable plate; microwave at HIGH (100%) 1 minute or until cheese has melted. Let stand 2 to 3 minutes to allow crust to become slightly firm. *Makes 4 sandwiches*

Savory Stuffed Turkey Burgers

(Pictured below)

1 pound ground turkey
1/4 cup A.1.® Steak Sauce, divided
1/4 cup chopped onion
1/2 teaspoon dried thyme leaves
1/4 teaspoon ground black pepper
1/2 cup prepared herb bread stuffing
1/2 cup whole berry cranberry sauce
4 slices whole wheat bread, toasted
4 lettuce leaves

Mix ground turkey, 2 tablespoons steak sauce, onion, thyme and pepper; shape into 8 thin patties. Place 2 tablespoons prepared stuffing in center of each of 4 patties. Top with remaining patties. Seal edges to form 4 patties; set aside.

Blend remaining 2 tablespoons steak sauce and cranberry sauce; set aside.

Grill burgers over medium heat for 10 minutes on each side or until done. Top each bread slice with lettuce leaf and burger. Serve immediately topped with prepared cranberry sauce mixture.

Makes 4 servings

Savory Stuffed Turkey Burgers

Grilled Vegetable & Cheese Sandwiches

(Pictured at right)

2 large zucchini, cut lengthwise into eight
1/4-inch slices
4 slices sweet onion (1/4 inch thick)
1 large yellow bell pepper, cut lengthwise into
quarters
6 tablespoons Caesar salad dressing, divided
8 oval slices sourdough bread
6 slices Muenster cheese (1 ounce each)

1. Prepare barbecue for grilling. Brush both sides
of vegetables with 1/4 cup salad dressing. Place
vegetables on grid over medium heat. Grill on
covered grill 5 minutes. Turn; grill 2 minutes longer.

2. Brush both sides of bread lightly with remaining
2 tablespoons salad dressing. Place bread on grid
around vegetables; grill 2 minutes or until bread is
lightly toasted. Turn bread; top 4 slices bread with
4 slices cheese. Tear remaining 2 slices cheese into
small pieces; place on bread around cheese. Grill
vegetables and bread 1 to 2 minutes more or until
cheese is melted, bread is toasted and vegetables
are crisp-tender.

3. Arrange vegetables over cheese side of bread;
top with remaining bread.   *Makes 4 servings*

Serving Suggestion: Serve with a fresh fruit salad.

Ranch Bacon and Egg Salad Sandwich

6 hard-cooked eggs, cooled and peeled
1/4 cup HIDDEN VALLEY® The Original Ranch®
Dressing
1/4 cup diced celery
3 tablespoons crisp-cooked, crumbled bacon*
1 tablespoon diced green onion
8 slices sandwich bread
Lettuce and tomato (optional)

Bacon pieces can be used.

Coarsely chop eggs. Combine with dressing, celery,
bacon and onion in a medium mixing bowl; mix well.
Chill until just before serving. Spread salad evenly
on 4 bread slices; arrange lettuce and tomato on egg
salad, if desired. Top with remaining bread slices.
      Makes 4 sandwiches (about 2 cups salad)

Six O'Clock Sandwich

1 package (16 ounces) BUTTERBALL® Lean
Turkey Smoked Sausage, cut into 1/2-inch
diagonal slices
2 tablespoons olive oil
1 large onion, cut into lengthwise strips
1 yellow bell pepper, cut into thin strips
1 red bell pepper, cut into thin strips
1 can (14 ounces) artichoke hearts, drained
and sliced thin
1/4 cup fresh basil, shredded
1 loaf Italian bread, halved lengthwise
1-1/2 cups (6 ounces) finely shredded Swiss cheese

Heat oil in large skillet over medium heat until hot.
Cook and stir onion and bell peppers until soft; add
sausage. Cook and stir 10 minutes. Stir in artichokes
and basil; remove from heat. Place bread halves on
baking sheet; top with half of cheese. Spoon vegetable
mixture over cheese; sprinkle with remaining
cheese. Place under broiler until cheese melts.
Cut into 6 to 8 open-face sandwiches.
      Makes 6 to 8 sandwiches

Tip: The Six O'Clock Sandwich is also great to serve
to a crowd. Make several sandwiches ahead of time
and refrigerate until ready to broil and serve.

Tuna Torpedoes

1 loaf (1 pound) French or Italian bread,
halved lengthwise
1/4 to 1/3 cup mayonnaise
1/2 teaspoon Italian herb seasoning
Lettuce leaves
8 tomato slices
1 (7-ounce) pouch of STARKIST® Premium
Albacore or Chunk Light Tuna
2 tablespoons minced onion
1 cup shredded mozzarella cheese

In hot oven or broiler, toast bread; spread both
halves with mayonnaise. Sprinkle with herb
seasoning. On bottom half arrange lettuce leaves
and tomato slices. Top with tuna, onion and cheese.
In hot oven or broiler, heat bread until cheese melts.
Place halves together to make a torpedo; slice into
serving pieces.   *Makes 4 to 6 servings*

Grilled Vegetable & Cheese Sandwiches

Italian Combo Subs

(Pictured at right)

1 tablespoon vegetable oil
1 pound boneless beef round steak, cut into
    thin strips
1 pound bulk Italian sausage
1 medium green bell pepper, julienned
1 medium onion, thinly sliced
1 can (4 ounces) mushroom stems and pieces,
    drained
  Salt and black pepper
1 jar (26 ounces) meatless spaghetti sauce
2 loaves Italian bread, cut into 1-inch-thick slices

SLOW COOKER DIRECTIONS
Heat oil in large skillet over medium-high heat.
Brown meat on both sides. Drain and discard fat.
Transfer meat to slow cooker.

In same skillet, cook and stir sausage until no longer
pink. Drain and discard fat. Add sausage to slow
cooker.

Place bell pepper, onion and mushrooms over meat
in slow cooker. Season to taste with salt and black
pepper. Top with spaghetti sauce. Cover and cook
on LOW 4 to 6 hours.

Cut each bread loaf into 3 pieces to form individual
rolls; cut rolls in half horizontally. Spoon beef
mixture into each roll.   *Makes 6 servings*

Serving Suggestion: Top with freshly grated
Parmesan cheese.

Chili Corn Wraps

4 large flour tortillas
1 tablespoon vegetable oil
1 medium onion, chopped
1 green bell pepper, diced
1 pound lean ground beef or turkey
2 tablespoons TABASCO® brand Green
    Pepper Sauce
1 tablespoon chili powder
1 teaspoon salt
1 (11-ounce) can corn, drained
1 (4-ounce) jar diced pimentos, drained
1/2 cup (2 ounces) shredded Monterey Jack cheese

Preheat oven to 375°F. Wrap tortillas in foil; place in
oven 10 minutes to warm. Heat oil in 12-inch skillet
over medium heat. Add onion and green bell
pepper; cook 5 minutes or until tender-crisp.
Remove vegetables to plate with slotted spoon.

Add beef to drippings remaining in skillet; cook
over medium-high heat until well browned, stirring
occasionally. Stir in TABASCO® Green Pepper Sauce,
chili powder and salt; cook 1 minute, stirring
frequently. Remove from heat. Stir in vegetable
mixture, corn, pimentos and Monterey Jack
cheese. To assemble wraps, place 1/4 of mixture
on each tortilla; roll up tortillas, tucking in sides.
   Makes 4 servings

Blue Cheese Burgers
with Red Onion

2 pounds ground beef chuck
2 cloves garlic, minced
1 teaspoon salt
1/2 teaspoon black pepper
4 ounces blue cheese
1/3 cup coarsely chopped walnuts, toasted
1 torpedo (long) red onion *or* 2 small red onions,
    sliced into 3/8-inch-thick rounds
2 baguettes (each 12 inches long)
  Olive or vegetable oil

Combine beef, garlic, salt and pepper in medium
bowl. Shape meat mixture into 12 oval patties. Mash
cheese and blend with walnuts in small bowl. Divide
cheese mixture equally; place onto centers of
6 meat patties. Top with remaining meat patties;
tightly pinch edges together to seal in filling.

Oil hot grid to help prevent sticking. Grill patties
and onion, if desired, on covered grill, over medium
KINGSFORD® Briquets, 7 to 12 minutes for medium
doneness, turning once. Cut baguettes into 4-inch
lengths; split each piece and brush cut side with
olive oil. Move cooked burgers to edge of grill to
keep warm. Grill bread, oil side down, until lightly
toasted. Serve burgers on toasted baguettes.
   Makes 6 servings

Basil Chicken and Vegetables on Focaccia

(Pictured at right)

1/2 cup mayonnaise
1/4 teaspoon garlic powder
1/2 teaspoon black pepper, divided
1 loaf (16 ounces) focaccia or Italian bread
4 boneless skinless chicken breast halves
(about 1-1/4 pounds)
3 tablespoons olive or vegetable oil
2 garlic cloves, minced
1-1/2 teaspoons dried basil
1/2 teaspoon salt
1 medium green bell pepper, cut into quarters
1 medium zucchini, cut lengthwise into 4 slices
2 plum tomatoes, sliced

Combine mayonnaise, garlic powder and 1/4 teaspoon black pepper in small bowl.

Cut focaccia into quarters. Cut each quarter horizontally in half; set aside.

Combine chicken, oil, garlic, basil, salt and remaining 1/4 teaspoon black pepper in large resealable plastic food storage bag. Seal bag; knead to combine. Add bell pepper and zucchini; knead to coat.

Grill or broil chicken, bell pepper and zucchini 4 inches from heat source 6 to 8 minutes on each side or until chicken is no longer pink in center. (Bell pepper and zucchini may take less time.)

Layer bottom half of each focaccia quarter with mayonnaise mixture, tomatoes, bell pepper, zucchini and chicken. Top with focaccia tops.

Makes 4 servings

Helpful Hint

When grilling, grease the grid with oil or cooking spray before using it to minimize food sticking and to assist in cleanup. (Do not spray the grill directly over the fire as this could cause a flare-up.) Grill-cleaning utensils such as wire brushes and steel wool pads can also make cleanup after grilling much easier.

Asian Pockets

1 pound BOB EVANS® Original Recipe
Roll Sausage
1/4 cup chopped green onions
2 teaspoons minced fresh ginger
3/4 teaspoon garlic powder
1 tablespoon vegetable oil
1 large green bell pepper, sliced lengthwise
1 large red bell pepper, sliced lengthwise
6 small white pita bread pockets
12 tablespoons apple butter, divided

Combine sausage, green onions, ginger and garlic powder in medium bowl; mix well. Shape mixture into 6 patties. Cook patties in medium skillet over medium heat until browned and cooked through. Set aside and keep warm. Add oil and bell peppers to same skillet; cook and stir 1 to 2 minutes over medium heat just until peppers are slightly tender.

Open each pita bread pocket; fill with sausage patty, 2 tablespoons pepper mixture and 2 tablespoons apple butter. Serve warm. Refrigerate leftovers.

Makes 6 servings

Meatball Parmesan Heroes

1 pound lean ground beef
1/2 cup Italian seasoned bread crumbs
1 egg
1 jar (1 pound 10 ounces) RAGÚ® Old World
Style® Pasta Sauce
4 Italian rolls (about 6 inches long each),
halved lengthwise
1 cup shredded mozzarella cheese
(about 4 ounces)

1. In medium bowl, combine ground beef, bread crumbs and egg; shape into 12 meatballs.

2. In 3-quart saucepan, bring Ragú Old World Style Pasta Sauce to a boil over medium-high heat. Gently stir in meatballs.

3. Reduce heat to low and simmer covered, stirring occasionally, 20 minutes or until meatballs are done. Serve meatballs and sauce in rolls. Top with cheese.

Makes 4 servings

Cowboy Burger

Hearty BBQ Beef Sandwiches

(Pictured on page 90)

1 envelope LIPTON® RECIPE SECRETS®
   Onion Soup Mix
2 cups water
1/2 cup chili sauce
1/4 cup firmly packed light brown sugar
1 (3-pound) boneless chuck roast
8 kaiser rolls or hamburger buns, toasted

1. Preheat oven to 325°F. In Dutch oven or 5-quart heavy ovenproof saucepot, combine soup mix, water, chili sauce and sugar; add roast.

2. Cover and bake 3 hours or until roast is tender.

3. Remove roast; reserve juices. Bring reserved juices to a boil over high heat. Boil 4 minutes.

4. Meanwhile, with fork, shred roast. Stir roast into reserved juices and simmer, stirring frequently, 1 minute. Serve on rolls.   *Makes 8 servings*

Recipe Tip: Always measure brown sugar in a dry measure cup and pack down firmly. To soften hardened brown sugar, place in glass dish with 1 slice of bread. Cover with plastic wrap and microwave at HIGH 30 to 40 seconds. Let stand 30 seconds; stir. Remove bread.

Cowboy Burgers

(Pictured above)

1 pound ground beef or turkey
1/2 teaspoon LAWRY'S® Seasoned Salt
1/2 teaspoon LAWRY'S® Seasoned Pepper
3 tablespoons butter or margarine
1 large onion, thinly sliced
1 package (1 ounce) LAWRY'S® Taco Spices &
   Seasonings
4 slices cheddar cheese
4 Kaiser rolls
   Lettuce leaves
   Tomato slices

In medium bowl, combine ground beef, Seasoned Salt and Seasoned Pepper; shape into four patties. Grill or broil to desired doneness. Meanwhile, in medium skillet, melt butter. Mix in onion and Taco Spices & Seasoning. Cook onion until soft and transparent. Top each patty with onions and cheese. Return to grill or broiler until cheese is melted. Place each patty on roll; top with lettuce and tomato.   *Makes 4 servings*

Meal Idea: Serve with your favorite baked beans.

Pocket Meals on the Run

8 boneless, skinless chicken tenderloins,
   cut into 1-inch pieces
1 cup UNCLE BEN'S® Instant Rice
1/3 cup oil and vinegar or Italian salad dressing
1/2 cup crumbled feta cheese
4 pita breads, halved
1 cup shredded lettuce
2 plum tomatoes, chopped
1/4 cup sliced ripe olives

1. Spray large skillet with nonstick cooking spray. Add chicken; cook over medium-high heat 6 to 8 minutes or until lightly browned and no longer pink. Add 1 cup water. Bring to a boil; add rice. Cover; remove from heat and let stand 5 minutes or until liquid is absorbed. Stir in salad dressing and cheese.

2. Fill pita bread halves with lettuce and chicken-rice mixture. Top with tomatoes and olives.

Makes 4 servings

Shrimp and Black Bean Wraps

(Pictured below)

- 4 large flour tortillas
- 1 tablespoon olive oil
- 8 ounces small shrimp, peeled and deveined
- 1 (15-ounce) can black beans, drained and rinsed
- 1 large tomato, chopped
- 2 green onions, sliced
- 1-1/2 teaspoons TABASCO® brand Pepper Sauce
- 1/2 teaspoon salt

Preheat oven to 375°F. Wrap tortillas in foil; place in oven 10 minutes to warm. Heat oil in 10-inch skillet over medium-high heat. Add shrimp; cook and stir until pink. Mash 1/2 cup beans in medium bowl; stir in remaining beans, shrimp, tomato, green onions, TABASCO® Sauce and salt. To assemble, place 1/4 of mixture on each tortilla; roll up tortillas, tucking in sides. *Makes 4 servings*

Cuban-Style Steak Sandwiches

- 1-1/2 pounds beef round tip steaks (thinly sliced sandwich steaks)
- 3 tablespoons olive or vegetable oil, divided
- 1 tablespoon lime juice
- 1-1/2 teaspoons minced garlic
- 1/2 teaspoon dried thyme
- 1/4 teaspoon salt
- 1/4 teaspoon pepper
- 1 large onion, cut in half and thinly sliced
- 4 (8-inch) hoagie or submarine sandwich rolls, split
  Lettuce leaves
- 1 medium tomato, sliced

Cut steaks into 3- to 4-inch pieces. Combine steaks with 2 tablespoons oil, lime juice, garlic, thyme, salt and pepper in shallow dish; toss to coat.

Heat skillet over high heat 1 minute. Cook steaks in 2 batches, 1-1/2 minutes per side. Remove from pan and cover to keep warm.

Add remaining 1 tablespoon oil and onion to skillet. Cook 3 minutes or until tender and lightly browned. Fill rolls with lettuce, tomato, steak and onion. *Makes 4 servings*

Shrimp and Black Bean Wraps

California Veggie Rolls

(Pictured at right)

1 package (8 ounces) cream cheese, softened
1/2 teaspoon LAWRY'S® Garlic Powder With Parsley
1/2 teaspoon LAWRY'S® Lemon Pepper
6 large (burrito size) *or* 12 soft taco size flour tortillas, warmed to soften
1 large bunch fresh spinach leaves, cleaned and stems removed
1-1/2 cups (6 ounces) shredded cheddar cheese
1-1/2 cups shredded carrot
     Fresh salsa

In small bowl, mix together cream cheese, Garlic Powder With Parsley and Lemon Pepper. On each flour tortilla, spread a layer of cream cheese mixture. Layer on spinach leaves, cheddar cheese and carrot. Roll up tortilla and secure with toothpicks. Slice each roll into 1-1/2-inch pieces. Serve with fresh salsa. *Makes 3 dozen rolls*

Variation: Adding sliced deli meat or stirring Dijon mustard into the cream cheese will add variety to these rolls.

Hint: To keep tortillas soft until slicing, wrap tightly in plastic wrap or cover with damp towel.

Chile Rellenos Monte Cristos

(Pictured on page 90)

1 can (4 ounces) whole roasted green chiles
8 large slices sourdough bread
4 slices SARGENTO® Deli Style Sliced Monterey Jack Cheese
4 slices SARGENTO® Deli Style Sliced Colby Cheese
2 eggs
1/4 cup milk
1 teaspoon ground cumin
1/4 cup butter or margarine
     Powdered sugar, optional
     Thick and chunky salsa, optional

1. Cut open chiles and remove any remaining seeds. Equally divide the chiles over 4 slices of bread. Top each with Monterey Jack and Colby cheeses. Place remaining bread slices on top.

2. In shallow bowl, beat eggs, milk and cumin until blended. Dip each sandwich in the egg mixture, turning carefully to coat until all liquid is absorbed by all sandwiches equally.

3. Melt butter in large skillet over medium heat. Place sandwiches in skillet. Grill (in batches if necessary) 3 to 4 minutes per side, or until browned and cheese has melted. Serve immediately. Serve with powdered sugar sprinkled on top and spoonful of salsa, if desired. *Makes 4 servings*

Easy Chicken & Rice Wraps

1 (6.8-ounce) package RICE-A-RONI® Spanish Rice
2 tablespoons margarine or butter
1 (16-ounce) jar salsa*
12 ounces boneless, skinless chicken breasts, cut into thin strips (about 3 breasts)
1 cup canned black or red kidney beans, drained and rinsed
1 cup frozen or canned corn, drained
8 (6-inch) flour tortillas, warmed
     Shredded Cheddar cheese and sour cream (optional)

Or, use 2 cups chopped fresh tomatoes or 1 (14-1/2-ounce) can tomatoes, undrained and chopped, if desired.

1. In large skillet over medium-high heat, sauté rice-vermicelli mix with margarine until vermicelli is golden brown.

2. Slowly stir in 2 cups water, salsa, chicken and Special Seasonings; bring to a boil. Reduce heat to low. Cover; simmer 15 to 20 minutes or until rice is tender and chicken is no longer pink inside.

3. Stir in beans and corn; let stand 5 minutes before serving. Serve in tortillas with cheese and sour cream, if desired. *Makes 4 servings*

Tip: To warm tortillas, wrap them in aluminum foil and bake in a 350°F oven for about 5 minutes. Turn off the heat and keep them in the oven until ready to serve.

California Veggie Rolls

Breads

Blueberry Coffeecake

(Pictured at left)

2 cups blueberries, fresh or frozen and partially thawed
1 tablespoon all-purpose flour
1/2 cup honey
2 tablespoons fresh lemon juice

CAKE
1-1/2 cups all-purpose flour
2 teaspoons baking powder
1/2 teaspoon baking soda
1/2 teaspoon salt
1/2 cup honey
2 eggs
1/4 cup milk
2 tablespoons fresh lemon juice
1 teaspoon freshly grated lemon peel
1 teaspoon vanilla extract
6 tablespoons butter, melted

Place blueberries in bottom of greased 9-inch round cake pan; distribute evenly. Sprinkle with flour; drizzle with honey and lemon juice. Set aside.

In small bowl, combine flour, baking powder, baking soda and salt; set aside. In medium bowl, combine honey, eggs, milk, lemon juice, lemon peel and vanilla; beat with fork until well mixed. Add flour mixture; mix well. Stir in melted butter; mix well. Pour batter over blueberries in pan; spread to cover evenly. Bake at 350°F for 30 to 35 minutes or until toothpick inserted in center of cake comes out clean. Cool in pan on wire rack 10 minutes. Invert cake onto large plate; cool.

Makes 8 servings

Favorite recipe from **National Honey Board**

Clockwise from top left: Blueberry Coffeecake, Cranberry Oat Bread (p. 118), Sunday Morning Upside-Down Rolls (p. 114) and Potato Rosemary Rolls (p. 122)

Creamy Cinnamon Rolls

2 (1-pound) loaves frozen bread dough, thawed
2/3 cup (one-half 14-ounce can) EAGLE BRAND®
    Sweetened Condensed Milk*
    (NOT evaporated milk), divided
1 cup chopped pecans
2 teaspoons ground cinnamon
1 cup sifted powdered sugar
1/2 teaspoon vanilla extract
    Additional chopped pecans, if desired

Use remaining Eagle Brand as a dip for fruit. Pour into storage container and store tightly covered in refrigerator for up to 1 week.

1. On lightly floured surface, roll each bread dough loaf into 12×9-inch rectangle. Spread 1/3 cup Eagle Brand over dough rectangles. Sprinkle rectangles with 1 cup pecans and cinnamon. Roll up jelly-roll style starting from short side. Cut each log into 6 slices.

2. Generously grease 13×9-inch baking pan. Place rolls cut sides down in pan. Cover loosely with greased waxed paper and then with plastic wrap. Chill overnight. Cover and chill remaining Eagle Brand.

3. To bake, let pan of rolls stand at room temperature 30 minutes. Preheat oven to 350°F. Bake 30 to 35 minutes or until golden brown. Cool in pan 5 minutes; loosen edges and remove rolls from pan.

4. Meanwhile for frosting, in small mixing bowl, combine powdered sugar, remaining 1/3 cup Eagle Brand and vanilla. Drizzle frosting over warm rolls. Sprinkle with additional chopped pecans, if desired.

Makes 12 rolls

Oatmeal Bread

2-1/4 teaspoons quick-rising active dry yeast
    (one 1/4-ounce package)
3 cups bread flour
1 cup QUAKER® Oats (quick or old fashioned, uncooked)
2 tablespoons granulated sugar
1 teaspoon salt
1-1/4 to 1-1/3 cups milk or water
2 tablespoons butter or margarine, melted, or
    1 tablespoon vegetable oil

Bring all ingredients to room temperature by letting them stand on the counter for about 30 minutes.* Place yeast in bread machine according to directions in manual. Combine flour, oats, sugar and salt in bowl; mix well. In separate bowl, combine milk and butter; mix well. Place in bread machine according to manual. When baking, use white bread and light crust setting.

Makes one 1-1/2-pound loaf

This can be done quickly by microwaving the ingredients for 15 to 20 seconds.

Maple Fruit Variation: Combine 1/3 cup pancake syrup with margarine and only 1 cup milk. Proceed as directed above. Add 1/2 cup dried fruit to bread dough partially through kneading cycle according to manual.

Whole Wheat Variation: Combine 1-1/2 cups bread flour with 1-1/2 cups whole wheat flour. Proceed as directed above.

Orange-Currant Scones

(Pictured at right)

1-1/2 cups all-purpose flour
1/4 cup plus 1 teaspoon sugar, divided
1 teaspoon baking powder
1/4 teaspoon salt
1/4 teaspoon baking soda
1/3 cup currants
1 tablespoon grated fresh orange peel
6 tablespoons cold butter, cut into small pieces
1/2 cup buttermilk

1. Preheat oven to 425°F. Combine flour, 1/4 cup sugar, baking powder, salt and baking soda in large bowl. Stir in currants and orange peel.

2. Cut in butter with pastry blender or 2 knives until mixture resembles coarse crumbs. Stir in buttermilk. Stir until mixture forms soft dough that clings together. (Dough will be sticky.)

3. Lightly flour hands and shape dough into a ball. Pat dough into 8-inch round on lightly greased baking sheet. Cut dough into 8 wedges with floured knife.

4. Sprinkle wedges with remaining 1 teaspoon sugar. Bake 18 to 20 minutes or until lightly browned.

Makes 8 scones

Orange-Currant Scones

Orange Cinnamon Swirl Bread

(Pictured below)

BREAD
- 1 package DUNCAN HINES® Bakery-Style Cinnamon Swirl Muffin Mix
- 1 egg
- 2/3 cup orange juice
- 1 tablespoon grated orange peel

ORANGE GLAZE
- 1/2 cup confectioners' sugar
- 2 to 3 teaspoons orange juice
- 1 teaspoon grated orange peel
- Quartered orange slices for garnish (optional)

1. Preheat oven to 350°F. Grease and flour 8-1/2×4-1/2×2-1/2-inch loaf pan.

2. For bread, combine muffin mix and contents of topping packet from mix in large bowl. Break up any lumps. Add egg, 2/3 cup orange juice and 1 tablespoon orange peel. Stir until moistened, about 50 strokes. Knead swirl packet from mix for 10 seconds before opening. Squeeze contents on top of batter. Swirl into batter with knife or spatula, folding from bottom of bowl to get an even swirl. *Do not completely mix in.* Pour into prepared pan. Bake at 350°F for 55 to 60 minutes or until toothpick inserted in center comes out clean. Cool in pan 10 minutes. Loosen loaf from pan. Invert onto cooling rack. Turn right side up. Cool completely.

3. For orange glaze, place confectioners' sugar in small bowl. Add orange juice, 1 teaspoon at a time, stirring until smooth and of desired consistency. Stir in 1 teaspoon orange peel. Drizzle over loaf. Garnish with orange slices, if desired.

Makes 1 loaf (12 slices)

Tip: If glaze becomes too thin, add additional confectioners' sugar. If glaze is too thick, add more orange juice.

Italian Herb Biscuit Loaf

- 1-1/2 cups all-purpose flour
- 1/4 cup grated Parmesan cheese
- 2 tablespoons cornmeal
- 2 teaspoons baking powder
- 1/2 teaspoon salt
- 1/4 cup cold butter or margarine, cut into pieces
- 2 eggs
- 1/2 cup heavy whipping cream
- 3/4 teaspoon dried basil
- 3/4 teaspoon dried oregano
- 1/8 teaspoon garlic powder
- Additional grated Parmesan cheese (optional)

1. Preheat oven to 425°F. Spray large baking sheet with nonstick cooking spray; set aside.

2. Combine flour, 1/4 cup cheese, cornmeal, baking powder and salt in large bowl. Cut in butter with pastry blender or 2 knives until mixture resembles coarse crumbs. Beat eggs in medium bowl. Add cream, basil, oregano and garlic powder; beat until well blended. Add cream mixture to flour mixture; stir until mixture forms ball.

3. Turn out dough onto well-floured surface. Knead 10 to 12 times; place on prepared cookie sheet. Roll or pat dough into 7-inch round, about 1 inch thick. Score top of dough into 8 wedges with tip of sharp knife; do not cut completely through dough. Sprinkle with additional cheese, if desired.

4. Bake 20 to 25 minutes or until toothpick inserted into center comes out clean. Cool on baking sheet on wire rack 10 minutes. Serve warm.

Makes 8 servings

Orange Cinnamon Swirl Bread

Cherry and Almond Coffeecake

Cherry and Almond Coffee Cake

(Pictured above)

1 sheet (1/2 of 17-1/4-ounce package) frozen
   puff pastry
1 package (3 ounces) cream cheese, softened
1/3 cup plus 2 tablespoons confectioners' sugar,
   divided
1 egg, separated
1/4 teaspoon almond extract
1 tablespoon water
1/2 cup dried cherries or cranberries, coarsely
   chopped
1/2 cup sliced almonds, divided

1. Thaw pastry sheet according to package directions.

2. Preheat oven to 375°F. Spray baking sheet with
nonstick cooking spray.

3. Combine cream cheese, 1/3 cup confectioners'
sugar, egg yolk and almond extract in large bowl.

Beat with electric mixer at medium speed until
smooth; set aside. In separate small bowl, beat
egg white and water; set aside.

4. On lightly floured surface, roll out pastry into
14×10-inch rectangle. Spread cream cheese mixture
over dough to within 1 inch of edges. Sprinkle evenly
with cherries. Reserve 2 tablespoons almonds;
sprinkle remaining almonds over cherries.

5. Starting with long side, loosely roll up dough
jelly-roll style. Place roll on baking sheet, seam
side down. Form into circle, pinching ends together.
Using scissors, cut at 1-inch intervals from outside
of ring toward (but not through) center. Twist each
section half a turn, allowing filling to show.

6. Brush top of ring with egg white mixture. Sprinkle
with reserved almonds. Bake 25 to 30 minutes or until
light brown. Using large spatula, carefully remove ring
to wire rack. Cool 15 minutes; sprinkle with remaining
2 tablespoons confectioners' sugar.

Makes 1 (12-inch) coffee cake

Sage Buns

(Pictured at right)

1-1/2 cups milk
2 tablespoons shortening
3 to 4 cups all-purpose flour, divided
2 tablespoons sugar
1 package (1/4 ounce) active dry yeast
2 teaspoons rubbed sage
1 teaspoon salt
1 tablespoon olive or vegetable oil (optional)

Heat milk and shortening in small saucepan over medium heat, stirring constantly, until shortening is melted and temperature reaches 120° to 130°F. Remove from heat.

Combine 2 cups flour, sugar, yeast, sage and salt in large bowl. Add milk mixture; beat vigorously 2 minutes. Add remaining flour, 1/4 cup at a time, until dough begins to pull away from side of bowl.

Turn out dough onto floured surface; flatten slightly. Knead 10 minutes or until dough is smooth and elastic, adding flour if necessary to prevent sticking.

Shape dough into ball. Place in large lightly greased bowl; turn dough over once to grease top. Cover with towel; let rise in warm place 1 hour or until doubled in bulk. Grease 13×9-inch pan.

Turn out dough onto lightly greased surface. Divide into 24 equal pieces. Form each piece into ball; space balls evenly in prepared pan. Cover and let rise 45 minutes.

Preheat oven to 375°F. Bake 15 to 20 minutes or until golden brown. Immediately remove bread from pan and cool on wire rack. Brush rolls with oil for soft shiny tops, if desired. *Makes 24 rolls*

Helpful Hint

How can you tell if yeast bread dough has doubled in bulk? One way to test this is to press two fingertips about 1/2 inch into the dough; the indentations should remain when you remove your fingers. (If the recipe requires the dough to rise twice, this test can be used only with the first rising.)

Sunday Morning Upside-Down Rolls

(Picture on page 108)

1/4 cup warm water (105°F to 115°F)
1 envelope quick-rising yeast
1/4 teaspoon sugar
1 cup scalded milk, slightly cooled
1/2 cup WESSON® Canola Oil
1/2 cup sugar
3 eggs, beaten
1-1/2 teaspoons salt
4-1/2 cups all-purpose flour
3/4 cup (1-1/2 sticks) butter, softened
2 cups packed brown sugar
1 cup maraschino cherries, chopped
1 (16-ounce) jar KNOTT'S BERRY FARM®
Light Apricot Pineapple Preserves

Pour water into a large bowl. Sprinkle yeast, then 1/4 teaspoon sugar into water; stir well. Let stand 5 to 8 minutes or until mixture is slightly foamy. Meanwhile, in a small bowl, whisk milk, Wesson® Oil, 1/2 cup sugar, eggs and salt until well blended. Pour milk mixture into yeast mixture; blend well. Gradually add flour to mixture; mix until smooth. Knead dough in bowl (about 5 minutes) until smooth. Add more flour if dough is sticky. Cover with towel and let rise in warm place for 30 minutes or until dough nearly doubles in size. Punch down dough once; cover.

Meanwhile, in small bowl, cream together butter and brown sugar. Spoon (be careful not to pack) 2 teaspoons of creamed sugar mixture into *each* of 24 muffin cups. Sprinkle maraschino cherries over creamed sugar mixture; then add 2 teaspoons Knott's® preserves to *each* muffin cup. Tear small pillows of dough and place on preserves, filling *each* muffin cup to the rim. Cover; let rise about 15 to 20 minutes. Preheat oven to 375°F. Bake for 12 to 15 minutes or until golden brown. Immediately invert muffin pans onto cookie sheet. *Do not remove rolls from muffin cups.* Allow a few minutes for preserves to drip down the sides. Lift muffin pans from rolls; cool 5 minutes. Remove muffins to wire rack. Serve warm. *Makes 2 dozen rolls*

Sweet Potato Biscuits

(Pictured at right)

2-1/2 cups all-purpose flour
1/4 cup packed brown sugar
3 teaspoons baking powder
3/4 teaspoon salt
3/4 teaspoon ground cinnamon
1/4 teaspoon ground ginger
1/4 teaspoon ground allspice
1/2 cup shortening
1/2 cup chopped pecans
3/4 cup mashed sweet potatoes
1/2 cup milk

Preheat oven to 450°F.

Combine flour, sugar, baking powder, salt, cinnamon, ginger and allspice in medium bowl. Cut in shortening with pastry blender or 2 knives until mixture resembles coarse crumbs. Stir in pecans.

Combine sweet potatoes and milk in separate medium bowl with wire whisk until smooth.

Make well in center of flour mixture. Add sweet potato mixture; stir until mixture forms soft dough that clings together and forms a ball.

Turn out dough onto well-floured surface. Knead dough gently 10 to 12 times.

Roll or pat dough to 1/2-inch thickness. Cut out dough with floured 2-1/2-inch biscuit cutter.

Place biscuits 2 inches apart on ungreased large baking sheet. Bake 12 to 14 minutes or until golden brown. Serve warm.   *Makes about 12 biscuits*

Poppy Seed Breadsticks

1 cup hot milk (about 120°F)
1/4 CRISCO® Stick or 1/4 cup CRISCO®
  all-vegetable shortening
1 tablespoon sugar
1 teaspoon salt
1 package active dry yeast
3 to 3-1/2 cups all-purpose flour, divided
1 egg
2 tablespoons water
  Poppy seeds

1. Combine milk, 1/4 cup shortening, sugar and salt. Cool slightly.

2. Combine yeast and 2-1/2 cups flour in large bowl. Stir in milk mixture until well blended. Beat in enough remaining flour to make a stiff dough.

3. Turn dough onto lightly floured surface. Knead for 5 minutes or until smooth and elastic. Let rest for 5 minutes.

4. Cut dough into 72 equal pieces with sharp knife. Roll out each piece between palms of hands or on flat surface to make a 6-inch strip. Place on greased cookie sheets.

5. Combine egg and water. Brush breadsticks with egg mixture and sprinkle with poppy seeds. Cover; let rest for 20 minutes.

6. Heat oven to 300°F.

7. Bake at 300°F for 45 to 50 minutes or until golden brown. *Do not overbake.* Cool on racks.

Makes 72 breadsticks

Savory Cheddar Bread

2 cups all-purpose flour
4 teaspoons baking powder
1 tablespoon sugar
1/2 teaspoon onion salt
1/2 teaspoon dried oregano, crushed
1/4 teaspoon dry mustard
1 cup (4 ounces) SARGENTO® Fancy Mild or
  Sharp Cheddar Shredded Cheese
1 cup milk
1 egg, beaten
1 tablespoon butter or margarine, melted

In large bowl, stir together flour, baking powder, sugar, onion salt, oregano, dry mustard and cheese. In separate bowl, combine milk, egg and butter; add to dry ingredients, stirring just until moistened. Spread batter in greased 8×4-inch loaf pan. Bake at 350°F 45 minutes or until wooden pick inserted in center comes out clean. Cool 10 minutes on wire rack. Remove from pan.   *Makes 16 slices*

Grandma's® Bran Muffins

Cranberry Oat Bread

(Pictured on page 108)

      3/4 cup honey
        2 eggs
      1/2 cup milk
      1/3 cup vegetable oil
  2-1/2 cups all-purpose flour
        1 cup quick-cooking rolled oats
        1 teaspoon baking soda
        1 teaspoon baking powder
      1/2 teaspoon salt
      1/2 teaspoon ground cinnamon
        2 cups fresh or frozen cranberries
        1 cup chopped nuts

Combine honey, eggs, milk and oil in large bowl; mix well. Combine flour, oats, baking soda, baking powder, salt and cinnamon in medium bowl; mix well. Stir into honey mixture. Fold in cranberries and nuts. Spoon into two 8-1/2×4-1/2×2-1/2-inch greased and floured loaf pans.

Bake in preheated 350°F oven 40 to 45 minutes or until wooden toothpick inserted near centers comes out clean. Cool in pans on wire racks 15 minutes. Remove from pans; cool completely on wire racks.
Makes 2 loaves

Favorite recipe from **National Honey Board**

Clover Tea Rolls

        2 cups sifted all-purpose flour
      1/4 cup sugar
      3/4 teaspoon ARM & HAMMER® Baking Soda
      1/2 teaspoon salt
      1/3 cup vegetable shortening
      1/2 cup milk
        3 tablespoons lemon juice

Sift together flour, sugar, baking soda and salt into large bowl. Cut in shortening until mixture resembles coarse meal. Combine milk and lemon juice; quickly stir into flour mixture to form a soft dough.

Turn dough onto lightly floured board; knead slightly. Form into 36 small balls about the size of marbles. Place three balls into each greased muffin cup (about 2-1/4-inch diameter). Bake in 450°F oven 15 minutes or until lightly browned.
Makes about 1 dozen rolls

Grandma's® Bran Muffins

(Pictured above)

  2-1/2 cups bran flakes, divided
        1 cup raisins
        1 cup boiling water
        2 cups buttermilk
        1 cup GRANDMA'S® Molasses
      1/2 cup canola oil
        2 eggs, beaten
  2-3/4 cups all-purpose flour
  2-1/2 teaspoons baking soda
      1/2 teaspoon salt

Heat oven to 400°F. In medium bowl, mix 1 cup bran flakes, raisins and water. Set aside. In large bowl, combine remaining ingredients. Mix in bran-raisin mixture. Pour into greased muffin pan cups. Fill 2/3 full and bake for 20 minutes. Remove muffins and place on rack to cool.   *Makes 48 muffins*

Apple Cinnamon Rolls

(Pictured below)

5 to 5-1/2 cups all-purpose flour
1/2 cup sugar
2 envelopes FLEISCHMANN'S® RapidRise™ Yeast
1 teaspoon salt
1/2 cup water
1/2 cup milk
1/4 cup butter or margarine
3 large eggs
Apple Filling (recipe follows)
Cinnamon-Sugar Topping (recipe follows)

In large bowl, combine 1 cup flour, sugar, undissolved yeast and salt. Heat water, milk and butter until very warm (120° to 130°F). Gradually add to dry ingredients. Beat 2 minutes at medium speed of electric mixer, scraping bowl occasionally. Add eggs and 1 cup flour; beat 2 minutes at high speed, scraping bowl occasionally. Stir in enough remaining flour to make soft dough. Knead on lightly floured surface until smooth and elastic, about 8 to 10 minutes. Cover; let rest 10 minutes.

Divide dough into 2 equal portions. Roll each portion into 12×8-inch rectangle. Spread Apple Filling evenly over dough. Beginning at long end of each rectangle, roll up tightly jelly-roll style. Pinch seams to seal. Cut each roll into 12 equal pieces. Place, cut sides up, in greased 9-inch round pans. Cover and let rise in warm, draft-free place until doubled in size, about 45 minutes. Sprinkle with Cinnamon-Sugar Topping.

Bake at 375°F for 25 to 30 minutes or until done. Remove from pans; serve warm. *Makes 24 rolls*

Apple Filling: Combine 2 large cooking apples, chopped, 3/4 cup sugar, 1/4 cup butter or margarine and 2 tablespoons all-purpose flour in medium saucepan; bring to a boil over medium high heat. Cook 3 minutes. Reduce heat to medium-low; cook 10 minutes, stirring constantly until thick. Stir in 1 teaspoon ground cinnamon and 1/2 teaspoon nutmeg. Cool completely.

Cinnamon-Sugar Topping: Combine 3/4 cup sugar, 1 teaspoon ground cinnamon and 1/2 teaspoon nutmeg. Stir until well blended.

Apple Cinnamon Rolls

Farmer-Style Sour Cream Bread

(Pictured at right)

1 cup (8 ounces) sour cream
3 tablespoons water
2-1/2 to 3 cups all-purpose flour, divided
1 package (1/4 ounce) active dry yeast
2 tablespoons sugar
1-1/2 teaspoons salt
1/4 teaspoon baking soda
Vegetable oil
1 tablespoon poppy or sesame seeds

Stir together sour cream and water in small saucepan. Heat over low heat until temperature reaches 120° to 130°F. *Do not boil.* Combine 2 cups flour, yeast, sugar, salt and baking soda in large bowl. Add sour cream mixture; stir until well blended. Turn out dough onto lightly floured surface. Knead about 5 minutes, adding remaining flour as necessary, until dough is smooth and elastic.

Grease large baking sheet. Shape dough into ball; place on prepared sheet. Flatten into 8-inch circle. Brush with oil; sprinkle with poppy seeds. Invert large bowl over dough and let rise in warm place 1 hour or until doubled in bulk.

Preheat oven to 350°F. Bake 22 to 27 minutes or until golden brown. Remove immediately from baking sheet; cool on wire rack.   *Makes 8 to 12 servings*

Honey Roasted Ham Biscuits

1 (10-ounce) can refrigerated buttermilk biscuits
2 cups (12 ounces) diced CURE 81® ham
1/2 cup honey mustard
1/4 cup finely chopped honey roasted peanuts, divided

Heat oven to 400°F. Separate biscuits. Place in muffin pans, pressing gently into bottom and up sides of pans. In bowl, combine ham, honey mustard and 2 tablespoons peanuts. Spoon ham mixture evenly into biscuit cups. Sprinkle with remaining 2 tablespoons peanuts. Bake 15 to 17 minutes.
      Makes 10 servings

Blueberry White Chip Muffins

2 cups all-purpose flour
1/2 cup granulated sugar
1/4 cup packed brown sugar
2-1/2 teaspoons baking powder
1/2 teaspoon salt
3/4 cup milk
1 large egg, lightly beaten
1/4 cup butter or margarine, melted
1/2 teaspoon grated lemon peel
2 cups (12-ounce package) NESTLÉ® TOLL HOUSE® Premier White Morsels, *divided*
1-1/2 cups fresh or frozen blueberries
Streusel Topping (recipe follows)

PREHEAT oven to 375°F. Paper-line 18 muffin cups.

COMBINE flour, granulated sugar, brown sugar, baking powder and salt in large bowl. Stir in milk, egg, butter and lemon peel. Stir in *1-1/2 cups* morsels and blueberries. Spoon into prepared muffin cups, filling almost full. Sprinkle with Streusel Topping.

BAKE for 22 to 25 minutes or until wooden pick inserted in center comes out clean. Cool in pans for 5 minutes; remove to wire racks to cool slightly.

PLACE *remaining* morsels in small, *heavy-duty* resealable plastic food storage bag. Microwave on MEDIUM-HIGH (70%) power for 30 seconds; knead. Microwave at additional 10- to 15-second intervals, kneading until smooth. Cut tiny corner from bag; squeeze to drizzle over muffins. Serve warm.
      Makes 18 muffins

Streusel Topping: COMBINE 1/3 cup granulated sugar, 1/4 cup all-purpose flour and 1/4 teaspoon ground cinnamon in small bowl. Cut in 3 tablespoons butter or margarine with pastry blender or two knives until mixture resembles coarse crumbs.

Helpful Hint

Frozen blueberries should not be thawed before using in baked goods. Add them to the batter in their solid state at the last minute to prevent them from "bleeding" into the batter.

Sesame-Onion Twists

(Pictured at right)

2 tablespoons butter or margarine
1-1/2 cups finely chopped onions
1/4 teaspoon paprika
1 loaf (16 ounces) frozen bread dough, thawed
1 egg, beaten
1 tablespoon sesame seeds

Grease large baking sheet; set aside. Melt butter in medium skillet over medium heat until foamy. Add onions and paprika; cook until onions are tender, stirring occasionally. Remove from heat.

Spray work surface with nonstick cooking spray. Roll thawed bread dough into 14×12-inch rectangle.

Spread onion mixture on one side of dough. Fold dough over onion mixture to form 14×6-inch rectangle. Pinch 14-inch side of dough to seal. Cut dough into 14 lengthwise strips.

Gently twist dough strip two times and place on prepared sheet. Press both ends of strip down on cookie sheet. Repeat with remaining strips.

Cover with towel. Let twists rise in warm place about 40 minutes or until doubled in bulk. Brush with egg; sprinkle with sesame seeds.

Preheat oven to 375°F. Bake 15 to 18 minutes or until golden brown. Serve immediately.

Makes 14 twists

Potato Rosemary Rolls

(Pictured on page 108)

DOUGH
1 cup plus 2 tablespoons water (70° to 80°F)
2 tablespoons olive oil
1 teaspoon salt
3 cups bread flour
1/2 cup instant potato flakes or buds
2 tablespoons nonfat dry milk powder
1 tablespoon sugar
1 teaspoon SPICE ISLANDS® Rosemary, crushed
1-1/2 teaspoons FLEISCHMANN'S® Bread Machine Yeast

TOPPING
1 egg, lightly beaten
Sesame or poppy seeds or additional dried rosemary, crushed

Measure all dough ingredients into bread machine pan in the order suggested by manufacturer, adding potato flakes with flour. Select dough/manual cycle. When cycle is complete, remove dough to floured surface. If necessary, knead in additional flour to make dough easy to handle.

Divide dough into 12 equal pieces. Roll each piece to 10-inch rope; coil each rope and tuck end under coil. Place rolls 2 inches apart on large greased baking sheet. Cover; let rise in warm, draft-free place until doubled in size, about 45 to 60 minutes. Brush tops with beaten egg; sprinkle with sesame seeds. Bake at 375°F for 15 to 20 minutes or until done. Remove from pan; cool on wire rack.

Makes 12 rolls

Note: Dough can be prepared in 1-1/2 and 2-pound bread machines.

Southern Hush Puppies

CRISCO® Oil,* for frying
3/4 cup yellow cornmeal
1/3 cup unsifted all-purpose flour
1-1/2 teaspoons baking powder
1/2 teaspoon salt
1/2 cup buttermilk
1 egg
1/4 cup finely chopped onion

*Use your favorite Crisco Oil product.

1. Heat 2 to 3 inches of oil in deep-fryer or large saucepan. Heat over high heat to 375°F.

2. Mix cornmeal, flour, baking powder and salt in medium mixing bowl. Add remaining ingredients; mix well.

3. Drop batter by tablespoonfuls into hot oil. Fry a few hush puppies at a time, 3 to 4 minutes, or until golden brown. Remove with slotted spoon.

4. Drain on paper towels. Repeat with remaining batter. Serve immediately or keep warm in 175°F oven.

Makes about 1 dozen hush puppies

Focaccia

(Pictured at right)

1 package (1/4 ounce) active dry yeast
1 teaspoon sugar
1-1/2 cups warm water (105 to 110°F)
4 cups all-purpose flour, divided
7 tablespoons olive or vegetable oil, divided
1 teaspoon salt
1/4 cup roasted red peppers, drained and
     cut into strips
1/4 cup pitted ripe olives

To proof yeast, sprinkle yeast and sugar over warm water in large bowl; stir until dissolved. Let stand 5 minutes or until mixture is bubbly. Add 3-1/2 cups flour, 3 tablespoons oil and salt, stirring until soft dough forms. Turn out dough onto lightly floured surface. Knead 5 minutes or until smooth and elastic, gradually adding remaining flour to prevent sticking, if necessary. Shape dough into ball; place in large, lightly greased bowl. Turn dough over so top is greased. Cover and let rise in warm place 1 hour or until doubled in bulk.

Brush 15-1/2×10-1/2-inch jelly-roll pan with 1 tablespoon oil. Punch down dough. Turn out dough onto lightly floured surface. Flatten into rectangle; roll out almost to size of pan. Place dough in pan; gently press dough to edges of pan. Poke surface of dough with end of wooden spoon handle, making indentations every 1 or 2 inches. Brush with remaining 3 tablespoons oil. Gently press peppers and olives into dough, forming decorative pattern. Cover with towel; let rise in warm place 30 minutes or until doubled in bulk.

Preheat oven to 450°F. Bake 12 to 15 minutes or until golden brown. Cut into squares or rectangles. Serve warm. *Makes 12 servings*

Helpful Hint

Yeast doughs need to be set in a warm (80° to 85°F), draft-free spot to rise. A gas oven with the pilot light on, or an electric oven that has been heated for one minute and then turned off are good places.

Chocolate Chunk Banana Bread

1 cup mashed ripe bananas
2 eggs, lightly beaten
1/3 cup oil
1/4 cup milk
2 cups flour
1 cup sugar
2 teaspoons CALUMET® Baking Powder
1/4 teaspoon salt
1 package (4 ounces) BAKER'S® GERMAN'S®
     Sweet Baking Chocolate, coarsely chopped
1/2 cup chopped nuts

HEAT oven to 350°F.

STIR bananas, eggs, oil and milk until well blended. Add flour, sugar, baking powder and salt; stir until just moistened. Stir in chocolate and nuts. Pour into greased 9×5-inch loaf pan.

BAKE for 55 minutes or until toothpick inserted into center comes out clean. Cool in pan 10 minutes. Remove from pan; cool completely on wire rack.
Makes 18 (1/2-inch) servings

Note: For easier slicing, wrap bread and store overnight.

Old-Fashioned Corn Bread

1 cup sifted all-purpose flour
1 teaspoon salt
3/4 teaspoon ARM & HAMMER® Baking Soda
1-1/2 cups cornmeal
1-1/2 cups buttermilk
2 eggs, beaten
3 tablespoons shortening, melted

Sift together flour, salt and baking soda. Stir in cornmeal. Combine buttermilk, eggs and melted shortening. Add liquid ingredients to dry ingredients, stirring only until smooth. Turn into well-greased 8×8-inch pan. Bake at 425°F 25 to 30 minutes.
Makes 16 servings

Main Dishes

Ham and Egg Enchiladas

(Pictured at left)

2 tablespoons butter or margarine
1 small red bell pepper, chopped
3 green onions with tops, sliced
1/2 cup diced fully cooked ham
8 eggs
8 flour tortillas (7- to 8-inch)
2 cups (8 ounces) shredded Colby-Jack cheese or
    pepper-Jack cheese, divided
1 can (10 ounces) enchilada sauce
1/2 cup prepared salsa
    Sliced avocado, fresh cilantro and red bell pepper slices
    (optional)

1. Preheat oven to 350°F.

2. Melt butter in large nonstick skillet over medium heat. Add bell pepper and onions; cook and stir 2 minutes. Add ham; cook and stir 1 minute.

3. Lightly beat eggs with wire whisk in medium bowl. Add eggs to skillet; cook until eggs are set but still soft, stirring occasionally.

4. Spoon about 1/3 cup egg mixture evenly down center of each tortilla; top with 1 tablespoon cheese. Roll tortillas up and place seam side down in shallow 11×7-inch baking dish.

5. Combine enchilada sauce and salsa in small bowl; pour evenly over enchiladas.

6. Cover enchiladas with foil; bake 20 minutes. Uncover and sprinkle with remaining cheese. Bake, uncovered, 10 minutes longer or until cheese is melted. Garnish with avocado, cilantro and bell pepper, if desired. Serve immediately. *Makes 4 servings*

Clockwise from top left: Pizza Meat Loaf (p. 128), Sausage and Broccoli Noodle Casserole (p. 168), Carolina Baked Beans & Pork Chop (p. 148) and Ham and Egg Enchiladas

Maple-Mustard-Glazed Spareribs

(Pictured at right)

4 pounds pork spareribs
1/2 teaspoon salt
1/2 teaspoon pickling spices*
2 teaspoons vegetable oil
1 small onion, coarsely chopped
1/2 cup maple-flavored syrup
1/4 cup cider vinegar
2 tablespoons water
1 tablespoon Dijon mustard
Dash salt
1/4 teaspoon black pepper

Pickling spices is a blend of seasonings used for pickling foods. It can include allspice, bay leaves, cardamom, coriander, cinnamon, cloves, ginger, mustard seeds and/or pepper. Most supermarkets carry prepackaged pickling spices in the spice aisle.

Sprinkle spareribs with 1/2 teaspoon salt. Place pickling spices in several thicknesses of cheesecloth; tie up to make a bouquet garni. Set aside. For glaze, heat oil in small saucepan; add onion. Cook and stir until tender. Add bouquet garni. Stir in syrup, vinegar, water, mustard, dash salt and pepper. Bring to a boil over medium-high heat; reduce heat to low and simmer 20 minutes. Discard bouquet garni.

Prepare grill with rectangular foil drip pan. Bank briquets on either side of drip pan for indirect cooking. Place ribs on grid over drip pan. Grill, on covered grill, over low coals 1-1/2 hours or until ribs are tender, turning and basting occasionally with glaze. (Do not baste during last 5 minutes of grilling.)   *Makes 4 servings*

Favorite recipe from **National Pork Board**

Helpful Hint

The indirect grilling method (food is set over a drip pan with hot coals banked on one or both sides of the pan) is used for slow, even cooking of foods, such as large cuts of meat and whole chickens. When grilling for more than 45 minutes, extra briquets will have to be added to the grill to maintain a constant temperature.

Pizza Meat Loaf

(Pictured on page 126 and on back cover)

1 envelope LIPTON® RECIPE SECRETS®
    Onion Soup Mix*
2 pounds ground beef
1-1/2 cups fresh bread crumbs
2 eggs
1 small green bell pepper, chopped (optional)
1/4 cup water
1 cup RAGÚ® Old World Style® Pasta Sauce,
    divided
1 cup shredded mozzarella cheese (about
    4 ounces), divided

Also terrific with LIPTON® RECIPE SECRETS® Savory Herb with Garlic Soup Mix.

Preheat oven to 350°F. In large bowl, combine all ingredients except 1/2 cup pasta sauce and 1/2 cup cheese.

In 13×9-inch baking or roasting pan, shape into loaf. Top with remaining 1/2 cup pasta sauce.

Bake uncovered 50 minutes.

Sprinkle top with remaining 1/2 cup cheese. Bake an additional 10 minutes or until done. Let stand 10 minutes before serving.   *Makes 8 servings*

Tip: When grating cheese, spray your box grater with nonstick cooking spray and place on a sheet of waxed paper. When you finish grating, clean-up is a breeze. Simply discard the waxed paper and rinse the grater clean.

Cure 81® Ham with Honey Mustard Glaze

1 CURE 81® half ham
1 cup packed brown sugar
1/2 cup honey
2 tablespoons prepared mustard

Bake ham according to package directions. Meanwhile, combine brown sugar, honey and mustard. Thirty minutes before ham is done, remove from oven. Score surface; spoon on glaze. Return to oven and continue basting with glaze during last 30 minutes of baking.   *Makes 8 to 10 servings*

Lemon Catfish Bake

(Pictured at right)

2 tablespoons butter or margarine, melted
2 tablespoons lemon juice
1/4 cup dry breadcrumbs
3/4 teaspoon LAWRY'S® Lemon Pepper
1/2 teaspoon LAWRY'S® Seasoned Salt
1/4 teaspoon dill weed
1 pound catfish fillets
 Paprika
4 lemon slices (garnish)

In shallow dish, combine butter and lemon juice; set aside. In another shallow dish, combine breadcrumbs, Lemon Pepper, Seasoned Salt and dill weed. Pat fillets dry. Dip in butter mixture, then in breadcrumb mixture. Place in ungreased 12×8×2-inch baking dish. Pour remaining butter mixture over fillets; sprinkle lightly with paprika. Bake, uncovered, in 350°F oven for 25 to 30 minutes or until fish begins to flake easily with fork.

Makes 4 servings

Tip: Garnish with lemon slices. Serve with fresh steamed vegetables, potatoes or rice.

Variation: Any type of fish fillets may be substituted.

Stuffed Acorn Squash

1 pound BOB EVANS® Zesty Hot Roll Sausage
2 eggs, lightly beaten
1/2 cup finely chopped onion
1 teaspoon salt
1/2 teaspoon ground black pepper
5 slices white bread
2 medium acorn squash

Preheat oven to 375°F. Combine sausage, eggs, onion, salt and pepper in medium bowl; mix well. Cut bread into cubes and combine with sausage mixture. Cut each squash in half crosswise and remove seeds. Cut small slice off ends so squash will sit flat in pan. Pierce inside of squash with fork; fill with sausage mixture. Place filled squash in 13×9-inch baking pan; place 1/2 cup water in bottom of pan. Bake 1 hour 15 minutes or until squash is tender and sausage is cooked through. Refrigerate leftovers. *Makes 4 servings*

Shrimp Alfredo with Sugar Snap Peas

1/2 cup milk
3 tablespoons margarine or butter
1 (4.7-ounce) package PASTA RONI®
 Fettuccine Alfredo
1 (9-ounce) package frozen sugar snap peas,
 thawed
8 ounces cooked, deveined, peeled medium
 shrimp
1/2 teaspoon ground lemon pepper

1. In large saucepan, bring 1-1/4 cups water, milk, margarine, pasta and Special Seasonings to a boil. Reduce heat to low. Gently boil 4 minutes, stirring occasionally.

2. Stir in snap peas, shrimp and lemon pepper; cook 1 to 2 minutes or until pasta is tender. Let stand 3 minutes before serving. *Makes 4 servings*

Tip: If you don't have lemon pepper in your cupboard, try Italian seasoning instead.

Deviled Chicken

3 tablespoons butter or margarine
1 package (about 2-3/4 pounds) PERDUE®
 Fresh Split Chicken Breasts
 Salt and ground pepper to taste
2 tablespoons chili sauce or ketchup
2 tablespoons Worcestershire sauce
2 teaspoons grainy, "country-style" mustard
1/8 teaspoon ground red pepper

Prepare outdoor grill for cooking or preheat broiler. In small saucepan over low heat, melt butter. Brush chicken breasts with butter and season with salt and pepper. To butter remaining in pan, add chili sauce, Worcestershire sauce, mustard and ground red pepper; stir to combine. Over medium heat, bring to a boil; set aside. Grill or broil chicken 6 to 8 inches from heat source 10 to 15 minutes per side, until nicely browned, cooked through and a meat thermometer inserted in thickest part of breast registers 170°F. During last 10 minutes of cooking time, baste 2 to 3 times with butter mixture.

Makes 4 servings

Onion-Baked Pork Chops

(Pictured at right)

1 envelope LIPTON® RECIPE SECRETS®
    Golden Onion Soup Mix*
1/3 cup plain dry bread crumbs
4 pork chops, 1 inch thick (about 3 pounds)
1 egg, well beaten

Also terrific with LIPTON® RECIPE SECRETS® Onion or Savory Herb with Garlic Soup Mix.

1. Preheat oven to 400°F. In small bowl, combine soup mix and bread crumbs. Dip chops in egg, then bread crumb mixture until evenly coated.

2. In lightly greased 13×9-inch baking or roasting pan, arrange chops.

3. Bake uncovered 20 minutes or until barely pink in center, turning once.   *Makes 4 servings*

Florentine Strata

8 ounces BARILLA® Spaghetti or Linguine
1 jar (26 ounces) BARILLA® Roasted Garlic and Onion Pasta Sauce, divided
1 package (12 ounces) frozen spinach soufflé, thawed
2 cups (8 ounces) shredded mozzarella cheese, divided
1/4 cup (1 ounce) grated Parmesan cheese, divided

1. Cook spaghetti according to package directions until partially done but still firm, 5 to 8 minutes. Drain.

2. Meanwhile, coat microwave-safe 13×9×2-inch baking dish with nonstick cooking spray. Pour 1-1/2 cups pasta sauce into baking dish; top with half of drained spaghetti, spinach soufflé, 1 cup mozzarella cheese and 2 tablespoons Parmesan. Repeat layers of spaghetti, pasta sauce and cheeses.

3. Cover with plastic wrap and microwave on HIGH, turning every 4 minutes, until strata is bubbly and cheese is melted, 8 to 10 minutes. Let stand 3 minutes before serving.   *Makes 8 servings*

Tip: When preparing pasta that will be used in a casserole, it's important to reduce the suggested cooking time on the package by about one third. The pasta will continue to cook and absorb liquid while the casserole is cooking.

Spaghetti Pie

6 ounces spaghetti, cooked and well drained
2 eggs, lightly beaten
8 ounces ground beef
1/2 cup chopped onion
3/4 cup spaghetti sauce
1/3 cup A.1.® Steak Sauce
8 ounces POLL-Y® Ricotta Cheese
2 tablespoons KRAFT® Grated Parmesan Cheese

1. Mix spaghetti with eggs until well blended; press on bottom and side of lightly greased 9-inch pie plate with spoon to form crust. Set aside.

2. Cook ground beef and onion in skillet over medium-high heat until meat is no longer pink, stirring to break up meat; pour off fat. Stir in spaghetti sauce and steak sauce. Heat to a boil; reduce heat to low. Cook, uncovered, for 1 to 2 minutes or until slightly thickened. Remove from heat.

3. Spread ricotta cheese into prepared crust; top with meat mixture.

4. Bake at 350°F for 25 to 30 minutes or until hot. Sprinkle with Parmesan cheese; bake for 5 minutes more. Let stand for 5 minutes before serving.   *Makes 6 servings*

Honey Roasted Chicken

3 tablespoons FILIPPO BERIO® Olive Oil
2 tablespoons orange juice
2 tablespoons honey
1-1/4 teaspoons paprika
2-1/2 pounds chicken quarters

Preheat oven to 425°F. In small bowl, whisk together olive oil, orange juice, honey and paprika. Brush chicken pieces generously with olive oil mixture. Arrange chicken in roasting pan. Roast 15 minutes. Reduce oven temperature to 400°F. Baste chicken again with olive oil mixture. Roast chicken, basting occasionally, 30 to 40 minutes or until chicken is no longer pink in center and juices run clear.   *Makes 4 servings*

Teriyaki Beef

Teriyaki Beef

(Pictured above)

3/4 pound sirloin tip steak, cut into thin strips
1/2 cup teriyaki sauce
1/4 cup water
  1 tablespoon cornstarch
  1 teaspoon sugar
  1 bag (16 ounces) BIRDS EYE® frozen Farm Fresh
    Mixtures Broccoli, Carrots and Water
    Chestnuts

• Spray large skillet with nonstick cooking spray; cook beef over medium-high heat 7 to 8 minutes, stirring occasionally.

• Combine teriyaki sauce, water, cornstarch and sugar; mix well.

• Add teriyaki sauce mixture and vegetables to beef. Bring to boil; quickly reduce heat to medium.

• Cook 7 to 10 minutes or until broccoli is heated through, stirring occasionally.

Makes 4 to 6 servings

Tip: Serve this Oriental favorite on a bed of rice and garnish with chow mein noodles or toasted sesame seeds.

Italian Sausage and Rice Frittata

  7 large eggs
3/4 cup milk
1/2 teaspoon salt
1/2 pound mild or hot Italian sausage,
    casing removed and sausage broken
    into small pieces
1-1/2 cups uncooked UNCLE BEN'S® Instant
    Brown Rice
  1 can (14-1/2 ounces) Italian-style stewed
    tomatoes, undrained
1/4 teaspoon Italian herb seasoning
1-1/2 cups (6 ounces) shredded Italian cheese blend,
    divided

1. Whisk together eggs, milk and salt in medium bowl. Set aside.

2. Preheat oven to 325°F. Cook sausage about 7 minutes in 11-inch ovenproof nonstick skillet over high heat until no longer pink.

3. Reduce heat to medium-low. Stir in rice, stewed tomatoes with their juices, breaking up any large pieces, and Italian seasoning. Sprinkle evenly with 1 cup cheese.

4. Pour egg mixture into skillet; stir gently to distribute egg. Cover and cook 15 minutes or until eggs are just set.

5. Remove from heat. Sprinkle remaining 1/2 cup cheese over frittata. Bake about 10 minutes or until puffed and cheese is melted.

6. Remove skillet from oven. Cover and let stand 5 minutes. Cut into 6 wedges before serving.
Makes 6 servings

Tip: Choose a blend of shredded mozzarella and provolone for this frittata, or the blend of your choice.

3-Cheese Baked Ham and Tortellini

(Pictured below)

2 tablespoons minced onion
2 cloves garlic, minced
1-1/2 tablespoons butter or margarine
2 tablespoons all-purpose flour
1-1/2 cups milk
1/4 cup shredded mozzarella cheese
1/4 cup shredded Parmesan cheese
1/4 cup shredded Swiss cheese
1 cup (6 ounces) finely chopped CURE 81® ham
1/4 teaspoon white pepper
4 cups cooked cheese-filled tortellini
Chopped fresh parsley

In small saucepan over medium-low heat, cook onion and garlic in butter until tender. Stir in flour. Cook 2 minutes, stirring constantly. Gradually stir in milk. Simmer 10 to 15 minutes or until thickened, stirring frequently. Add cheeses. Stir until melted. Stir in ham and white pepper. Spoon pasta into 4 to 6 individual gratin dishes. Spoon sauce over pasta. Broil 4 inches from heat source 3 to 5 minutes or until topping is slightly golden. Sprinkle with chopped parsley. *Makes 4 to 6 servings*

Barbecued Chicken

2-1/2 to 3-pound broiler-fryer chicken, cut up
BARBECUE SAUCE
1 cup catsup
1/4 cup GRANDMA'S® Molasses Unsulphured
1/4 cup cider vinegar
1/4 cup Dijon mustard
2 tablespoons Worcestershire sauce
1 teaspoon garlic powder
1 teaspoon hickory flavor liquid smoke
1/4 teaspoon cayenne pepper
1/4 teaspoon hot pepper sauce

In 12×8-inch (2-quart) microwave-safe baking dish, arrange chicken pieces with thickest portions to outside. In small bowl, combine all sauce ingredients; set aside.

Prepare barbecue grill. Cover chicken with waxed paper. Microwave on HIGH (100%) for 10 minutes. Immediately place chicken on grill over medium heat. Brush with sauce. Cook 20 to 25 minutes or until no longer pink, turning once and brushing frequently with sauce. *Makes 4 to 6 servings*

Note: This Barbecue Sauce is equally delicious on ribs.

3-Cheese Baked Ham and Tortellini

Campbell's® Garlic Mashed Potatoes & Beef Bake

(Pictured at right)

1 pound ground beef
1 can (10-3/4 ounces) CAMPBELL'S®
    Condensed Cream of Mushroom
    with Roasted Garlic Soup
1 tablespoon Worcestershire sauce
1 bag (16 ounces) frozen vegetable combination
    (broccoli, cauliflower, carrots), thawed
3 cups hot mashed potatoes

1. In medium skillet over medium-high heat, cook beef until browned, stirring to separate meat. Pour off fat.

2. In 2-quart shallow baking dish mix beef, *1/2 can* soup, Worcestershire and vegetables.

3. Stir remaining soup into potatoes. Spoon potato mixture over beef mixture. Bake at 400°F. for 20 minutes or until hot.   *Makes 4 servings*

Velveeta® Tex-Mex Chicken & Rice

4 small boneless skinless chicken breast halves
    (about 1 pound)
1 can (15 ounces) pinto beans, drained or
    1-1/2 cups cooked pinto beans
1 can (14-1/2 ounces) chicken broth
1 cup TACO BELL® HOME ORIGINALS®*
    Thick 'N Chunky Salsa
2 cups MINUTE® White Rice, uncooked
1/2 pound (8 ounces) VELVEETA® Pasteurized
    Prepared Cheese Product, cut up

TACO BELL and HOME ORIGINALS are registered trademarks owned and licensed by Taco Bell Corp.

1. Spray large skillet with no stick cooking spray. Add chicken; cover. Cook on medium-high heat 4 minutes on each side or until cooked through. Remove chicken from skillet.

2. Add beans, broth and salsa to skillet; stir. Bring to boil.

3. Stir in rice and VELVEETA. Top with chicken; cover. Cook on low heat 5 minutes. Sprinkle with chopped cilantro, if desired, before serving.
    Makes 4 servings

Skillet Fillets

1 medium tomato, seeded and chopped
2 tablespoons sliced ripe olives
1 tablespoon chopped parsley
1 tablespoon red wine vinegar
1 package (16 ounces) frozen sole fillets, thawed
1/4 cup Dijon mustard, divided
1 can (14-1/2 ounces) chicken broth
1 clove garlic, minced
1 cup uncooked white rice
1 package (10 ounces) frozen chopped spinach,
    thawed and very well drained

1. Combine tomato, olives, parsley and vinegar in small bowl, stir well and set aside.

2. Pat fillets dry with paper towels. Divide 1 tablespoon mustard between fillets, spreading thin layer on one side of fillets. Combine broth, garlic and remaining 3 tablespoons mustard in large skillet; bring to a boil over high heat. Stir in rice. Cover and reduce heat to low; simmer 10 minutes. Stir in spinach. Arrange fillets on top of rice mixture; cover and simmer about 8 minutes or until liquid is absorbed and fish flakes easily with a fork. Spoon tomato mixture over top of fish before serving.
    Makes 4 servings

Favorite recipe from **National Fisheries Institute**

Seafood Quiche

1 package (8 ounces) PHILADELPHIA®
    Cream Cheese, softened
1 can (6 ounces) crabmeat, drained, flaked
4 eggs
1/2 cup sliced green onions
1/2 cup milk
1/2 teaspoon dill weed
1/2 teaspoon lemon and pepper seasoning salt
1 (9-inch) baked pastry shell

MIX all ingredients except pastry shell with electric mixer on medium speed until well blended.

POUR into pastry shell.

BAKE at 350°F for 40 minutes or until knife inserted in center comes out clean. Let stand 10 minutes before serving.   *Makes 6 to 8 servings*

*Campbell's® Garlic Mashed
Potatoes & Beef Bake*

Baja Fish Tacos

(Pictured at right)

1/2 cup sour cream
1/2 cup mayonnaise
1/4 cup chopped fresh cilantro
1 package (1.25 ounces) ORTEGA® Taco
  Seasoning Mix, *divided*
1 pound (about 4) cod or other white fish fillets,
  cut into 1-inch pieces
2 tablespoons vegetable oil
2 tablespoons lemon juice
1 package (12) ORTEGA® Taco Shells

TOPPINGS
  Shredded cabbage, chopped tomato, lime
  juice, ORTEGA® Thick & Smooth Taco Sauce

COMBINE sour cream, mayonnaise, cilantro and
2 tablespoons seasoning mix in small bowl.

COMBINE cod, vegetable oil, lemon juice and
remaining taco seasoning mix in medium bowl;
pour into large skillet. Cook, stirring constantly,
over medium-high heat for 4 to 5 minutes or until
fish flakes easily when tested with fork.

FILL taco shells with fish mixture. Top with desired
toppings.   *Makes 6 servings*

Tip: Try a variety of fish and seafood such as shark,
shrimp, crab or lobster in these fresh-tasting tacos.

Mexicali Cornbread Casserole

2-1/2 cups frozen mixed vegetables, thawed
1-1/2 cups cubed HILLSHIRE FARM® Ham
  1 package (10 ounces) cornbread stuffing mix
  2 cups milk
  3 eggs, lightly beaten
  Salt and black pepper to taste
1/2 cup (2 ounces) shredded taco-flavored cheese

Preheat oven to 375°F.

Combine mixed vegetables, Ham and stuffing mix
in small casserole; set aside. Combine milk, eggs,
salt and pepper in medium bowl; pour over ham
mixture. Bake, covered, 45 minutes. Top with
cheese; bake, uncovered, 3 minutes or until
cheese is melted.   *Makes 4 servings*

Spicy-Sweet Brisket

4 to 5 pounds boneless beef brisket, well
  trimmed
1 pound fresh mushrooms, cleaned but not
  sliced
3 carrots, cut into 2-inch pieces
3 onions, thinly sliced
1 rib celery, cut into 2-inch pieces
1 (26-ounce) jar NEWMAN'S OWN®
  Diavolo Sauce
1/2 cup water
1/2 cup packed brown sugar
1 tablespoon garlic powder
1/2 teaspoon black pepper

Preheat oven to 350°F. Brown meat in large ungreased
skillet. Remove to large Dutch oven. Add vegetables
to meat. In separate bowl, combine Diavolo Sauce,
water and brown sugar; stir and pour over meat.
Sprinkle with garlic powder and pepper.

Cover tightly and bake 3 hours. Remove cover and
allow meat to slightly brown 30 minutes.

Brisket should be made a day ahead of time and
refrigerated overnight to allow flavors to blend.
Thinly slice brisket across the grain.
                                    Makes 12 servings

Swanson® 25-Minute Chicken & Noodles

1 can (14-3/4 ounces) SWANSON® Chicken
  Broth (1-3/4 cups)
1/2 teaspoon dried basil leaves, crushed
1/8 teaspoon pepper
  2 cups frozen vegetable combination
    (broccoli, cauliflower, carrots)
  2 cups *uncooked* medium egg noodles
  2 cups cubed cooked chicken

1. In medium skillet mix broth, basil, pepper and
vegetables. Over medium-high heat, heat to a boil.
Reduce heat to medium. Cover and cook 5 minutes.

2. Stir in noodles. Cover and cook 5 minutes, stirring
often. Add chicken and heat through.
                                    Makes 4 servings

Franco-American® Quick Pepper Steak

(Pictured at right)

1 pound boneless beef sirloin *or* top round steak, 3/4 inch thick
2 tablespoons vegetable oil
2 medium green *or* red peppers, cut into 2-inch-long strips (about 3 cups)
1 medium onion, cut into wedges
1/2 teaspoon garlic powder
1 can (10-1/4 ounces) FRANCO-AMERICAN® Beef Gravy
1 tablespoon Worcestershire sauce
4 cups hot cooked rice

1. Slice beef into thin strips.

2. In medium skillet over medium-high heat, heat *half* the oil. Add beef in 2 batches and stir-fry until browned. Set beef aside.

3. Reduce heat to medium. Add remaining oil. Add peppers, onion and garlic powder and stir-fry until tender-crisp. Pour off fat.

4. Add gravy and Worcestershire. Heat to a boil. Return beef to pan. Reduce heat to low and heat through. Serve over rice.   *Makes 4 servings*

Tip: Instead of choosing either green or red peppers, try both together to vary the flavor and create a colorful dish!

Moroccan Supper

1 (7.2-ounce) package RICE-A-RONI® Rice Pilaf
1/2 cup chopped onion
2 cloves garlic, minced
2 tablespoons margarine or olive oil
1 teaspoon ground cumin
1/4 teaspoon ground cinnamon
1 (15-ounce) can garbanzo beans or chick peas, rinsed and drained
1-1/2 cups broccoli flowerets
1/4 cup dried apricots, slivered or raisins
1/3 cup slivered or sliced almonds, toasted
1/4 cup chopped cilantro (optional)

1. In large skillet over medium heat, sauté rice-pasta mix, onion and garlic with margarine until pasta is light golden brown.

2. Slowly stir in 2 cups water, cumin, cinnamon and Special Seasonings; bring to a boil. Cover; reduce heat to low. Simmer 10 minutes.

3. Stir in beans, broccoli and apricots. Cover; simmer 10 to 12 minutes or until rice is tender. Serve topped with almonds and cilantro, if desired.
Makes 4 servings

Tip: For a Southwestern flair, use black beans, 1-1/2 cups corn and 1/4 teaspoon chili powder instead of garbanzo beans, apricots and cinnamon.

Tomato Chutney Chicken

4 boneless, skinless chicken breast halves
1 can (16 ounces) tomatoes with juice, cut up
1 cup peeled and chopped cooking apple
1/4 cup chopped onion
1/4 cup chopped green pepper
1/4 cup golden raisins
2 tablespoons brown sugar
2 tablespoons lemon juice
1 teaspoon grated lemon peel
1 clove garlic, minced
1/2 teaspoon ground cinnamon
1/4 teaspoon red pepper flakes
1/4 teaspoon salt

In large skillet, place tomatoes with juice, apple, onion, green pepper, raisins, brown sugar, lemon juice, lemon peel, garlic, cinnamon and red pepper flakes; stir to mix. Cook, stirring, over medium-high heat until mixture boils. Sprinkle salt over chicken breasts. Place chicken over tomato mixture. Reduce heat to medium-low; cover and cook, stirring and turning frequently, about 15 minutes or until chicken is fork-tender. Arrange chicken on serving platter; spoon sauce over chicken.   *Makes 4 servings*

Favorite recipe from **Delmarva Poultry Industry, Inc.**

Helpful Hint

All-purpose apples, such as Cortland, Fuji, Granny Smith, Jonathan and McIntosh, are good for both cooking and eating raw.

Franco-American® Quick Pepper Steak

Short Rib Contadina®

Family Baked Bean Dinner

1 can (20 ounces) DOLE® Pineapple Chunks
1/2 DOLE® Green Bell Pepper, julienne-cut
1/2 cup chopped onion
1 pound Polish sausage or frankfurters,
   cut into 1-inch chunks
1/3 cup packed brown sugar
1 teaspoon dry mustard
2 cans (16 ounces each) baked beans

MICROWAVE DIRECTIONS

Drain pineapple chunks; reserve juice for beverage. Add green pepper and onion to 13×9-inch microwavable dish.

Cover; microwave on HIGH (100% power) 3 minutes. Add sausage, arranging around edges of dish. Cover; continue microwaving on HIGH 6 minutes.

In bowl, combine brown sugar and mustard; stir in beans and pineapple. Add to sausage mixture. Stir to combine. Microwave, uncovered, on HIGH 8 to 10 minutes, stirring after 4 minutes.

Makes 6 servings

Short Ribs Contadina®

(Pictured above)

2 tablespoons olive or vegetable oil
4 pounds beef short ribs
1 onion, coarsely chopped
1 can (12 ounces) CONTADINA® Italian Paste
   with Italian Seasonings
2-2/3 cups water
1/2 teaspoon salt
1/4 teaspoon ground black pepper
2 carrots, peeled, cut into 2-inch pieces

1. Heat oil in large saucepan over medium heat. Add ribs; cook until browned on both sides. Add onion; cook for 1 minute.

2. Combine tomato paste, water, salt and pepper in small bowl. Pour over ribs; cover.

3. Simmer for 1-1/2 hours. Add carrots; simmer, covered, for additional 30 minutes or until ribs are tender. *Makes 6 servings*

Beef Tips and Egg Noodles

2 packages (0.88 ounce each) LAWRY'S®
   Brown Gravy Mix
1 can (6 ounces) tomato paste
1/2 teaspoon LAWRY'S® Seasoned Salt
2 tablespoons vegetable or olive oil
1-1/2 pounds boneless top sirloin or sirloin tip,
   cut into 1/2-inch cubes
1/4 cup chopped green bell pepper
8 ounces wide egg noodles, cooked

In medium bowl, whisk together Brown Gravy Mix, 2 cups water, tomato paste and Seasoned Salt until smooth; set aside. In large skillet, heat oil over high heat. Add beef and bell pepper; cook until beef is browned, about 5 minutes. Stir in gravy mixture. Bring to a boil; reduce heat to low, cover and cook 8 minutes, stirring occasionally. Serve over hot egg noodles. *Makes 4 to 6 servings*

Meal Idea: Add 1 package (8 ounces) sliced fresh mushrooms or 1 can (4 ounces) sliced mushrooms; cook with gravy and bell pepper for extra flavor.

Hint: Sirloin is recommended since less tender cuts of beef need longer cooking times.

Mile-High Enchilada Pie

(Pictured below)

5 corn tortillas (6-inch)
1 jar (12 ounces) salsa
1 can (16 ounces) kidney beans, rinsed and
  drained
1 cup shredded cooked chicken
1 cup (4 ounces) shredded pepper Jack cheese

SLOW COOKER DIRECTIONS

Prepare foil handles for slow cooker (see below);
place in slow cooker. Place one tortilla in slow
cooker. Top with small amount of salsa, beans,
chicken and cheese. Continue layering using
remaining ingredients, ending with cheese. Cover
and cook on LOW 6 to 8 hours or on HIGH 3 to
4 hours. Using foil handles, remove from slow
cooker.   *Makes 4 to 6 servings*

Foil Handles: Tear off three 18×2-inch strips
of heavy foil or use regular foil folded to double
thickness. Crisscross foil strips in spoke design
and place in slow cooker to make lifting of tortilla
stack easier.

Hunter-Style Lamb Stew

1 pound boneless American lamb, cut into
  3/4-inch cubes
2 cloves garlic, minced
3/4 cup apple juice or dry red wine
1 cup reduced-sodium chicken broth, divided
1/2 teaspoon dried rosemary, crushed
1/4 teaspoon ground black pepper
1/8 teaspoon ground sage
2 tablespoons all-purpose flour
3 cups cooked linguini
1 to 2 tablespoons chopped fresh parsley

Spray skillet or large saucepan with nonstick
cooking spray. Cook and stir lamb cubes and
garlic over medium-high heat until lamb is evenly
browned. Add apple juice, 1/2 cup broth, rosemary,
pepper and sage. Bring to a boil; reduce heat. Cover
and simmer about 1 hour or until lamb is tender.
Combine remaining 1/2 cup broth and flour. Stir
into lamb mixture; cook and stir until thickened
and bubbly. Cook and stir 1 minute more. Serve
lamb mixture over hot cooked linguini. Sprinkle
with parsley.   *Makes 4 servings*

Favorite recipe from **American Lamb Council**

Mile-High Enchilada Pie

Sweet & Zesty Fish with Fruit Salsa

(Pictured at right)

1/4 cup *French's*® Bold n' Spicy Brown Mustard
1/4 cup honey
  2 cups chopped assorted fresh fruit (pineapple, kiwi, strawberries and mango)
  1 pound sea bass or cod fillets or other firm-fleshed white fish

1. Preheat broiler or grill. Combine mustard and honey. Stir *2 tablespoons* mustard mixture into fruit; set aside.

2. Brush remaining mustard mixture on both sides of fillets. Place in foil-lined broiler pan. Broil (or grill) fish 6 inches from heat for 8 minutes or until fish is opaque.

3. Serve fruit salsa with fish. *Makes 4 servings*

Tip: To prepare this meal even faster, purchase cut-up fresh fruit from the supermarket salad bar.

🍇 🍇 🍇

Easy Chicken Pot Pie

  2 cups cut-up cooked chicken
  1 package (10 ounces) frozen mixed vegetables, thawed
1-1/4 cups milk
  1 envelope LIPTON® RECIPE SECRETS® Golden Onion Soup Mix*
  1 pie crust or pastry for single-crust pie

Also terrific with LIPTON® RECIPE SECRETS® Savory Herb with Garlic Soup Mix.

1. Preheat oven to 400°F. In 9-inch pie plate, combine chicken and vegetables; set aside.

2. In small saucepan, bring milk and soup mix to a boil over medium heat, stirring occasionally. Cook 1 minute. Stir into chicken mixture.

3. Top with pie crust. Press pastry around edge of pie plate to seal; trim excess pastry, then flute edges. With tip of knife, make small slits in pastry.

4. Bake uncovered 35 minutes or until crust is golden. *Makes about 4 servings*

Menu Suggestion: Serve with your favorite LIPTON® Soup and LIPTON® Iced Tea.

Southern-Style Chicken and Greens

  1 teaspoon salt
  1 teaspoon paprika
1/2 teaspoon pepper
  1 broiler/fryer chicken (3-1/2 pounds), cut up
  4 thick slices smoked bacon, cut widthwise into 1/4-inch strips
  1 cup uncooked rice
  1 can (14-1/2 ounces) stewed tomatoes, undrained
1-1/4 cups chicken broth
  2 cups packed coarsely chopped fresh collard or mustard greens or kale (3 to 4 ounces)

1. Preheat oven to 350°F.

2. Combine salt, paprika and pepper in small bowl. Sprinkle meaty side of chicken pieces with salt mixture; set aside.

3. Place bacon in ovenproof Dutch oven; cook over medium heat until crisp. Remove from Dutch oven; drain on paper towels. Reserve drippings.

4. Heat drippings in Dutch oven over medium-high heat until hot. Arrange chicken in single layer in Dutch oven and cook 3 minutes on each side or until chicken is browned. Transfer to plate; set aside. Repeat with remaining pieces. Reserve 1 tablespoon drippings in Dutch oven.

5. Add rice to drippings; cook and stir 1 minute. Add tomatoes with juice, broth, collard greens and half of bacon; bring to a boil over high heat. Remove from heat; arrange chicken over rice mixture.

6. Bake, covered, about 40 minutes or until juices run clear and most of liquid is absorbed. Let stand 5 minutes before serving. Transfer to serving platter; sprinkle with remaining bacon.
  Makes 4 to 6 servings

Serving Suggestion: Serve with corn bread or corn muffins.

Sweet & Zesty Fish with Fruit Salsa

Cheddar Broccoli Tart

(Pictured at right)

1-1/2 cups milk
3 eggs
1 package KNORR® Recipe Classics™ Leek Soup, Dip and Recipe Mix
1 package (10 ounces) frozen chopped broccoli, thawed and drained
1-1/2 cups shredded Cheddar, Swiss or Monterey Jack cheese (about 6 ounces)
1 9-inch unbaked or frozen deep-dish pie crust*

If using 9-inch deep-dish frozen prepared pie crust, do not thaw. Preheat oven and cookie sheet. Pour filling into pie crust; bake on cookie sheet.

Preheat oven to 375°F. In large bowl, with fork, beat milk, eggs and recipe mix until blended. Stir in broccoli and cheese; spoon into pie crust.

Bake 40 minutes or until knife inserted 1 inch from edge comes out clean. Let stand 10 minutes before serving.   *Makes 6 servings*

Tip: Cheddar Broccoli Tart is perfect for brunch or lunch. Or serve it with a mixed green salad and soup for a hearty dinner.

Spinach-Feta Rice & Ham

1 cup uncooked rice
1 cup reduced-sodium chicken broth
1 onion, chopped
1 cup sliced fresh mushrooms
2 cloves garlic, minced
1 tablespoon lemon juice
2 teaspoons chopped fresh oregano
6 cups (about 1/4 pound) shredded fresh spinach leaves
1 cup chopped HILLSHIRE FARM® Ham
3 ounces feta cheese, crumbled
Freshly ground black pepper

Combine rice, chicken broth and 1 cup water in medium saucepan over high heat. Bring to a boil; stir once or twice. Reduce heat; simmer, covered, 15 minutes or until rice is tender and liquid is absorbed. Spray large skillet with nonstick cooking spray. Sauté onion, mushrooms and garlic over medium-high heat until onion is tender. Stir in lemon juice and oregano. Add rice, spinach, Ham, cheese and pepper; toss lightly until spinach is wilted.   *Makes 6 to 8 servings*

Roast Leg of Lamb

3 tablespoons coarse-grained mustard
2 garlic cloves, minced*
1-1/2 teaspoons dried rosemary, crushed
1/2 teaspoon black pepper
1 boneless leg of lamb, (about 4 pounds)
Mint jelly (optional)

For more intense garlic flavor inside the meat, cut garlic into slivers. Cut small pockets at random intervals throughout roast with tip of sharp knife; insert garlic slivers.

Preheat oven to 400°F. Combine mustard, garlic, rosemary and pepper. Rub mustard mixture over lamb.** Place lamb on meat rack in shallow, foil-lined roasting pan. Bake, uncovered, 15 minutes. *Reduce oven temperature to 325°F;* bake, uncovered, about 20 minutes per pound for medium or until internal temperature reaches 145°F when tested with meat thermometer inserted into thickest part of lamb.

Transfer lamb to cutting board; cover with foil. Let stand 10 to 15 minutes before carving. Internal temperature will continue to rise 5° to 10°F during stand time. Serve roast with mint jelly, if desired.   *Makes 10 to 12 servings*

**At this point lamb may be covered and refrigerated up to 24 hours before roasting.*

Turkey with Chili Cranberry Sauce

1 pound ground raw turkey
1/4 cup seasoned dry bread crumbs
1/4 cup thinly sliced green onions
1 egg, slightly beaten
1/4 teaspoon salt
1/4 teaspoon pepper
1 tablespoon vegetable oil
2/3 cup whole-berry cranberry sauce
1/3 cup HEINZ® Chili Sauce
2 tablespoons water
1/8 teaspoon ground cinnamon

Combine turkey, bread crumbs, green onions, egg, salt and pepper. Shape into 4 patties, about 1/2 inch thick. Slowly sauté patties in oil, about 4 to 5 minutes per side or until cooked through. Stir in cranberry sauce, chili sauce, water and cinnamon. Simmer, uncovered, 1 minute.   *Makes 4 servings*

Cheddar Broccoli Tart

Nutty Oven-Fried Chicken Drumsticks

(Pictured at right)

1 cup cornflake crumbs
1/3 cup finely chopped pecans
1 tablespoon sugar
1-1/2 teaspoons salt
1/2 teaspoon onion powder
1/2 teaspoon pepper
12 chicken drumsticks or 6 legs (about 3 pounds)
1 egg, beaten
1/4 cup butter or margarine, melted

1. Preheat oven to 400°F.

2. Combine cornflake crumbs, pecans, sugar, salt, onion powder and pepper in large resealable plastic food storage bag. Coat chicken with beaten egg. Add chicken drumsticks, two at a time, to cornflake mixture; seal bag and shake to coat.

3. Place chicken on foil-lined baking sheet; drizzle with butter. Bake, uncovered, 40 to 45 minutes or until juices run clear.   *Makes 4 to 6 servings*

French Beef Stew

1-1/2 pounds stew beef, cut into 1-inch cubes
1/4 cup all-purpose flour
2 tablespoons vegetable oil
2 cans (14-1/2 ounces each) DEL MONTE®
    Diced Tomatoes with Garlic & Onion
1 can (14 ounces) beef broth
4 medium carrots, peeled and cut into
    1-inch chunks
2 medium potatoes, peeled and cut into
    1-inch chunks
3/4 teaspoon dried thyme, crushed
2 tablespoons Dijon mustard (optional)

1. Combine meat and flour in large plastic food storage bag; toss to coat evenly.

2. Brown meat in hot oil in 6-quart saucepan. Season with salt and pepper, if desired.

3. Add all remaining ingredients except mustard. Bring to a boil; reduce heat to medium-low. Cover; simmer 1 hour or until beef is tender.

4. Blend in mustard. Garnish and serve with warm crusty French bread, if desired.

Makes 6 to 8 servings

Carolina Baked Beans & Pork Chops

(Pictured on page 126)

2 cans (16 ounces each) pork and beans
1/2 cup chopped onion
1/2 cup chopped green bell pepper
1/4 cup *French's® Classic Yellow®* Mustard
1/4 cup packed light brown sugar
2 tablespoons *French's®* Worcestershire Sauce
1 tablespoon *Frank's® RedHot®* Original Cayenne
    Pepper Sauce
6 boneless pork chops (1 inch thick)

1. Preheat oven to 400°F. Combine all ingredients *except pork chops* in 3-quart shallow baking dish; mix well. Arrange chops on top, turning once to coat with sauce.

2. Bake, uncovered, 30 to 35 minutes or until pork is no longer pink in center. Stir beans around chops once during baking. Serve with green beans or mashed potatoes, if desired.   *Makes 6 servings*

Poached Salmon & Asparagus

2 tablespoons butter
1 cup onion, sliced
2 stalks celery, sliced
1 cup asparagus stems, sliced
2 packages UNCLE BEN'S NATURAL SELECT®
    Garlic & Butter Flavor Rice
3 cups water
6 pieces salmon fillets
1 cup asparagus tips

1. In large skillet with tight-fitting lid, melt butter over medium heat and sauté onion, celery and asparagus stems for about 3 minutes.

2. Add rice and water and bring to a boil. Carefully place fillets on top of rice, reduce heat, cover and simmer about 4 minutes.

3. Arrange asparagus tips around the salmon fillets, cover and simmer 6 to 8 minutes longer.

Makes 6 servings

Nutty Oven Fried Chicken Drumsticks

Shrimp Creole

2 tablespoons olive oil
1 medium onion, chopped
1 medium green bell pepper, chopped
1 jar (1 pound 10 ounces) RAGÚ® Chunky
    Gardenstyle Pasta Sauce
1/2 cup bottled clam juice
2 to 3 teaspoons hot pepper sauce
1-1/2 pounds medium shrimp, peeled and deveined

1. In 12-inch skillet, heat olive oil over medium-high heat and cook onion and green pepper, stirring frequently, 6 minutes or until tender.

2. Stir in Ragú Chunky Gardenstyle Pasta Sauce, clam juice and hot pepper sauce. Bring to a boil over high heat. Reduce heat to medium and continue cooking, stirring occasionally, 5 minutes. Stir in shrimp and cook, stirring occasionally, 3 minutes or until shrimp turn pink.

3. Serve, if desired, over hot cooked rice.

Makes 4 servings

Tip: For a more classic dish, stir in 1 package (9 ounces) chopped frozen okra with Ragú Chunky Gardenstyle Pasta Sauce. Okra is a vegetable native to the Southeastern United States and is used in cooking for thickening and flavor.

Ham and Swiss Quiche

1 *unbaked* 9-inch (4-cup volume) deep-dish
    pie shell
1 cup (4 ounces) shredded Swiss cheese, *divided*
1 cup finely chopped cooked ham
2 green onions, sliced
1 can (12 fluid ounces) NESTLÉ® CARNATION®
    Evaporated Milk
3 large eggs
1/4 cup all-purpose flour
1/4 teaspoon salt
1/8 teaspoon ground black pepper

PREHEAT oven to 350°F.

SPRINKLE *1/2 cup* cheese, ham and green onions into pie crust. Whisk together evaporated milk, eggs, flour, salt and pepper in large bowl. Pour mixture into pie shell; sprinkle with *remaining* cheese.

BAKE for 45 to 50 minutes or until knife inserted near center comes out clean. Cool on wire rack for 10 minutes before serving. *Makes 8 servings*

For Mini-Quiche Appetizers: Use 1-1/2 packages (3 crusts) refrigerated pie crusts. Grease miniature muffin pans. Unfold crust on lightly floured surface. Cut fourteen 2-1/2-inch circles from each crust. Press 1 circle of dough into bottom and up side of each cup. Repeat with *remaining* crusts. Combine cheese, ham, green onions, *2/3 cup (5-fluid-ounce can)* evaporated milk, 2 eggs (lightly beaten), *2 tablespoons* flour, salt and pepper in large bowl; mix well. Spoon mixture into crusts, filling 3/4 full. Bake in preheated 350°F. oven for 20 to 25 minutes or until crusts are golden brown. Cool slightly; lift quiche from cup with tip of knife. Serve warm or cool and freeze for later entertaining. Makes 3-1/2 dozen.

Campbell's® Chicken Broccoli Divan

(Pictured at right)

1 pound fresh broccoli, cut into spears, cooked
    and drained, *or* 1 package (about 10 ounces)
    frozen broccoli spears, cooked and drained
1-1/2 cups cubed cooked chicken *or* turkey
1 can (10-3/4 ounces) CAMPBELL'S® Condensed
    Broccoli Cheese Soup *or* Cream of Chicken
    Soup
1/3 cup milk
1/2 cup shredded Cheddar cheese (2 ounces),
    optional
2 tablespoons dry bread crumbs
1 tablespoon margarine *or* butter, melted

1. In 9-inch pie plate or 2-quart shallow baking dish arrange broccoli and chicken. In small bowl mix soup and milk and pour over broccoli and chicken.

2. Sprinkle cheese over soup mixture. Mix bread crumbs with margarine and sprinkle over cheese.

3. Bake at 400°F. for 25 minutes or until hot.

Makes 4 servings

Campbell's® Chicken Broccoli Divan

Campbell's® Shortcut Beef Stew

(Pictured below)

1 tablespoon vegetable oil
1 pound boneless beef sirloin steak, cut into
    1-inch cubes
1 can (10-3/4 ounces) CAMPBELL'S® Condensed
    Tomato Soup
1 can (10-3/4 ounces) CAMPBELL'S® Condensed
    Beefy Mushroom Soup
1 tablespoon Worcestershire sauce
1 bag (24 ounces) frozen vegetables for stew
    (potatoes, carrots, celery)

1. In Dutch oven over medium-high heat, heat oil.
Add beef and cook until browned, stirring often.
Set beef aside.

2. Add soups, Worcestershire and vegetables. Heat
to a boil. Return beef to pan. Reduce heat to low.
Cover and cook 10 minutes or until vegetables are
tender, stirring occasionally.   *Makes 4 servings*

Campbell's® Shortcut Beef Stew

Chicken and Black Bean Chili

1 tablespoon vegetable oil
1 medium onion, chopped
3-1/2 cups shredded, cooked chicken
2 cans (14-1/2 ounces each) diced tomatoes,
    with juice
1 can (15 ounces) black beans, rinsed and
    drained
1 can (4 ounces) diced green chiles
1/2 cup water
1 package (1.48 ounces) LAWRY'S® Spices
    & Seasonings for Chili
1/2 teaspoon LAWRY'S® Garlic Powder With
    Parsley
1/2 teaspoon hot pepper sauce (optional)
1 tablespoon chopped cilantro

In large deep skillet, heat oil over medium-high
heat and cook onion. Add remaining ingredients
except cilantro. Bring to a boil; reduce heat to
low and cook, uncovered for 20 minutes, stirring
occasionally. Stir in cilantro.   *Makes 5-1/2 cups*

Meal Idea: Serve with sour cream and tortilla chips.
Diced avocados make a great garnish, too.

Variation: Instead of shredded chicken, try
1-1/2 pounds ground turkey, browned.

Chicken Vesuvio

1 broiler/fryer chicken (3 to 3-1/2 pounds)
1/4 cup olive or vegetable oil
3 tablespoons lemon juice
4 garlic cloves, minced
3 large baking potatoes
    Salt and lemon-pepper seasoning

Preheat oven to 375°F. Place chicken, breast
side down, on rack in large shallow roasting pan.
Combine olive oil, lemon juice and garlic; brush half
of oil mixture over chicken. Set aside remaining oil
mixture. Bake chicken, uncovered, 30 minutes.

Meanwhile, peel potatoes; cut lengthwise into
quarters. Turn chicken breast side up. Arrange
potatoes around chicken in pan. Brush chicken
and potatoes with remaining oil mixture; sprinkle
with salt and lemon pepper seasoning to taste. Roast
chicken and potatoes, basting occasionally with pan
juices, 50 minutes or until meat thermometer inserted
into thigh registers 180°F and potatoes are tender.
Makes 4 to 6 servings

Lasagna Florentine

Lasagna Florentine

(Pictured above)

2 tablespoons olive oil
3 medium carrots, finely chopped
1 package (8 to 10 ounces) sliced mushrooms
1 medium onion, finely chopped
2 cloves garlic, finely chopped
1 jar (1 pound 10 ounces) RAGÚ® Robusto!
   Pasta Sauce
1 container (15 ounces) ricotta cheese
2 cups shredded mozzarella cheese, divided
1 box (10 ounces) frozen chopped spinach,
   thawed and squeezed dry
1/4 cup grated Parmesan cheese
2 eggs
1 teaspoon salt
1 teaspoon dried Italian seasoning
16 lasagna noodles, cooked and drained

Preheat oven to 375°F. In 12-inch skillet, heat olive oil over medium heat and cook carrots, mushrooms, onion and garlic until carrots are almost tender, about 5 minutes. Stir in Ragú Robusto! Pasta Sauce; heat through.

Meanwhile, in medium bowl, combine ricotta cheese, 1-1/2 cups mozzarella cheese, spinach, Parmesan cheese, eggs, salt and Italian seasoning; set aside.

In bottom of 13×9-inch baking dish, evenly spread 1/2 cup sauce mixture. Arrange 4 lasagna noodles lengthwise over sauce, overlapping edges slightly. Spread 1/3 of the ricotta mixture over noodles; repeat layers, ending with noodles. Top with remaining sauce and 1/2 cup mozzarella cheese. Cover with foil and bake 40 minutes. Remove foil and continue baking 10 minutes or until bubbling.

Makes 8 servings

Cheesy Garlic Chicken

(Pictured at right)

4 boneless, skinless chicken breast halves
    (about 1-1/4 pounds)
1 medium tomato, coarsely chopped
1 envelope LIPTON® RECIPE SECRETS®
    Savory Herb with Garlic Soup Mix
1/3 cup water
1 tablespoon BERTOLLI® Olive Oil
1 cup shredded mozzarella cheese
    (about 4 ounces)
1 tablespoon grated Parmesan cheese

1. Preheat oven to 400°F. In 13×9-inch baking dish, arrange chicken; top with tomato.

2. Pour soup mix blended with water and oil over chicken.

3. Bake uncovered 20 minutes. Top with cheeses and bake 5 minutes or until cheese is melted and chicken is thoroughly cooked. Serve, if desired, with crusty Italian bread.   *Makes 4 servings*

Recipe Tip: Turn leftover Cheesy Garlic Chicken into a quick and delicious lunch or dinner. Simply heat and serve on hot store-bought garlic bread.

Creamy Shells with Spinach and Mushrooms

1 package (16 ounces) BARILLA® Medium or
    Large Shells
1 can (12 ounces) evaporated milk
1 cup (4 ounces) grated Parmesan cheese,
    divided
4 ounces brick cheese, cubed (about 3/4 cup)
4 tablespoons butter or margarine
2 tablespoons olive or vegetable oil
1 small onion, chopped
3 cloves garlic, minced
2 packages (10 ounces each) frozen chopped
    spinach, thawed and well drained
1-1/2 cups (4 ounces) sliced mushrooms

1. Cook pasta shells according to package directions; drain.

2. Meanwhile, heat evaporated milk, Parmesan (reserving 2 tablespoons for topping) and brick cheese in small saucepan over medium heat until cheeses melt, stirring frequently. Set aside.

3. Heat butter and oil in large skillet over medium-high heat. Add onion and garlic; cook about 5 minutes, stirring occasionally, until onion is transparent. Add spinach and mushrooms; cook 5 minutes, stirring occasionally.

4. Stir cheese mixture into skillet; mix well. Pour over hot drained pasta shells on platter; sprinkle with reserved Parmesan.   *Makes 8 servings*

Sausage Apple Quiche

1 (9-inch) refrigerated pie crust
3/4 cup (3 ounces) shredded Swiss cheese
2 tablespoons Parmesan cheese
1 tablespoon chopped fresh chives
1 tablespoon chopped fresh parsley
1 (12-ounce) package BOB EVANS® Original
    or Maple Links
4 eggs
1-1/2 cups milk
3/4 teaspoon salt
3/4 teaspoon sugar
    Dash cayenne pepper (optional)
1 medium apple, cut into 1/4-inch slices

Preheat oven to 425°F. Line 10-inch quiche or pie pan with pie crust. Sprinkle cheeses, chives and parsley over bottom of crust. Cook sausage in large skillet over medium heat until browned. Arrange in spoke fashion over cheese layer. Beat eggs in medium bowl with wire whisk until light in color. Whisk in milk, salt and sugar until well blended. Carefully pour egg mixture over sausage layer; sprinkle with cayenne pepper, if desired. Arrange apple slices around outside edge of quiche, pressing down slightly into egg mixture to coat apples. Bake 20 minutes. Reduce oven temperature to 350°F; bake 15 to 20 minutes more or until knife inserted into center comes out clean. Refrigerate leftovers.   *Makes 8 servings*

Note: This basic quiche recipe works well with any combination of cheeses and vegetables.

Taco Pot Pie

(Pictured at right)

1 pound ground beef
1 package (1-1/4 ounces) taco seasoning
1/4 cup water
1 can (8 ounces) kidney beans, rinsed and drained
1 cup chopped tomato
3/4 cup frozen corn, thawed
3/4 cup frozen peas, thawed
1-1/2 cups (6 ounces) shredded cheddar cheese
1 tube (11-1/2 ounces) refrigerated corn bread twists

1. Preheat oven to 400°F. Brown meat in medium ovenproof skillet over medium-high heat, stirring to separate; drain drippings. Add taco seasoning and water to skillet. Cook over medium-low heat 3 minutes or until most of liquid is absorbed, stirring occasionally.

2. Stir in beans, tomato, corn and peas. Cook 3 minutes or until mixture is hot. Remove from heat; stir in cheese.

3. Unwrap corn bread dough; separate into 16 strips. Twist strips, cutting to fit skillet. Arrange in spoke pattern over meat mixture. Press ends of dough lightly to edge of skillet to secure. Bake 15 minutes or until corn bread is golden brown and meat mixture is bubbly. *Makes 4 to 6 servings*

Skillet Spaghetti Pizza

1 pound bulk Italian sausage
1 tablespoon minced garlic
1/2 pound uncooked thin spaghetti, broken into 2-inch lengths
1 jar (26 ounces) spaghetti sauce
1-1/2 cups water
1 cup (4 ounces) shredded mozzarella cheese
1/2 cup diced green bell pepper
1-1/3 cups *French's®* French Fried Onions

1. Cook sausage and garlic in large nonstick skillet over medium heat until browned, stirring frequently; drain.

2. Stir in uncooked spaghetti, spaghetti sauce and water. Bring to a boil; reduce heat to medium-low. Cover and simmer 15 minutes or until spaghetti is cooked, stirring occasionally.

3. Top spaghetti mixture with cheese, bell pepper and French Fried Onions; remove from heat. Cover and let stand 3 minutes until cheese is melted. Serve immediately. *Makes 8 servings*

Tip: You may substitute link sausage; remove from casing before cooking.

Variation: Substitute other pizza toppings such as mushrooms, eggplant, olives or pepperoni for green peppers.

Baked Salmon in Foil

2 tablespoons FILIPPO BERIO® Olive Oil, divided
1 (10-ounce) package frozen chopped spinach, thawed
1 (8-ounce) can stewed tomatoes
1 onion, chopped
1 clove garlic, minced
4 salmon steaks, 1 inch thick (about 2 pounds)
4 pieces heavy-duty aluminum foil, each 12 inches square
4 thin lemon slices
1 tablespoon coarsely chopped fresh parsley
Salt and freshly ground black pepper

Preheat oven to 375°F. In medium saucepan, heat 1 tablespoon olive oil over medium heat until hot. Add spinach, tomatoes, onion and garlic. Cook, stirring occasionally, 5 minutes or until mixture is thick and onion is tender.

In medium skillet, heat remaining 1 tablespoon olive oil over medium-high heat until hot. Add salmon; cook 1 to 2 minutes on each side or until lightly browned. Remove from heat. Place one-fourth of spinach mixture in center of each piece of foil; top with one salmon steak. Drizzle liquid from skillet over salmon. Top each with lemon slice and parsley. Fold edges of each foil square together. Pinch well to seal, completely enclosing filling. Place on baking sheet. Bake 15 minutes or until salmon flakes easily when tested with fork. To serve, cut an "X" on top of each packet; carefully peel back foil. Season to taste with salt and pepper. *Makes 4 servings*

Taco Pot Pie

Beefy Nacho Crescent Bake

(Pictured at right)

    1 pound ground beef
  1/2 cup chopped onion
  1/4 teaspoon salt
  1/8 teaspoon pepper
    1 tablespoon chili powder
    1 teaspoon ground cumin
    1 teaspoon dried oregano leaves
    1 can (11 ounces) condensed nacho cheese
      soup, undiluted
    1 cup milk
    1 can (8 ounces) refrigerated crescent roll dough
  1/4 cup (1 ounce) shredded cheddar cheese
      Minced fresh cilantro or parsley (optional)
      Salsa (optional)

1. Preheat oven to 375°F. Spray 13×9-inch baking dish with nonstick cooking spray.

2. Place beef and onion in large skillet; season with salt and pepper. Brown beef over medium-high heat until no longer pink, stirring to separate meat. Drain fat. Stir in chili powder, cumin and oregano. Cook and stir 2 minutes; remove from heat.

3. Combine soup and milk in medium bowl, stirring until smooth. Pour soup mixture into prepared dish, spreading evenly.

4. Separate crescent dough into 4 rectangles; press perforations together firmly. Roll each rectangle to 8×4 inches. Cut each rectangle in half widthwise to form eight 4-inch squares.

5. Spoon about 1/4 cup beef mixture into center of each square. Lift 4 corners of dough up over filling to meet in center; pinch and twist firmly to seal. Place squares in dish.

6. Bake, uncovered, 20 to 25 minutes or until golden brown. Sprinkle with cheese. Bake 5 minutes longer or until cheese is melted. To serve, spoon soup mixture over each serving; sprinkle with cilantro. Serve with salsa, if desired.   *Makes 4 servings*

Helpful Hint

Ground beef should be stored in the coldest part of the refrigerator for up to two days after purchasing. Ground beef can also be frozen for up to three months; wrap it airtight for the best results.

Mediterranean Torta

    5 flour tortillas (8 inches)
    1 package (10 ounces) frozen creamed spinach,
      thawed
    1 cup crumbled feta cheese
    1 jar (12 ounces) roasted red peppers, drained
      and chopped
    1 large tomato, chopped
1-1/3 cups *French's*® French Fried Onions, divided
    3 tablespoons chopped pitted kalamata or ripe
      black olives
  1/2 cup (2 ounces) shredded mozzarella cheese

1. Preheat oven to 350°F. Coat 8- or 9-inch springform pan with vegetable cooking spray. Place 1 tortilla in bottom of pan. Spread tortilla with 3 tablespoons spinach. Top with about 2 tablespoons each feta cheese, roasted peppers, tomato, French Fried Onions and 2 teaspoons olives.

2. Repeat to make 3 more layers. Place remaining tortilla on top; coat with vegetable cooking spray. Bake 25 minutes or until heated through.

3. Sprinkle with mozzarella cheese and remaining onions; bake 5 minutes or until onions are golden. Cut into wedges to serve.
    Makes 8 appetizer or 4 main-dish servings

Mushroom-Sauced Steak

  1/2 cup sliced onion
    2 tablespoons margarine or butter
1-1/2 cups sliced mushrooms
    1 cup A.1.® BOLD & SPICY Steak Sauce
  1/2 cup dairy sour cream
    2 (8-ounce) beef club or strip steaks, about
      1 inch thick

Sauté onion in margarine in medium skillet over medium heat until tender, about 5 minutes. Add mushrooms; sauté 5 minutes more. Stir in steak sauce; heat to a boil. Reduce heat and simmer 5 minutes; stir in sour cream. Cook and stir until heated through (do not boil); keep warm.

Grill steaks over medium heat 5 minutes on each side or until done. Serve steaks topped with mushroom sauce.   *Makes 4 servings*

Beefy Nacho Crescent Bake

Herbed Chicken & Vegetables

Ropa Vieja

1 (1-1/2-pound) flank steak
1 tablespoon olive oil
1 medium green bell pepper, chopped
1 jar (1 pound 10 ounces) RAGÚ® Chunky
   Gardenstyle Pasta Sauce
1/2 cup beef broth or water
1 can (4 ounces) chopped green chilies, drained
1/4 teaspoon red pepper flakes

1. Season steak, if desired, with salt and ground black pepper. In 6-quart saucepot or Dutch oven, heat olive oil over medium-high heat and brown steak with green pepper.

2. Stir in Ragú Chunky Gardenstyle Pasta Sauce, broth, green chilies and red pepper flakes. Bring to a boil over high heat. Reduce heat to low and simmer covered 1 hour or until meat is fork-tender.

3. Remove meat from sauce; cool slightly. With two forks, shred meat. Return meat to sauce and heat through. Serve, if desired, over hot cooked rice.
Makes 6 servings

Tip: Rope vieja is a traditional Spanish dish. It translates to "old clothes," which the shredded meat in the recipe represents.

Herbed Chicken & Vegetables

(Pictured above)

2 medium all-purpose potatoes, thinly sliced
   (about 1 pound)
2 medium carrots, sliced
4 bone-in chicken pieces (about 2 pounds)
1 envelope LIPTON® RECIPE SECRETS®
   Savory Herb with Garlic Soup Mix
1/3 cup water
1 tablespoon BERTOLLI® Olive Oil

1. Preheat oven to 425°F. In broiler pan without the rack, place potatoes and carrots; arrange chicken on top. Pour soup mix blended with water and oil over chicken and vegetables.

2. Bake uncovered 40 minutes or until chicken is thoroughly cooked and vegetables are tender.
Makes 4 servings

Slow Cooker Method: Place all ingredients in slow cooker, arranging chicken on top; cover. Cook on HIGH 4 hours or LOW 6 to 8 hours.

Pork Chops with Apples and Stuffing

4 pork chops, 1/2 inch thick
   Salt and pepper
1 tablespoon oil
2 medium apples, cored, cut into 8 wedges
1 cup apple juice
2 cups STOVE TOP® Cornbread Stuffing Mix
   in the Canister
1/4 cup chopped pecans

SPRINKLE chops with salt and pepper. Heat oil in large skillet on medium-high heat. Add chops and apples; cook until chops are browned on both sides.

STIR in apple juice. Bring to a boil. Reduce heat to low; cover and simmer 8 minutes or until chops are cooked through. Remove chops from skillet.

STIR Stuffing Mix Pouch and pecans into skillet. Return chops to skillet; cover. Remove from heat. Let stand 5 minutes. *Makes 4 servings*

Summer Sausage 'n' Egg Wedges

(Pictured below)

4 eggs, beaten
1/3 cup milk
1/4 cup all-purpose flour
1/2 teaspoon baking powder
1/8 teaspoon garlic powder
2-1/2 cups (10 ounces) shredded Cheddar or
  mozzarella cheese, divided
1-1/2 cups diced HILLSHIRE FARM® Summer
  Sausage
1 cup cream-style cottage cheese with chives

Preheat oven to 375°F.

Combine eggs, milk, flour, baking powder and garlic powder in medium bowl; beat until combined. Stir in 2 cups Cheddar cheese, Summer Sausage and cottage cheese. Pour into greased 9-inch pie plate. Bake, uncovered, 25 to 30 minutes or until golden and knife inserted into center comes out clean. To serve, cut into 6 wedges. Sprinkle wedges with remaining 1/2 cup Cheddar cheese.

Makes 6 servings

Farm Fresh Tip: Here's a simple do-ahead garlic bread and a great accompaniment to your favorite Hillshire Farm meal: Cut a 1-pound loaf of French bread into 1-inch slices. Spread with a mixture of 1/2 cup soft butter and 1/4 teaspoon garlic powder. Sprinkle with salt, pepper and paprika. Reassemble the loaf and wrap in heavy-duty foil. Heat in a 350°F oven for 15 to 20 minutes.

Helpful Hint

Be sure to check the date stamped on the bottom of the cottage cheese carton before purchasing it. Cottage cheese is a fresh cheese made from pasteurized milk and is more perishable than other cheeses; it should be stored in the coldest part of the refrigerator for up to 10 days past the stamped date.

Summer Sausage 'n' Egg Wedge

Citrus Grove Marinated Salmon

(Pictured at right)

4 salmon fillets or steaks
1/3 cup lemonade concentrate, thawed
1/4 cup WESSON® Vegetable Oil
1/4 cup orange juice concentrate, thawed
1/2 tablespoon fresh dill weed *or* 1/2 teaspoon dried dill weed
PAM® No-Stick Cooking Spray

1. Rinse salmon and pat dry; set aside.

2. In small bowl, combine *remaining* ingredients *except* PAM Cooking Spray.

3. Place salmon in large resealable plastic food storage bag; pour *3/4* marinade over fish; set *remaining* marinade aside. Seal bag and gently turn to coat; refrigerate 2 hours, turning fish several times during marinating.

4. Preheat broiler. Foil-line jelly-roll pan; spray with PAM Cooking Spray.

5. Place fish on pan; discard used marinade. Broil until fish flakes easily with fork, basting frequently with *remaining* marinade.   *Makes 4 servings*

Turkey Cottage Pie

1/4 cup butter or margarine
1/4 cup all-purpose flour
1 envelope LIPTON® RECIPE SECRETS® Golden Onion Soup Mix
2 cups water
2 cups cut-up cooked turkey or chicken
1 package (10 ounces) frozen mixed vegetables, thawed
1-1/4 cups shredded Swiss cheese (about 5 ounces), divided
1/8 teaspoon pepper
5 cups hot mashed potatoes

1. Preheat oven to 375°F.

2. In large saucepan, melt butter and add flour; cook, stirring constantly, 5 minutes or until golden. Stir in golden onion soup mix thoroughly blended with water. Bring to a boil, then simmer 15 minutes or until thickened. Stir in turkey, vegetables, 1 cup cheese and pepper. Turn into lightly greased 2-quart casserole; top with hot potatoes, then remaining 1/4 cup cheese. Bake 30 minutes or until bubbling.
        Makes about 8 servings

Microwave Directions: In 2-quart casserole, heat butter at HIGH (100% power) 1 minute. Stir in flour and heat uncovered, stirring frequently, 2 minutes. Stir in golden onion soup mix thoroughly blended with water. Heat uncovered, stirring occasionally, 4 minutes or until thickened. Stir in turkey, vegetables, 1 cup cheese and pepper. Top with hot potatoes, then remaining 1/4 cup cheese. Heat uncovered, turning casserole occasionally, 5 minutes or until bubbling. Let stand uncovered 5 minutes. For additional color, sprinkle, if desired, with paprika.

Ortega® Huevos Rancheros

2 tablespoons vegetable oil
2 medium green, red and/or yellow bell peppers, thinly sliced
1 small red onion, thinly sliced
1 package (1.25 ounces) ORTEGA® Taco Seasoning Mix
1 can (12 fluid ounces) NESTLÉ® CARNATION® Evaporated Milk
6 large eggs, lightly beaten
1 cup (4 ounces) shredded 4-cheese Mexican blend
12 (6-inch) fajita-size flour tortillas, warmed

GARNISH SUGGESTIONS
ORTEGA® Salsa, sour cream, additional cheese

HEAT oil in large nonstick skillet over medium-high heat. Add bell peppers, onion and seasoning mix; stir well. Cook, stirring frequently, for 3 to 5 minutes or until vegetables are crisp-tender. Transfer to bowl; cover.

COMBINE evaporated milk and eggs in medium bowl. Pour into heated skillet and scramble until soft curds form. Move eggs to center of skillet. Arrange vegetables around eggs. Sprinkle cheese over eggs and vegetables.

SERVE with tortillas. Garnish as desired.
        Makes 6 servings

Citrus Grove Marinated Salmon

Yankee Pot Roast and Vegetables

(Pictured at right)

1 beef chuck roast (2-1/2 pounds)
  Salt and pepper
3 medium baking potatoes (about 1 pound),
  unpeeled and cut into quarters
2 large carrots, cut into 3/4-inch slices
2 celery ribs, cut into 3/4-inch slices
1 medium onion, sliced
1 large parsnip, peeled and cut into
  3/4-inch slices
2 bay leaves
1 teaspoon dried rosemary, crushed
1/2 teaspoon dried thyme
1/2 cup beef broth

SLOW COOKER DIRECTIONS

1. Trim excess fat from meat and discard. Cut meat into serving pieces; sprinkle with salt and pepper.

2. Combine vegetables, bay leaves, rosemary and thyme in 5-quart slow cooker. Place beef over vegetables. Pour broth over beef. Cover and cook on LOW 8-1/2 to 9 hours or until beef is fork-tender. Remove beef to serving platter. Arrange vegetables around beef. Discard bay leaves.

Makes 10 to 12 servings

Tip: To make gravy, ladle the juices into a 2-cup measure; let stand 5 minutes. Skim off and discard fat. Measure remaining juices and heat to a boil in small saucepan. For each cup of juice, mix 2 tablespoons of flour with 1/4 cup of cold water until smooth. Stir mixture into boiling juices, stirring constantly 1 minute or until thickened.

Helpful Hint

Vegetables such as potatoes and carrots can sometimes take longer to cook in a slow cooker than meat; this is why recipes often suggest placing them on the bottom or along the sides of the slow cooker when possible. It is also helpful to cut these ingredients into uniform pieces so that everything cooks evenly.

Campbell's® Cod Vera Cruz

1 pound fresh *or* thawed frozen cod *or* haddock
  fillets
1 can (10-3/4 ounces) CAMPBELL'S® Condensed
  Tomato Soup
1 can (10-1/2 ounces) CAMPBELL'S® Condensed
  Chicken Broth
1/3 cup PACE® Chunky Salsa *or* Picante Sauce
1 tablespoon lime juice
2 teaspoons chopped fresh cilantro
1 teaspoon dried oregano leaves, crushed
1/8 teaspoon garlic powder *or* 1 clove garlic,
  minced
4 cups hot cooked rice

1. Place fish in 2-quart shallow baking dish.

2. Mix soup, broth, salsa, lime juice, cilantro, oregano and garlic powder. Pour over fish. Bake at 400°F. for 20 minutes or until fish flakes easily when tested with a fork. Serve over rice.

Makes 4 servings

Perfect Crispy Catfish

2 tablespoons LAWRY'S® Perfect Blend
  Seasoning and Rub for Fish & Seafood
3/4 cup yellow cornmeal
1 pound catfish fillets, cut into bite-size pieces
1/2 cup milk
1/4 cup flour
1/3 cup vegetable oil

In large Ziploc® bag, combine Perfect Blend with cornmeal. Dip fish into milk; shake off excess milk. Add fish pieces to bag of seasoned cornmeal; shake to coat. Place flour in shallow pan, then press coated fish into flour. Dip fish again in milk, then shake in bag of seasoned cornmeal again. In large electric fry pan, heat oil to 350°F; fry fish about 5 minutes on each side, depending upon thickness, or until fish begins to flake easily.

Makes 5 servings (about 8 pieces each)

Hint: Coat fish ahead of time, then place on a tray; cover and refrigerate until ready to fry.

Chicken and Black Bean Enchiladas

(Pictured below)

2 jars (16 ounces each) mild picante sauce
1/4 cup chopped fresh cilantro
2 tablespoons chili powder
1 teaspoon ground cumin
2 cups (10 ounces) chopped cooked chicken
1 can (15 ounces) black beans, drained and
    rinsed
1-1/3 cups *French's®* French Fried Onions, divided
1 package (about 10 ounces) flour tortillas
    (7 inches)
1 cup (4 ounces) shredded Monterey Jack cheese
    with jalapeño peppers

Preheat oven to 350°F. Grease 15×10-inch jelly-roll baking pan. Combine picante sauce, cilantro, chili powder and cumin in large saucepan. Bring to a boil. Reduce heat to low; simmer 5 minutes.

Combine 1-1/2 cups sauce mixture, chicken, beans and *2/3 cup* French Fried Onions in medium bowl. Spoon a scant 1/2 cup filling over bottom third of

Chicken and Black Bean Enchiladas

each tortilla. Roll up tortillas enclosing filling and arrange, seam-side down, in single layer in bottom of prepared baking pan. Spoon remaining sauce evenly over tortillas.

Bake, uncovered, 20 minutes or until heated through. Sprinkle with remaining *2/3 cup* onions and cheese. Bake 5 minutes or until cheese is melted and onions are golden. Serve immediately.

Makes 5 to 6 servings
(4 cups sauce, 4-1/2 cups filling)

Tip: This is a great make-ahead party dish.

Sauerbraten

1 boneless beef rump roast (1-1/4 pounds)
3 cups baby carrots
1-1/2 cups fresh or frozen pearl onions
1/4 cup raisins
1/2 cup water
1/2 cup red wine or cider vinegar
1 tablespoon honey
1/2 teaspoon salt
1/2 teaspoon ground mustard
1/2 teaspoon garlic-pepper seasoning
1/4 teaspoon ground cloves
1/4 cup crushed crisp gingersnap cookies
    (5 cookies)

SLOW COOKER DIRECTIONS
Heat large nonstick skillet over medium heat until hot. Brown roast on all sides. Place roast, carrots, onions and raisins in slow cooker.

Combine water, vinegar, honey, salt, mustard, garlic-pepper seasoning and cloves in small bowl; mix well. Pour mixture over meat and vegetables. Cover and cook on LOW 4 to 6 hours or until internal temperature reaches 145°F when tested with meat thermometer inserted into thickest part of roast.

Transfer roast to cutting board; cover with foil and let stand 10 to 15 minutes before slicing. Internal temperature will continue to rise 5° to 10°F during stand time.

Remove vegetables with slotted spoon to bowl; cover to keep warm. Stir crushed cookies into sauce mixture in slow cooker. Cover and cook on HIGH 10 to 15 minutes or until sauce is thickened. Serve meat and vegetables with sauce.

Makes 5 servings

Campbell's® Cajun Fish

Campbell's® Cajun Fish

(Pictured above)

1 tablespoon vegetable oil
1 small green pepper, diced (about 2/3 cup)
1/2 teaspoon dried oregano leaves, crushed
1 can (10-3/4 ounces) CAMPBELL'S® Condensed
    Tomato Soup
1/3 cup water
1/8 teaspoon garlic powder
1/8 teaspoon black pepper
1/8 teaspoon ground red pepper
1 pound firm white fish fillets (cod, haddock or
    halibut)

1. In medium skillet over medium heat, heat oil. Add green pepper and oregano and cook until tender-crisp, stirring often. Add soup, water, garlic powder, black pepper and red pepper. Heat to a boil.

2. Place fish in soup mixture. Reduce heat to low. Cover and cook 5 minutes or until fish flakes easily when tested with a fork. Serve with rice if desired.

Makes 4 servings

Cabbage Rolls

8 large cabbage leaves
1 pound BOB EVANS® Original Recipe
    Roll Sausage
1 cup cooked rice
1/4 cup chopped onion
1 egg, lightly beaten
1/2 teaspoon salt
1/8 teaspoon black pepper
2 (10-3/4-ounce) cans condensed tomato soup,
    divided

Cook cabbage leaves in boiling water 2 to 3 minutes to soften. Drain and set aside. Combine remaining ingredients except soup in large bowl. Moisten mixture with 2 tablespoons soup. Place equal amounts of sausage mixture on each cabbage leaf; roll up and secure with wooden toothpicks. Arrange cabbage rolls in heavy skillet; pour remaining soup over rolls. Cover and cook 45 minutes over low heat, turning occasionally. Remove toothpicks and serve with sauce remaining in skillet. Refrigerate leftovers.

Makes 4 to 6 servings

Chesapeake Crab Strata

(Pictured at right)

1/4 cup butter or margarine
4 cups unseasoned croutons
2 cups (8 ounces) shredded cheddar cheese
2 cups (8 ounces) milk
8 eggs, beaten
1/2 teaspoon ground mustard
1/2 teaspoon seafood seasoning
    Salt and pepper to taste
1 pound crabmeat, flaked and cartilage removed

1. Preheat oven to 325°F. Place butter in 11×7-inch baking dish. Heat in oven until melted, tilting to coat dish. Remove dish from oven; sprinkle croutons over butter. Top with cheese; set aside.

2. Combine milk, eggs, mustard, seafood seasoning, salt and pepper; mix well. Pour egg mixture over cheese in dish; sprinkle with crab. Bake, uncovered, 50 minutes or until mixture is set. Let stand about 10 minutes. *Makes 6 to 8 servings*

Sausage and Broccoli Noodle Casserole

(Pictured on page 126)

1 jar (1 pound) RAGÚ® Cheese Creations!®
    Classic Alfredo Sauce
1/3 cup milk
1 pound sweet Italian sausage, cooked and
    crumbled
1 package (9 ounces) frozen chopped broccoli,
    thawed
8 ounces egg noodles, cooked and drained
1 cup shredded Cheddar cheese (about
    4 ounces), divided
1/4 cup chopped roasted red peppers

1. Preheat oven to 350°F. In large bowl, combine Ragú Cheese Creations! Sauce and milk. Stir in sausage, broccoli, noodles, 3/4 cup cheese and roasted peppers.

2. In 13×9-inch baking dish, evenly spread sausage mixture. Sprinkle with remaining 1/4 cup cheese.

3. Bake 30 minutes or until heated through. *Makes 6 servings*

Tip: Substitute sausage with equal amounts of vegetables for a hearty vegetarian entrée.

Easy Three Cheese Tuna Soufflé

4 cups large croutons*
2-1/2 cups milk
4 large eggs
1 can (10-3/4 ounces) cream of celery soup
3 cups shredded cheese, use a combination
    of Cheddar, Monterey Jack and Swiss
1 (7-ounce) pouch of STARKIST® Premium
    Albacore or Chunk Light Tuna
1 tablespoon butter or margarine
1/2 cup chopped celery
1/2 cup finely chopped onion
1/4 pound mushrooms, sliced

Use garlic and herb or ranch-flavored croutons.

In bottom of lightly greased 13×9-inch baking dish, arrange croutons. In medium bowl, beat together milk, eggs and soup; stir in cheeses and tuna. In small skillet, melt butter over medium heat. Add celery, onion and mushrooms; sauté until onion is soft.

Spoon sautéed vegetables over croutons; pour egg-tuna mixture over top. Cover; refrigerate overnight. Remove from refrigerator 1 hour before baking; bake in 325°F oven 45 to 50 minutes or until hot and bubbly. *Makes 8 servings*

Simply Delicious Pasta Primavera

1/4 cup margarine or butter
1 envelope LIPTON® RECIPE SECRETS®
    Vegetable Soup Mix
1-1/2 cups milk
8 ounces linguine or spaghetti, cooked and
    drained
1/4 cup grated Parmesan cheese (about 1 ounce)

1. In medium saucepan, melt margarine over medium heat and stir in soup mix and milk. Bring just to a boil over high heat.

2. Reduce heat to low and simmer uncovered, stirring occasionally, 10 minutes or until vegetables are tender. Toss hot linguine with sauce and Parmesan cheese. *Makes 4 servings*

Chesapeake Crab Strata

Ravioli Stew

(Pictured at right)

1 tablespoon olive oil
3 medium carrots, chopped
2 medium ribs celery, chopped
1 medium onion, chopped
1 jar (1 pound 10 ounces) RAGÚ® Robusto!
    Pasta Sauce
1 can (14-1/2 ounces) chicken broth
1 cup water
1 package (12 to 16 ounces) fresh or frozen
    mini ravioli, cooked and drained

1. In 6-quart saucepot, heat olive oil over medium-high heat and cook carrots, celery and onion, stirring occasionally, 8 minutes or until golden.

2. Stir in Ragú Robusto! Pasta Sauce, broth and water. Bring to a boil over high heat. Reduce heat to low and simmer covered 15 minutes.

3. Just before serving, stir in hot ravioli and season, if desired, with salt and ground black pepper. Garnish, if desired, with fresh basil.

Makes 6 servings

Spinach and Mushroom Enchiladas

2 packages (10 ounces each) frozen chopped
    spinach, thawed
1-1/2 cups sliced fresh mushrooms
1 can (15 ounces) pinto beans, rinsed and
    drained
3 teaspoons chili powder, divided
1/4 teaspoon crushed red pepper flakes
1 can (8 ounces) tomato sauce
2 tablespoons water
1/2 teaspoon hot pepper sauce
8 corn tortillas (8-inch)
1 cup (4 ounces) shredded Monterey Jack cheese
    Shredded lettuce (optional)
    Chopped tomatoes (optional)
    Sour cream (optional)

1. Combine spinach, mushrooms, beans, 2 teaspoons chili powder and red pepper flakes in large skillet over medium heat. Cook and stir 5 minutes; remove from heat.

2. Combine tomato sauce, water, remaining 1 teaspoon chili powder and pepper sauce in skillet. Dip tortillas into tomato sauce mixture; stack tortillas on waxed paper.

3. Divide spinach filling into 8 portions. Spoon down center of tortillas; roll up and place in 11×8-inch microwavable dish. Secure rolls with toothpicks, if desired. Spread remaining tomato sauce mixture over enchiladas.

4. Cover with vented plastic wrap. Microwave, uncovered, at MEDIUM (50% power) 10 minutes or until heated through. Sprinkle with cheese. Microwave at MEDIUM 3 minutes or until cheese is melted. Serve with lettuce, tomatoes and sour cream, if desired.

Makes 4 servings

Pesto Turkey & Pasta

1/4 cup milk
1 tablespoon margarine or butter
1 (4.7-ounce) package PASTA RONI® Chicken &
    Broccoli Flavor with Linguine
1 pound boneless, skinless turkey or chicken
    breasts, cut into thin strips
1 medium red or green bell pepper, sliced
1/2 medium onion, chopped
1/2 cup prepared pesto sauce
1/4 cup pine nuts or chopped walnuts, toasted
    Grated Parmesan cheese (optional)

1. In large saucepan, bring 1-1/2 cups water, milk and margarine to a boil. Stir in pasta and Special Seasonings. Reduce heat to medium. Gently boil 1 minute.

2. Add turkey, bell pepper and onion. Return to a boil. Gently boil 8 to 9 minutes or until pasta is tender and turkey is no longer pink inside, stirring occasionally.

3. Stir in pesto. Let stand 3 to 5 minutes before serving. Sprinkle with nuts and cheese, if desired.

Makes 4 servings

Tip: To make your own pesto, blend 2 cups fresh parsley or basil, 2 cloves garlic and 1/3 cup walnuts in a blender or food processor. Slowly add 1/2 cup olive oil and 1/4 cup Parmesan cheese.

Jambalaya

(Pictured at right)

　1 pound large shrimp, shelled and deveined
1/2 pound kielbasa or smoked sausage, sliced
　2 ribs celery, diagonally sliced
　1 green bell pepper, cut into strips
　1 can (14-1/2 ounces) whole tomatoes,
　　undrained
　1 can (10-1/2 ounces) condensed chicken broth
　2 tablespoons *Frank's® RedHot®* Original
　　Cayenne Pepper Sauce
1/2 teaspoon dried thyme leaves
1-1/3 cups uncooked instant rice
1-1/3 cups *French's®* French Fried Onions, divided

Generously spray large nonstick skillet with nonstick cooking spray; heat over high heat. Add shrimp and sausage; cook about 3 minutes or until shrimp are opaque.

Stir in celery, bell pepper, tomatoes with liquid, chicken broth, **Frank's RedHot** Sauce, thyme, rice and *2/3 cup* French Fried Onions. Bring to a boil, stirring occasionally. Cover; remove from heat. Let stand 5 to 8 minutes or until all liquid is absorbed. Sprinkle with remaining *2/3 cup* onions just before serving. 　　　*Makes 6 servings*

Stuffed Mexican Pizza Pie

　　1 pound ground beef
　　1 large onion, chopped
　　1 large green bell pepper, chopped
1-1/2 cups UNCLE BEN'S® Instant Rice
　　2 cans (14-1/2 ounces each) Mexican-style
　　　stewed tomatoes, undrained
2/3 cup water
　　2 cups (8 ounces) shredded Mexican-style
　　　seasoned Monterey Jack-Colby cheese blend,
　　　divided
　　1 container (10 ounces) refrigerated pizza crust
　　　dough

1. Preheat oven to 425°F. Spray 13×9-inch baking pan with nonstick cooking spray; set aside.

2. Spray large nonstick skillet with nonstick cooking spray; heat over high heat until hot. Add beef, onion and bell pepper; cook and stir 5 minutes or until beef is no longer pink.

3. Add rice, stewed tomatoes and water. Bring to a boil. Pour beef mixture into prepared baking pan. Sprinkle with 1-1/4 cups cheese and stir until blended.

4. Unroll pizza crust dough on work surface. Place dough in one even layer over mixture in baking pan. Cut 6 to 8 slits in dough with sharp knife. Bake 10 minutes or until crust is lightly browned. Sprinkle top of crust with remaining 3/4 cup cheese; continue baking 4 minutes or until cheese is melted and crust is deep golden brown.

5. Let stand 5 minutes before cutting.
　　　Makes 6 servings

Maple Cider Basted Turkey

　　1 PERDUE® Fresh Whole Turkey Breast
　　　(4 to 7 pounds)
　　1 to 2 tablespoons canola oil
　　1 tablespoon grainy, "country-style" mustard
　　　Salt and ground pepper to taste
　　1 apple, cored but unpeeled, sliced thinly
1/4 cup maple syrup
　　2 tablespoons cider vinegar
　　　Dash Worcestershire sauce

Preheat oven to 350°F. Pat breast dry with paper towel. In small bowl, mix oil and mustard; rub over breast and under skin from neck end. (Do not detach skin at base.) Season with salt and pepper. Slide apple slices between skin and meat. If necessary, reinsert BIRD-WATCHER® Thermometer to original location. Place breast in roasting pan and roast, uncovered, 1-1/2 to 1-3/4 hours, until BIRD-WATCHER® Thermometer pops up and meat thermometer inserted in thickest part of breast registers 170°F.

Meanwhile, combine syrup, vinegar and Worcestershire sauce. During last 20 minutes of roasting, baste breast with mixture. If skin is browning too quickly, tent with foil. Remove breast to serving platter and let rest 10 to 15 minutes before carving.

　　　Makes 6 to 8 servings

Chili Meatloaf and Potato Bake

1-1/2 pounds ground turkey
  3/4 cup salsa
    1 tablespoon chili powder
    1 egg, beaten
1-1/3 cups *French's*® French Fried Onions, divided
  1/2 teaspoon salt
  1/4 teaspoon ground black pepper
    2 cups prepared hot mashed potatoes
    2 cups (8 ounces) shredded taco blend cheese, divided

1. Preheat oven to 375°F. Combine ground turkey, salsa, chili powder, egg, *2/3 cup* French Fried Onions, salt and pepper until blended. Press turkey mixture into 9-inch square baking dish.

2. Bake 25 minutes or until turkey is cooked through and juices run clear. Drain off fat.

3. Combine potatoes and 1 cup cheese. Spread evenly over meatloaf. Sprinkle with remaining cheese and onions; bake 5 minutes or until cheese is melted and onions are golden.

Makes 6 servings

Tip: Prepare instant mashed potatoes for 4 servings.

Variation: For added Cheddar flavor, substitute *French's*® Cheddar French Fried Onions for the original flavor.

Cherry-Glazed Chicken

    1 (2-1/2- to 3-pound) broiler-fryer chicken, cut up (or 6 chicken breast halves, skinned and boned)
1/2 cup milk
1/2 cup all-purpose flour
    1 teaspoon dried thyme
    Salt and pepper, to taste
    1 to 2 tablespoons vegetable oil
    1 (16-ounce) can unsweetened tart cherries
1/4 cup brown sugar
1/4 cup granulated sugar
    1 teaspoon prepared yellow mustard

Rinse chicken; pat dry with paper towels. Pour milk into shallow container. In another container, combine flour, thyme, salt and pepper. Dip chicken first in milk, then in flour mixture; coat evenly. Heat oil in large skillet. Add chicken; brown on all sides.

Place chicken in 13×9×2-inch baking dish. Bake, covered with aluminum foil, in preheated 350°F oven 30 minutes.

Meanwhile, drain cherries, reserving 1/2 cup juice. Combine cherry juice, brown sugar and granulated sugar in small saucepan; mix well. Bring mixture to a boil over medium heat. Add mustard; mix well. Cook 5 minutes or until sauce is syrupy. Stir in cherries.

After chicken has cooked 30 minutes, remove baking dish from oven and carefully remove foil cover. Spoon hot cherry mixture evenly over chicken. Bake, uncovered, 15 minutes or until chicken is done. Serve immediately.

Makes 6 servings

Favorite recipe from **Cherry Marketing Institute**

Turkey Mushroom Stew

(Pictured at right)

    1 pound turkey cutlets, cut into 4×1-inch strips
    1 small onion, thinly sliced
    2 tablespoons minced green onion with top
1/2 pound fresh mushrooms, sliced
    2 to 3 tablespoons all-purpose flour
    1 cup half-and-half cream or milk
    1 teaspoon salt
    1 teaspoon dried tarragon
    Pepper to taste
1/2 cup frozen peas
1/2 cup sour cream (optional)
    Prepared puff pastry shells

SLOW COOKER DIRECTIONS
Layer turkey, onions and mushrooms in slow cooker. Cover and cook on LOW 4 hours. Remove turkey and vegetables to serving bowl. Turn slow cooker to HIGH.

Blend flour into cream until smooth; pour into slow cooker. Stir in salt, tarragon and pepper. Return cooked vegetables and turkey to slow cooker. Stir in peas. Cover and cook 1 hour or until sauce is thickened and peas are heated through.

Stir in sour cream just before serving, if desired. Serve in puff pastry shells. *Makes 4 servings*

Turkey Mushroom Stew

Beef Kabobs over Lemon Rice

Caribbean Island Chicken

1 bottle (16 ounces) K.C. MASTERPIECE™
  Spiced Caribbean Jerk Marinade
1/3 cup frozen pineapple juice concentrate*,
  diluted with 1/3 cup water
4 to 6 boneless, skinless chicken breast halves
3 cups cooked rice
1 can (15 ounces) black beans, drained and
  rinsed
1 can (11 ounces) corn, drained
1 red bell pepper, diced
1/2 cup cucumber, peeled, seeded, and diced

You can substitute frozen orange juice concentrate.

Combine 1/3 cup Spiced Caribbean Jerk Marinade
with pineapple juice mixture; reserve. Combine
chicken with remaining marinade for 30 minutes,
up to 24 hours.

Discard excess marinade from chicken and broil
both sides of chicken until meat reaches 160°F.

Combine rice, black beans, corn, bell pepper, and
cucumber. Simmer reserved marinade mixture
2 minutes. *Do not boil.* Slice chicken diagonally into
thin strips. Place overlapping strips on top of rice
mixture; drizzle warm sauce over chicken and rice.

Makes 4 to 6 servings

Campbell's® Turkey & Broccoli Alfredo

1/2 package linguine (8 ounces)*
  1 cup fresh *or* frozen broccoli flowerets
  1 can (10-3/4 ounces) CAMPBELL'S® Condensed
    Cream of Mushroom Soup *or* 98% Fat Free
    Cream of Mushroom Soup
1/2 cup milk
1/2 cup grated Parmesan cheese
1/4 teaspoon freshly ground pepper
  1 cup cubed cooked turkey

Or substitute spaghetti for linguine.

1. Prepare linguine according to package directions.
Add broccoli for last 4 minutes of cooking time.
Drain.

2. In same pan mix soup, milk, cheese and pepper.
Add turkey and linguine mixture and heat through,
stirring occasionally. Serve with additional
Parmesan cheese. *Makes 4 servings*

Beef Kabobs over Lemon Rice

(Pictured above)

1/2 pound boneless beef sirloin steak, cut into
  1-inch cubes
1 small zucchini, sliced
1 small yellow squash, sliced
1 small red bell pepper, cut into squares
1 small onion, cut into chunks
1/4 cup Italian dressing
1 cup hot cooked rice
2 teaspoons fresh lemon juice
1 tablespoon snipped fresh parsley
1/4 teaspoon seasoned salt

Combine beef and vegetables in large resealable
plastic food storage bag; add dressing. Seal bag and
marinate 4 to 6 hours in refrigerator, turning bag
occasionally. Thread beef and vegetables alternately
onto 4 metal skewers. Grill over medium coals, or
broil, 5 to 7 minutes or to desired doneness, turning
occasionally. Combine rice and remaining
ingredients. Serve kabobs over rice mixture.

Makes 2 servings

Favorite recipe from **USA Rice Federation**

Hearty Manicotti

(Pictured below)

8 to 10 dry manicotti shells
1 package (10 ounces) frozen chopped spinach, thawed, squeezed dry
1 carton (15 ounces) ricotta cheese
1 egg, lightly beaten
1/2 cup (2 ounces) grated Parmesan cheese
1/8 teaspoon ground black pepper
2 cans (6 ounces each) CONTADINA® Italian Paste with Italian Seasonings
1-1/3 cups water
1/2 cup (2 ounces) shredded mozzarella cheese

1. Cook pasta according to package directions; drain.

2. Meanwhile, combine spinach, ricotta cheese, egg, Parmesan cheese and pepper in medium bowl; mix well.

3. Spoon into manicotti shells. Place in ungreased 12×7-1/2-inch baking dish.

4. Combine tomato paste and water in small bowl; pour over manicotti. Sprinkle with mozzarella cheese. Bake in preheated 350°F oven for 30 to 40 minutes or until heated through.   *Makes 4 to 5 servings*

Bratwurst Skillet

1 pound uncooked bratwurst links, cut into 1/2-inch slices
1-1/2 cups julienned green bell pepper
1-1/2 cups julienned red bell pepper
1-1/2 cups sliced onions
1 teaspoon paprika
1 teaspoon caraway seeds

1. Heat large skillet over medium heat until hot. Add bratwurst; cover and cook about 5 minutes or until browned and no longer pink. Transfer bratwurst to plate. Cover and keep warm.

2. Drain all but 1 tablespoon drippings from skillet. Add peppers, onions, paprika and caraway seeds. Cook and stir about 5 minutes or until vegetables are tender.

3. Combine bratwurst and vegetables. Serve immediately.   *Makes 4 servings*

Serving Suggestion: For a special touch, garnish dish with cherry tomato halves and celery leaves.

Tip: To make this even speedier, purchase a packaged stir-fry pepper and onion mix and use in place of the bell peppers and onions.

Hearty Manicotti

Chunky Vegetarian Chili

(Pictured at right)

1 tablespoon vegetable oil
1 medium green bell pepper, chopped
1 medium onion, chopped
3 cloves garlic, minced
2 cans (14-1/2 ounces each) Mexican-style
    tomatoes, undrained
1 can (15 ounces) kidney beans, rinsed, drained
1 can (15 ounces) pinto beans, rinsed, drained
1 can (11 ounces) whole-kernel corn, drained
2-1/2 cups water
1 cup uncooked rice
2 tablespoons chili powder
1-1/2 teaspoons ground cumin
    Sour cream (optional)

Heat oil in 3-quart saucepan or Dutch oven over medium-high heat. Add bell pepper, onion and garlic and cook and stir 5 minutes or until tender. Add tomatoes, beans, corn, water, rice, chili powder and cumin; stir well. Bring to a boil. Reduce heat; cover. Simmer 30 minutes, stirring occasionally. To serve, top with sour cream, if desired.

Makes 6 servings

Favorite recipe from **USA Rice Federation**

20 Minute Chicken & Brown Rice Pilaf

1 tablespoon vegetable oil
4 boneless skinless chicken breast halves
1 can (10-1/2 ounces) condensed chicken broth
1/2 cup water
1 cup sliced fresh mushrooms
1 small onion, chopped
1 cup frozen peas
2 cups MINUTE® Brown Rice, uncooked

HEAT oil in skillet. Add chicken; cook until browned. Remove chicken.

ADD chicken broth and water to skillet; stir. Bring to boil.

STIR in mushrooms, onion, peas and rice. Top with chicken; cover. Cook on low heat 5 minutes or until chicken is cooked through. Let stand 5 minutes.

Makes 4 servings

Take a Shortcut: Omit oil. Substitute 1 package (6 ounces) LOUIS RICH® Grilled Chicken Breast Strips for the cooked chicken breasts. Bring chicken broth and water to a boil in large skillet. Stir in chicken breast strips with the mushroom, onions, peas and rice. Cook over low heat until mixture is thoroughly heated, stirring occasionally.

Hearty Beef Barley Stew

1 tablespoon BERTOLLI® Olive Oil
1-1/2 pounds beef stew meat
2 cups baby carrots
1 package (8 ounces) fresh mushrooms, sliced
2 cups (14-1/2 ounces each) beef broth
2 cups water
1 can (14-1/2 ounces) diced tomatoes,
    undrained
3/4 cup barley
1 envelope LIPTON® RECIPE SECRETS®
    Onion Soup Mix
1 cup frozen peas

In 6-quart saucepot, heat oil over medium-high heat. Brown beef, stirring occasionally, 4 minutes.

Stir in carrots, mushrooms, broth, water, tomatoes, barley and soup mix.

Bring to a boil over high heat. Reduce heat to medium-low and simmer, covered, 1-1/2 hours, stirring occasionally. Stir in peas. Cook 5 minutes or until heated through. *Makes 6 servings*

Slow Cooker Method: Layer carrots, mushrooms and beef in slow cooker. Combine broth, water, tomatoes, barley and soup mix. Pour over beef and vegetables. Cover. Cook on HIGH 5 to 6 hours or LOW 8 to 10 hours. Stir in peas and cook until heated through, about 5 minutes. Season, if desired, with salt and pepper.

Campbell's® Chicken Asparagus Gratin

(Pictured at right)

1 can (10-3/4 ounces) CAMPBELL'S® Condensed
    Cream of Asparagus Soup
1/2 cup milk
1/4 teaspoon onion powder
1/8 teaspoon pepper
3 cups hot cooked corkscrew macaroni
    (about 2-1/2 cups uncooked)
1-1/2 cups cubed cooked chicken *or* turkey
1-1/2 cups cooked cut asparagus
1 cup shredded Cheddar *or* Swiss cheese
    (4 ounces)

1. In 2-quart casserole mix soup, milk, onion powder and pepper. Stir in macaroni, chicken, asparagus and *1/2 cup* cheese.

2. Bake at 400°F. for 25 minutes or until hot.

3. Stir. Sprinkle remaining cheese over chicken mixture. Bake 5 minutes more or until cheese is melted.   *Makes 4 servings*

Tip: For 1-1/2 cups cooked cut asparagus, cook 3/4 pound fresh asparagus, trimmed and cut into 1-inch pieces, or 1 package (about 9 ounces) frozen asparagus cuts.

Cornmeal and Sausage Layered Dinner

1-1/2 pounds BOB EVANS® Italian Roll Sausage
1 cup chopped onion
1 clove garlic, minced
1 (16-ounce) can diced tomatoes, undrained
1 (8-ounce) can tomato sauce
1 tablespoon chopped fresh basil *or* 1 teaspoon
    dried basil leaves
1/2 teaspoon ground black pepper
1-1/2 cups yellow cornmeal
3/4 teaspoon salt
3 cups water
1 cup grated Romano cheese

Crumble and cook sausage in large skillet until browned. Remove sausage from skillet and reserve. Pour off all but 1 tablespoon drippings. Add onion and garlic to skillet; cook until tender. Stir in tomatoes, tomato sauce, basil, pepper and sausage.

Bring to a boil; reduce heat to low and simmer, uncovered, 25 minutes. Preheat oven to 375°F.

While sausage mixture is cooking, combine cornmeal, salt and water in medium saucepan. Bring to a boil, stirring constantly; cook and stir until thickened. Remove from heat; let cool slightly. Pour half of cornmeal mixture into greased 2-1/2-quart casserole dish. Top with half of sausage mixture; sprinkle with half of cheese. Repeat with remaining cornmeal mixture, sausage mixture and cheese. Bake, uncovered, 30 minutes. Refrigerate leftovers.
    Makes 6 servings

Harvest Pork Roast

1/4 cup WESSON® Best Blend Oil
2-1/2 cups cubed onions (1/2-inch dice)
1-1/2 teaspoons fresh minced garlic
3/4 cup honey
1/4 cup Dijon mustard
1-1/2 teaspoons coarsely ground pepper
    PAM® No-Stick Cooking Spray
3-1/2 to 4 pounds boned pork shoulder roast,
    trimmed
    4 large Red Delicious apples, quartered and
        cored
    3 acorn squash, sliced horizontally 1-1/2 inches
        thick
    1 cup fresh cranberries

Preheat oven to 350°F. In large skillet, heat Wesson® Oil. Add onions and garlic; sauté until onions are crisp-tender. Remove from heat. Add honey, mustard and pepper to onions and garlic in skillet; mix well. Spray large roasting pan with PAM® Cooking Spray. Place pork roast in center of roasting pan. Pour onion mixture evenly over roast. Bake, covered, for 1-1/2 hours, basting often with pan juices. Arrange apples and squash around roast. Baste roast, apples and squash several times with pan juices; cover. Bake an additional hour, basting occasionally, or until apples and squash are tender. Sprinkle cranberries evenly over dish. Bake, uncovered, for 10 minutes.   *Makes 4 to 6 servings*

Tip: If fresh cranberries are not available, use 2/3 cup dried cranberries.

Campbell's® Chicken Asparagus Gratin

Desserts

Spicy Ginger Molasses Cookies

(Pictured at left)

2 cups all-purpose flour
1-1/2 teaspoons ground ginger
1 teaspoon baking soda
1/2 teaspoon ground cloves
1/4 teaspoon salt
1 cup sugar
3/4 cup butter or margarine, softened
1/4 cup molasses
1 egg
Additional sugar
1/2 cup yogurt-covered raisins

Preheat oven to 375°F.

Combine flour, ginger, baking soda, cloves and salt in small bowl; set aside.

Beat 1 cup sugar and butter in large bowl of electric mixer at medium speed until light and fluffy. Add molasses and egg; beat until well blended. Gradually beat in flour mixture on low speed just until blended.

Drop dough by level 1/4-cupfuls onto parchment-lined cookie sheets, spacing 3 inches apart. Flatten each ball of dough until 2 inches in diameter with bottom of glass that has been dipped in additional sugar. Press 7 to 8 yogurt-covered raisins onto each cookie.

Bake 11 to 12 minutes or until cookies are set. Cool cookies 2 minutes on cookie sheets; slide parchment paper and cookies onto wire rack to cool completely.

Makes about 1 dozen (4-inch) cookies

Clockwise from top left: *Spicy Ginger Molasses Cookies, Juicy Berry Sorbet (p. 203), Heavenly Chocolate Mousse Pie (p. 202) and Praline Bars (p. 186)*

Cider Apple Pie in Cheddar Crust

(Pictured at right)

CRUST

2 cups sifted all-purpose flour
1 cup shredded Cheddar cheese
1/2 teaspoon salt
2/3 CRISCO® Stick or 2/3 cup CRISCO®
    all-vegetable shortening
5 to 6 tablespoons ice water

FILLING

6 cups sliced peeled apples (about 2 pounds
    or 6 medium)
1 cup apple cider
2/3 cup granulated sugar
2 tablespoons cornstarch
2 tablespoons water
1/2 teaspoon ground cinnamon
1 tablespoon butter or margarine

GLAZE

1 egg yolk
1 tablespoon water

1. Heat oven to 400°F.

2. For crust, place flour, cheese and salt in food processor bowl. Add 2/3 cup shortening. Process 15 seconds. Sprinkle water through feed tube, 1 tablespoon at a time, until dough just forms (process time not to exceed 20 seconds). Shape into ball. Divide dough in half. Press between hands to form two 5- to 6-inch "pancakes." Roll and press bottom crust into 9-inch pie plate.

3. For filling, combine apples, apple cider and sugar in large saucepan. Cook and stir on medium-high heat until mixture comes to a boil. Reduce heat to low. Simmer 5 minutes. Combine cornstarch, water and cinnamon. Stir into apples. Cook and stir until mixture comes to a boil. Remove from heat. Stir in butter. Spoon into unbaked pie crust. Moisten pastry edge with water.

4. Roll top crust. Lift onto filled pie. Trim 1/2 inch beyond edge of pie plate. Fold top edge under bottom crust. Flute. Cut slits or design in top crust to allow steam to escape.

5. For glaze, beat egg yolk with fork. Stir in water. Brush over top.

6. Bake at 400°F for 35 to 40 minutes or until filling in center is bubbly and crust is golden brown. Cover edge with foil, if necessary, to prevent overbrowning. *Do not overbake.* Cool to room temperature before serving.   *Makes 1 (9-inch) pie (8 servings)*

Note: Golden Delicious, Granny Smith and Jonathan apples are all suitable for pie baking.

Blueberry Crisp Cupcakes

CUPCAKES

2 cups all-purpose flour
2 teaspoons baking powder
1/4 teaspoon salt
1-3/4 cups granulated sugar
1/2 cup butter or margarine, softened
3/4 cup milk
1-1/2 teaspoons vanilla extract
3 egg whites
3 cups fresh or frozen blueberries

STREUSEL

1/3 cup all-purpose flour
1/4 cup uncooked old-fashioned or quick oats
1/4 cup packed light brown sugar
1/2 teaspoon ground cinnamon
1/4 cup cold butter or margarine, softened
1/2 cup chopped walnuts or pecans

1. Preheat oven to 350°F. Line 30 regular-size (2-1/2-inch) muffin cups with paper baking cups.

2. For cupcakes, combine 2 cups flour, baking powder and salt in medium bowl; mix well. Beat granulated sugar and 1/2 cup butter with electric mixer at medium speed 1 minute. Add milk and vanilla. Beat at low speed 30 seconds.

3. Gradually beat in flour mixture; beat at medium speed 2 minutes. Add egg whites; beat 1 minute. Spoon batter into prepared muffin cups, filling half full. Spoon blueberries over batter. Bake 10 minutes.

4. Meanwhile, for streusel, combine 1/3 cup flour, oats, brown sugar and cinnamon in small bowl; mix well. Cut in 1/4 cup butter with pastry blender or two knives until mixture is well combined. Stir in chopped nuts.

5. Sprinkle streusel over partially baked cupcakes. Return to oven; bake 18 to 20 minutes or until golden brown and toothpick inserted into centers comes out clean. Cool in pans on wire racks 10 minutes. Remove cupcakes to racks; cool completely.   *Makes 30 cupcakes*

Cider Apple Pie in Cheddar Crust

Frozen Lemon Squares

(Pictured at right)

1-1/4 cups graham cracker crumbs
1/4 cup sugar
1/4 cup (1/2 stick) butter or margarine, melted
1 (14-ounce) can EAGLE BRAND® Sweetened Condensed Milk (NOT evaporated milk)
3 egg yolks
1/2 cup lemon juice from concentrate
Yellow food coloring, if desired
Whipped cream or non-dairy whipped topping

1. Preheat oven to 325°F. In small mixing bowl, combine crumbs, sugar and butter; press firmly on bottom of 8- or 9-inch square pan.

2. In small mixing bowl, beat Eagle Brand, egg yolks, lemon juice and food coloring, if desired. Pour into crust.

3. Bake 30 minutes. Cool completely. Top with whipped cream. Freeze 4 hours or until firm. Let stand 10 minutes before serving. Garnish as desired. Freeze leftovers. *Makes 6 to 9 servings*

Pepperidge Farm® Caramel Apple Tarts

1 package (10 ounces) PEPPERIDGE FARM® Frozen Puff Pastry Shells
6 tablespoons sugar
1/2 teaspoon ground cinnamon
1/2 teaspoon ground ginger
3 apples *or* pears, peeled, cored and thinly sliced (about 4 cups)
2/3 cup caramel sauce
Vanilla ice cream

1. Thaw pastry shells at room temperature 30 minutes. Preheat oven to 375°F. Mix sugar, cinnamon and ginger and set aside.

2. Roll pastry shells into 5-inch circles on lightly floured surface. Place on 2 shallow-sided baking sheets. Divide apple slices among pastry circles. Sprinkle each with ***1 tablespoon*** sugar mixture. Bake 25 minutes or until pastry is golden.

3. In small saucepan over medium heat, heat caramel sauce until warm. Spoon over tarts. Serve with ice cream. *Makes 6 servings*

Triple Chocolate Parfaits

2/3 cup granulated sugar
1/4 cup unsweetened cocoa powder
2-1/2 tablespoons cornstarch
2 cups milk
1 large egg
1 tablespoon butter
1 teaspoon vanilla extract
8 (1/2-inch) slices packaged chocolate or marbled pound cake
1-1/4 cups "M&M's"® Milk Chocolate Mini Baking Bits, divided
2 cups thawed frozen nondairy whipped topping

In medium saucepan combine sugar, cocoa powder and cornstarch; stir in milk. Cook over medium heat, stirring often, until mixture comes to a boil. Boil 1 minute, stirring constantly. Remove from heat. In small bowl beat egg lightly; stir in 1/2 cup hot milk mixture. Stir egg mixture into hot milk mixture in saucepan. Cook over medium heat 2 minutes, stirring constantly. Remove from heat; stir in butter and vanilla. Let pudding cool 15 minutes; stirring occasionally. Just before serving, cut cake into cubes. Divide half of cake cubes among 8 (8-ounce) parfait glasses. Evenly layer half of pudding, 1/2 cup "M&M's"® Milk Chocolate Mini Baking Bits and 1 cup whipped topping. Repeat layers. Decorate with remaining 1/4 cup "M&M's"® Milk Chocolate Mini Baking Bits. Serve immediately. *Makes 8 servings*

Tip: If you're short on time, prepare 2 packages (4-serving size each) instant chocolate pudding instead of making this stove-top version. Then assemble the parfaits as directed.

Helpful Hint

Unsweetened cocoa powder can be stored in a tightly closed container in a cool, dark place for up to two years. If it is lumpy, run it through a strainer before measuring.

Hershey's White Chip Brownies

(Pictured at right and on front cover)

4 eggs
1-1/4 cups sugar
1/2 cup (1 stick) butter or margarine, melted
2 teaspoons vanilla extract
1-1/3 cups all-purpose flour
2/3 cup HERSHEY'S Cocoa
1 teaspoon baking powder
1/2 teaspoon salt
1-2/3 cups (10-ounce package) HERSHEY'S Premier White Chips

1. Heat oven to 350°F. Grease 13×9×2-inch baking pan.

2. Beat eggs in large bowl until foamy; gradually beat in sugar. Add butter and vanilla; beat until blended. Stir together flour, cocoa, baking powder and salt; add to egg mixture, beating until blended. Stir in white chips. Spread batter into prepared pan.

3. Bake 25 to 30 minutes or until brownies begin to pull away from sides of pan. Cool completely in pan on wire rack. Cut into squares.

Makes about 36 brownies

Tip: Brownies and bar cookies cut into different shapes can add interest to a plate of simple square cookies. Cut cookies into different size rectangles or make triangles by cutting them into 2- to 2-1/2-inch squares; cut each square in half diagonally. To make diamond shapes, cut straight lines 1 or 1-1/2 inches apart the length of the baking pan, then cut straight lines 1-1/2 inches apart diagonally across the pan.

Cookies 'n' Cream Cake

1 package (18-1/4 ounces) white cake mix
1 package (3.4 ounces) instant vanilla-flavored pudding mix
1 cup vegetable oil
4 egg whites
1/2 cup milk
20 cream-filled chocolate sandwich cookies, coarsely chopped
1/2 cup semisweet chocolate chips
1 teaspoon shortening
4 cream-filled chocolate sandwich cookies, cut into quarters

1. Preheat oven to 350°F. Spray 10-inch fluted tube pan with nonstick cooking spray.

2. Beat cake mix, pudding mix, oil, egg whites and milk 2 minutes in large bowl with electric mixer at medium speed or until ingredients are well blended. Stir in chopped cookies; spread in prepared pan.

3. Bake 50 to 60 minutes or until cake springs back when lightly touched. Cool 1 hour in pan on wire rack. Invert cake onto serving plate; cool completely.

4. Combine chocolate chips and shortening in glass measuring cup. Heat in microwave on HIGH (100%) power 1 minute; stir. Continue heating at 15 second intervals, stirring, until melted and smooth. Drizzle glaze over cake and garnish with quartered cookies.

Makes 10 to 12 servings

Cool 'n' Easy® Pie

2/3 cup boiling water
1 package (4-serving size) JELL-O® Brand Gelatin, any flavor
1/2 cup cold juice, any flavor
Ice cubes
1 tub (8 ounces) COOL WHIP® Whipped Topping, thawed
1 prepared graham cracker crumb crust (6 ounces)
Assorted fruit (optional)

STIR boiling water into gelatin in large bowl 2 minutes or until completely dissolved. Mix cold juice and ice to make 1 cup. Add to gelatin, stirring until slightly thickened. Remove any remaining ice.

STIR in whipped topping with wire whisk until smooth. Refrigerate 10 to 15 minutes or until mixture is very thick and will mound. Spoon into crust.

REFRIGERATE 4 hours or until firm. Just before serving, garnish with fruit, if desired. Store leftover pie in refrigerator.
Makes 8 servings

Southern Banana Pudding

(Pictured at right)

1 package (4-serving size) JELL-O® Vanilla or
    Banana Cream Flavor Cook & Serve
    Pudding & Pie Filling *(not Instant)*
2-1/2 cups milk
2 egg yolks, well beaten
30 to 35 vanilla wafers
2 large bananas, sliced
2 egg whites
    Dash salt
1/4 cup sugar

HEAT oven to 350°F.

STIR pudding mix into milk in medium saucepan. Add egg yolks. Stirring constantly, cook on medium heat until mixture comes to full boil. Remove from heat.

ARRANGE layer of cookies on bottom and up side of 1-1/2-quart baking dish. Add layer of banana slices; top with 1/3 of the pudding. Repeat layers twice, ending with pudding.

BEAT egg whites and salt in medium bowl with electric mixer on high speed until foamy. Gradually add sugar, beating until stiff peaks form. Spoon meringue mixture lightly onto pudding, spreading to edge of dish to seal.

BAKE 10 to 15 minutes or until meringue is lightly browned. Serve warm or refrigerate until ready to serve.   *Makes 8 servings*

Best-Ever Baked Rice Pudding

3 eggs
1/3 cup sugar
1/4 teaspoon salt
2 cups milk
2 cups *cooked* rice
1/2 cup golden raisins
    Grated peel of 1 SUNKIST® lemon
    Warm Lemon Sauce (recipe follows)

In bowl, beat eggs slightly with sugar and salt. Stir in milk, rice, raisins and lemon peel. Pour into well-buttered 1-quart casserole. Bake, uncovered, at 325°F 50 to 60 minutes or until set. Serve with Warm Lemon Sauce. Refrigerate leftovers.   *Makes 6 servings (about 3-1/2 cups)*

Warm Lemon Sauce

1/3 cup sugar
2 tablespoons cornstarch
1/8 teaspoon salt
    Dash nutmeg (optional)
3/4 cup water
    Grated peel of 1/2 SUNKIST® lemon
    Juice of 1 SUNKIST® lemon
1 tablespoon butter or margarine
    Few drops yellow food coloring (optional)

In small saucepan, combine sugar, cornstarch, salt and nutmeg. Gradually blend in water, lemon peel and juice. Add butter. Cook over medium heat, stirring until thickened. Stir in food coloring. Serve warm.   *Makes about 1 cup*

Colorful Cookie Buttons

1-1/2 cups (3 sticks) butter, softened
1/2 cup granulated sugar
1/2 cup firmly packed light brown sugar
2 large egg yolks
1 teaspoon vanilla extract
3-1/2 cups all-purpose flour
1-1/2 teaspoons baking powder
1/2 teaspoon salt
1 cup "M&M's"® Chocolate Mini Baking Bits

Preheat oven to 350°F. In large bowl cream butter and sugars until light and fluffy; beat in egg yolks and vanilla. In medium bowl combine flour, baking powder and salt; add to creamed mixture. Shape dough into 72 balls. For each cookie, place one ball on ungreased cookie sheet and flatten. Place 8 to 10 "M&M's"® Chocolate Mini Baking Bits on dough. Flatten second ball and place over "M&M's"® Chocolate Mini Baking Bits, pressing top and bottom dough together. Decorate top with remaining "M&M's"® Chocolate Mini Baking Bits. Repeat with remaining dough balls and "M&M's"® Chocolate Mini Baking Bits, placing cookies about 2 inches apart on cookie sheet. Bake 17 to 18 minutes. Cool 2 minutes on cookie sheets; cool completely on wire racks. Store in tightly covered container.

                     Makes 3 dozen cookies

Southern Banana Pudding

Vermont Spice Cake

Vermont Spice Cake

(Pictured above)

CAKE

- 3 cups all-purpose flour
- 3-1/2 teaspoons baking powder
- 2 teaspoons pumpkin pie spice
- 1 teaspoon baking soda
- 3/4 teaspoon ground nutmeg
- 1/2 teaspoon salt
- 1-1/2 cups granulated sugar
- 3/4 cup (1-1/2 sticks) butter, softened
- 3 large eggs
- 1-1/2 cups LIBBY'S® 100% Pure Pumpkin
- 1/2 cup NESTLÉ® CARNATION® Evaporated Milk
- 1/4 cup water
- 1-1/2 teaspoons vanilla extract

MAPLE FROSTING

- 11 ounces cream cheese, softened
- 1/3 cup butter, softened
- 3-1/2 cups sifted powdered sugar
- 2 to 3 teaspoons maple flavoring
  Orange peel twists, fresh mint, chopped nuts or nut halves (optional)

PREHEAT oven to 325°F. Grease and flour two 9-inch-round cake pans.

FOR CAKE
COMBINE flour, baking powder, pumpkin pie spice, baking soda, nutmeg and salt in small bowl. Beat granulated sugar and butter in large mixer bowl until creamy. Add eggs; beat for 2 minutes. Beat in pumpkin, evaporated milk, water and vanilla extract. Gradually beat in flour mixture. Spread evenly into prepared cake pans.

BAKE for 35 to 40 minutes or until wooden pick inserted in center comes out clean. Cool in pans on wire racks for 15 minutes; remove to wire racks to cool completely.

FOR MAPLE FROSTING
BEAT cream cheese, butter and powdered sugar in large mixer bowl until fluffy. Add maple flavoring; mix well.

TO ASSEMBLE
CUT each layer in half horizontally with long, serrated knife. Frost between layers and on top of cake, leaving side unfrosted. Garnish as desired.
Makes 12 servings

Note: To make a 2-layer cake, frost between layers, over top and on side of cake.

Grandma's® Gingerbread

- 1/2 cup shortening or butter
- 1/2 cup sugar
- 1 cup GRANDMA'S® Molasses
- 2 eggs
- 2-1/2 cups all-purpose flour
- 2 teaspoons baking powder
- 2 teaspoons ground cinnamon
- 1 teaspoon salt
- 1 teaspoon ground ginger
- 1/2 teaspoon baking soda
- 1/2 teaspoon ground cloves
- 1 cup hot water

Heat oven to 350°F. In medium bowl, blend shortening with sugar; add molasses and eggs. Beat well. Sift dry ingredients; add alternately with water to molasses mixture. Bake in greased 9-inch square pan about 50 minutes.
Makes 8 servings

Grilled Peaches with Raspberry Sauce

(Pictured below)

1 package (10 ounces) frozen raspberries, thawed
1-1/2 teaspoons lemon juice
3 tablespoons brown sugar
1 teaspoons ground cinnamon
1 teaspoon rum extract (optional)
4 medium peaches, peeled, halved and pitted
2 teaspoons butter
Fresh mint sprigs (optional)

Combine raspberries and lemon juice in food processor fitted with metal blade; process until smooth. Chill in refrigerator.

Combine brown sugar, cinnamon and rum extract, if desired, in medium bowl; roll peach halves in mixture. Place peach halves, cut side up, on foil. Dot with butter. Fold foil over peaches and seal loosely. Grill over medium coals for 15 minutes.

To serve, spoon 2 tablespoons raspberry sauce over each peach half. Garnish with fresh mint sprig, if desired.   *Makes 4 servings*

Berry Squares

1 package (12 ounces) pound cake, cut into 10 slices
3 tablespoons orange juice
2 pints fresh seasonal berries (strawberries, raspberries or blueberries)
2 tablespoons sugar
2-1/2 cups cold milk
2 packages (4-serving size each) JELL-O® Vanilla or Lemon Flavor Instant Pudding & Pie Filling
1 tub (8 ounces) COOL WHIP® Whipped Topping, thawed, divided

ARRANGE cake slices in bottom of 13×9-inch pan. Drizzle cake with juice. Top with berries; sprinkle with sugar.

POUR milk into large bowl. Add pudding mixes. Beat with wire whisk 1 minute or until well blended. Gently stir in 1 cup whipped topping. Spoon mixture over berries in pan. Top with remaining whipped topping.

REFRIGERATE until ready to serve or overnight. Garnish as desired.   *Makes 15 servings*

Grilled Peaches with Raspberry Sauce

Sweet Potato Pecan Pie

(Pictured at right)

1 pound sweet potatoes or yams, cooked and
    peeled
1/4 cup (1/2 stick) butter or margarine, softened
1 (14-ounce) can EAGLE BRAND® Sweetened
    Condensed Milk (NOT evaporated milk)
1 egg
1 teaspoon grated orange peel
1 teaspoon ground cinnamon
1 teaspoon vanilla extract
1/2 teaspoon ground nutmeg
1/4 teaspoon salt
1 (6-ounce) graham cracker crumb pie crust
    Pecan Topping (recipe follows)

1. Preheat oven to 425°F. In large mixing bowl, beat
hot sweet potatoes and butter until smooth. Add
Eagle Brand and remaining ingredients except crust
and Pecan Topping; mix well. Pour into crust.

2. Bake 20 minutes. Meanwhile, prepare Pecan
Topping.

3. Remove pie from oven; *reduce oven temperature
to 350°F.* Spoon Pecan Topping over pie.

4. Bake 25 minutes longer or until set. Cool. Serve
warm or at room temperature. Garnish, if desired.
Refrigerate leftovers. *Makes 1 pie*

Pecan Topping: In small mixing bowl, beat 1 egg,
2 tablespoons firmly packed light brown sugar,
2 tablespoons dark corn syrup, 1 tablespoon
melted butter and 1/2 teaspoon maple flavoring.
Stir in 1 cup chopped pecans.

Strawberry Chantilly

1 box (10 ounces) BIRDS EYE® frozen
    Strawberries
1 cup heavy cream*
2 tablespoons sugar*
1/2 teaspoon vanilla extract*
    Belgian waffles or pound cake slices, toasted

*For extra-quick preparation, substitute 2 cups thawed frozen
whipped topping for cream, sugar and vanilla.*

• Thaw strawberries according to package directions
until partially thawed. Mash strawberries in bowl.

• Beat cream, sugar and vanilla in large bowl until
stiff peaks form. Gently fold in 1/4 cup mashed
strawberries.

• Spoon remaining strawberries over waffles. Top
with whipped cream mixture.
Makes about 4 servings

Cinnamon Roll Cookies

CINNAMON MIXTURE
4 tablespoons granulated sugar
1 tablespoon ground cinnamon

COOKIE DOUGH
1 Butter Flavor CRISCO® Stick or 1 cup Butter
    Flavor CRISCO® all-vegetable shortening
1 cup firmly packed light brown sugar
2 large eggs
1 teaspoon vanilla
3 cups all-purpose flour
2 teaspoons baking powder
1 teaspoon ground cinnamon
1/2 teaspoon salt

1. For cinnamon mixture, combine granulated sugar
and 1 tablespoon cinnamon in small bowl; mix well.
Set aside.

2. For cookie dough, combine 1 cup shortening and
brown sugar in large bowl. Beat at medium speed
with electric mixer until well blended. Beat in eggs
and vanilla until well blended.

3. Combine flour, baking powder, 1 teaspoon
cinnamon and salt in small bowl. Add to creamed
mixture; mix well.

4. Turn dough onto sheet of waxed paper. Spread
dough into 9×6-inch rectangle using rubber spatula.
Sprinkle with 4 tablespoons cinnamon mixture to
within 1 inch from edge. Roll up jelly-roll style into
log. Dust log with remaining cinnamon mixture.
Wrap tightly in plastic wrap; refrigerate 4 hours
or overnight.

5. Heat oven to 375°F. Spray cookie sheets with
CRISCO® No-Stick Cooking Spray.

6. Slice dough 1/4 inch thick. Place on prepared
cookie sheets. Bake at 350°F for 8 minutes or until
lightly browned on top. Cool on cookie sheets
4 minutes; transfer to cooling racks.
Makes about 5 dozen cookies

Kitchen Hint: Be careful when working with this
dough. It is a stiff dough and can crack easily
when rolling. Roll the dough slowly and smooth
any cracks with your finger as you go.

Sweet Potato Pecan Pie

Creamy Caramel Flan

(Pictured at right)

> 3/4 cup sugar
> 4 eggs
> 1-3/4 cups water
> 1 (14-ounce) can EAGLE BRAND® Sweetened Condensed Milk (NOT evaporated milk)
> 1 teaspoon vanilla extract
> 1/8 teaspoon salt
> Sugar Garnish (recipe follows), if desired

1. Preheat oven to 350°F. In heavy skillet over medium heat, cook and stir sugar until melted and caramel-colored. Carefully pour into 8 ungreased 6-ounce custard cups, tilting to coat bottoms.

2. In large mixing bowl, beat eggs; stir in water, Eagle Brand, vanilla and salt. Pour into prepared custard cups. Set cups in large shallow pan. Fill pan with 1 inch hot water.

3. Bake 25 minutes or until knife inserted near centers comes out clean. Cool. Chill. To serve, invert flans onto individual serving plates. Top with Sugar Garnish, if desired, or garnish as desired. Store covered in refrigerator.   *Makes 8 servings*

Sugar Garnish: Fill medium metal bowl half-full of ice. In medium saucepan over medium-high heat, combine 1 cup sugar with 1/4 cup water. Stir; cover and bring to a boil. Cook over high heat 5 to 6 minutes or until light brown in color. Immediately put pan in ice for 1 minute. Using spoon, carefully drizzle sugar decoratively over foil. Cool. To serve, peel sugar garnish from foil.

Peanutty Cranberry Bars

> 1/2 cup (1 stick) butter or margarine, softened
> 1/2 cup granulated sugar
> 1/4 cup packed light brown sugar
> 1 cup all-purpose flour
> 1 cup quick-cooking rolled oats
> 1/4 teaspoon baking soda
> 1/4 teaspoon salt
> 1 cup REESE'S® Peanut Butter Chips
> 1-1/2 cups fresh or frozen whole cranberries
> 2/3 cup light corn syrup
> 1/2 cup water
> 1 teaspoon vanilla extract

1. Heat oven to 350°F. Grease 8-inch square baking pan.

2. Beat butter, granulated sugar and brown sugar in medium bowl until fluffy. Stir together flour, oats, baking soda and salt; gradually add to butter mixture, mixing until mixture is consistency of coarse crumbs. Stir in peanut butter chips.

3. Reserve 1-1/2 cups mixture for crumb topping. Firmly press remaining mixture evenly into prepared pan. Bake 15 minutes or until set. Meanwhile, in medium saucepan, combine cranberries, corn syrup and water. Cook over medium heat, stirring occasionally, until mixture boils. Reduce heat; simmer 15 minutes, stirring occasionally. Remove from heat. Stir in vanilla. Spread evenly over baked layer. Sprinkle reserved 1-1/2 cups crumbs evenly over top.

4. Return to oven. Bake 15 to 20 minutes or until set. Cool completely in pan on wire rack. Cut into bars.
Makes about 16 bars

Lemon-Blueberry Pie Cups

> 6 vanilla wafer cookies
> 3/4 cup canned blueberry pie filling
> 1 cup boiling water
> 1 package (4-serving size) JELL-O® Brand Lemon Flavor Gelatin
> 3/4 cup cold water
> 1/2 tub (8 ounces) COOL WHIP® Whipped Topping, thawed

PLACE one vanilla wafer on bottom of each of 6 dessert cups. Top each wafer with 2 tablespoons pie filling. Set aside.

STIR boiling water into gelatin in large bowl at least 2 minutes until completely dissolved.

STIR in cold water. Refrigerate 10 to 15 minutes or until mixture is slightly thickened (consistency of unbeaten egg whites). Stir in 1/2 of the whipped topping until well blended. Spoon over pie filling in cups.

REFRIGERATE 2 hours or until firm. Garnish with remaining whipped topping, if desired.
Makes 6 servings

Great Substitutes: Try using cherry or pineapple pie filling instead of the blueberry pie filling.

Creamy Caramel Flan

Cappuccino Bon Bons

(Pictured at right)

1 (21-ounce) package DUNCAN HINES®
    Family-Style Chewy Fudge Brownie Mix
2 eggs
1/3 cup water
1/3 cup vegetable oil
1-1/2 tablespoons instant coffee
1 teaspoon ground cinnamon
    Whipped topping
    Cinnamon

1. Preheat oven to 350°F. Place 2-inch foil cupcake liners on cookie sheet.

2. Combine brownie mix, eggs, water, oil, instant coffee and cinnamon. Stir with spoon until well blended, about 50 strokes. Fill each cupcake liner with 1 measuring tablespoon batter. Bake 12 to 15 minutes or until wooden toothpick inserted in center comes out clean. Cool completely. Garnish with whipped topping and a dash of cinnamon. Refrigerate until ready to serve.

Makes about 40 bon bons

Tip: To make larger bon bons, use twelve 2-1/2-inch foil cupcake liners and fill with 1/4 cup batter. Bake 28 to 30 minutes.

Orange Pecan Refrigerator Cookies

2-1/3 cups all-purpose flour
1/2 teaspoon baking soda
1/4 teaspoon salt
1/2 cup butter or margarine, softened
1/2 cup packed brown sugar
1/2 cup granulated sugar
1 egg, lightly beaten
    Grated peel of 1 SUNKIST® orange
3 tablespoons fresh squeezed SUNKIST®
    orange juice
3/4 cup pecan pieces

In bowl, stir together flour, baking soda and salt. In large bowl, blend together butter, brown sugar and granulated sugar. Add egg, orange peel and juice; beat well. Stir in pecans. Gradually beat in flour mixture. (Dough will be stiff.) Divide mixture in half and shape each half (on long piece of waxed paper) into roll about 1-1/4 inches in diameter and 12 inches long. Roll up tightly in waxed paper. Chill several hours or overnight.

Cut into 1/4-inch slices and arrange on lightly greased cookie sheets. Bake at 350°F for 10 to 12 minutes or until lightly browned. Cool on wire racks.

Makes about 6 dozen cookies

Chocolate Filled Sandwich Cookies: Cut each roll into 1/8-inch slices and bake as above. When cool, to make each sandwich cookie, spread about 1 teaspoon canned chocolate fudge frosting on bottom side of 1 cookie; cover with second cookie of same shape. Makes about 4 dozen sandwich cookies.

Pepperidge Farm® Chocolate Walnut Strudel

1/2 package (17-1/4-ounce size) PEPPERIDGE
    FARM® Frozen Puff Pastry Sheets (1 sheet)
1 egg
1 tablespoon water
4 squares (1 ounce *each*) semi-sweet chocolate
2 tablespoons milk
1 tablespoon margarine *or* butter
1/2 cup chopped walnuts
    Sweetened whipped cream

1. Thaw pastry sheet at room temperature 30 minutes. Preheat oven to 375°F. Mix egg and water and set aside.

2. In large microwave-safe bowl microwave chocolate, milk and margarine on HIGH 1-1/2 minutes or until chocolate is almost melted, stirring halfway through heating. Stir until chocolate is completely melted.

3. Unfold pastry on lightly floured surface. Roll into 16- by 12-inch rectangle. Spread chocolate mixture evenly on pastry to within 1-1/2 inches of edges. Sprinkle walnuts over chocolate. Starting at short side, roll up like a jelly roll. Place seam-side down on baking sheet. Tuck ends under to seal. Brush with egg mixture.

4. Bake 35 minutes or until golden. Cool on baking sheet on wire rack at least 30 minutes. Slice and serve with whipped cream.

Makes 8 servings

Premier White Lemony Cheesecake

CRUST
6 tablespoons butter or margarine, softened
1/4 cup granulated sugar
1-1/4 cups all-purpose flour
1 large egg yolk
1/8 teaspoon salt

FILLING
6 bars (*two* 6-ounce boxes) NESTLÉ® TOLL HOUSE® Premier White Baking Bars, broken into pieces or 2 cups (12-ounce package) NESTLÉ® TOLL HOUSE® Premier White Morsels
1/2 cup heavy whipping cream
2 packages (8 ounces *each*) cream cheese, softened
1 tablespoon lemon juice
2 teaspoons grated lemon peel
1/4 teaspoon salt
3 large egg whites
1 large egg

PREHEAT oven to 350°F. Lightly grease 9-inch springform pan.

FOR CRUST
BEAT butter and sugar in small mixer bowl until creamy. Beat in flour, egg yolk and salt. Press mixture onto bottom and 1 inch up side of prepared pan.

BAKE for 14 to 16 minutes or until crust is set.

FOR FILLING
MICROWAVE baking bars and whipping cream in medium, uncovered, microwave-safe bowl on MEDIUM-HIGH (70%) power for 1 minute. Stir. Morsels may retain some of their original shape. If necessary, microwave at additional 10- to 15-second intervals, stirring just until morsels are melted.

BEAT cream cheese, lemon juice, lemon peel and salt in large mixer bowl until smooth. Gradually beat in melted baking bars. Beat in egg whites and egg. Pour into crust.

BAKE for 35 to 40 minutes or until edge is lightly browned. Run knife around edge of cheesecake. Cool completely in pan on wire rack. Refrigerate for several hours or overnight. Remove side of springform pan. Garnish as desired.

Makes 12 to 16 servings

Mini Chocolate Caramel Cupcakes

(Pictured at right)

1 package (21.5 ounces) brownie mix plus ingredients to prepare mix
1 cup chopped pecans, toasted, divided
1 cup prepared dark chocolate frosting
12 caramels
1 to 2 tablespoons heavy whipping cream

1. Heat oven to 350°F. Line 54 mini (1-1/2-inch) muffin cups with paper baking cups.

2. Prepare brownie batter according to package directions. Stir in 1/2 cup chopped pecans.

3. Spoon batter into prepared muffin cups filling two-thirds full. Bake 18 minutes or until toothpick inserted into centers comes out clean. Cool in pans on wire racks 5 minutes. Remove cupcakes to racks; cool completely. (Cupcakes may be frozen up to 3 months. Thaw at room temperature before frosting.)

4. Spread frosting over cooled cupcakes; top with remaining 1/2 cup chopped pecans.

5. Combine caramels and 1 tablespoon cream in small saucepan. Cook and stir over low heat until caramels are melted and mixture is smooth. Add additional 1 tablespoon cream if needed. Drizzle caramel over cupcakes. Store at room temperature up to 24 hours or cover and refrigerate for up to 3 days.

Makes 54 mini cupcakes

Helpful Hint

Toasting nuts before using them intensifies their flavor and crunch. To toast nuts, spread them on a baking sheet and place in a 350°F oven for 8 to 10 minutes. Or, toast nuts in an ungreased skillet over medium heat until golden brown, stirring frequently. Let them cool to room temperature before combining them with other ingredients.

Mini Chocolate Caramel Cupcakes

Moist and Tender Carrot Cake

Moist and Tender Carrot Cake

(Pictured above)

2 cups granulated sugar
1-1/2 cups vegetable oil
1 teaspoon vanilla extract
2-1/2 cups all-purpose flour
2 tablespoons ground cinnamon, divided
1 teaspoon baking soda
1 teaspoon salt
1/2 teaspoon ground ginger
4 eggs, beaten
2 cups grated carrots
1 cup canned crushed pineapple, drained and juice reserved
3/4 cup chopped pecans
1/2 cup golden raisins
Pineapple juice
Cream Cheese Frosting (recipe follows)

1. Preheat oven to 350°F. Grease and flour two 8-inch round cake pans. Set aside.

2. Combine sugar, oil and vanilla in large bowl. Sift flour, 1 tablespoon cinnamon, baking soda, salt and ginger into medium bowl. Add flour mixture to

sugar mixture alternately with eggs. Add carrots, pineapple, pecans and raisins; mix well. Pour evenly into prepared cake pans.

3. Bake 45 to 50 minutes or until toothpick inserted near centers comes out clean. Poke holes in warm cakes with wooden skewer. Add enough pineapple juice to reserved canned pineapple juice to measure 2 cups. Pour 1 cup over each cake layer. Allow cake layers to soak up juice and cool in pans.

4. Prepare Cream Cheese Frosting.

5. Invert one cake layer onto serving plate; frost top of cake. Top with second cake layer. Frost top and sides of cake. Sprinkle with remaining 1 tablespoon cinnamon. Store in refrigerator.

Makes 10 to 12 servings

Cream Cheese Frosting

2 cups butter or margarine, softened
1 package (8 ounces) cream cheese, softened
2 tablespoons vanilla extract
2 cups confectioners' sugar
Whipping cream

Beat butter, cream cheese and vanilla in large bowl with electric mixer until light and fluffy. Beat in confectioners' sugar until blended. If frosting is too thick, thin with whipping cream, 1 tablespoon at a time.

Heavenly Chocolate Mousse Pie

(Pictured on page 182)

4 (1-ounce) squares unsweetened chocolate, melted
1 (14-ounce) can EAGLE BRAND® Sweetened Condensed Milk (NOT evaporated milk)
1-1/2 teaspoons vanilla extract
1 cup (1/2 pint) whipping cream, whipped
1 (6-ounce) chocolate crumb pie crust

1. In medium mixing bowl, beat melted chocolate with Eagle Brand and vanilla until well blended.

2. Chill 15 minutes or until cooled; stir until smooth. Fold in whipped cream.

3. Pour into crust. Chill thoroughly. Garnish as desired. Refrigerate leftovers.

Makes 1 pie

Chocolate Cream Crêpes

(Pictured below)

1 (14-ounce) can EAGLE BRAND® Sweetened
    Condensed Milk (NOT evaporated milk)
1/4 cup cold water
1 (4-serving-size) package instant chocolate
    pudding and pie filling mix
1/4 cup unsweetened cocoa
1 cup whipping cream, whipped
1 (4-1/2-ounce) package ready-to-use crêpes
    (10 crêpes)
1-1/2 cups sliced or cut-up fresh fruit such as
    strawberries, peaches, nectarines or
    kiwifruit
    Sifted powdered sugar
    White chocolate curls, if desired

1. In large mixing bowl, beat Eagle Brand and water.
Beat in pudding mix and cocoa. Fold in whipped
cream. Cover and chill 15 minutes.

2. Pipe or spoon generous 1/3 cup filling into
center of each crêpe. Roll up each crêpe. Place
on serving plate. Spoon fruit over crêpes. Sprinkle
with powdered sugar. Garnish with white chocolate
curls, if desired. *Makes 5 servings*

Juicy Berry Sorbet

(Pictured on page 182)

1-1/4 cups boiling water
1 package (4-serving size) JELL-O® Brand
    Cranberry Flavor Gelatin
1/2 cup sugar
1-1/2 cups cold juice, any flavor

STIR boiling water into gelatin and sugar in large
bowl at least 2 minutes until completely dissolved.
Stir in cold juice. Pour into 9-inch square baking pan.

FREEZE about 1 hour or until ice crystals form
1 inch around edges. Spoon into blender container;
cover. Blend on high speed about 30 seconds or
until smooth. Return to pan.

FREEZE 6 hours or overnight until firm. Scoop into
dessert dishes. *Makes 8 to 10 servings*

Great Substitute: This recipe can be made with any
flavor JELL-O® Gelatin, so try them all!

Tip: For a really fun presentation, try pre-scooping
the sorbet onto a freezer-safe plate. Arrange
decoratively into a wreath, using lemon leaves
for garnish.

Chocolate Cream Crêpes

Plum Streusel

PLUM FILLING
1/2 cup firmly packed light brown sugar
3 tablespoons cornstarch
1/2 teaspoon ground nutmeg
2-1/2 pounds ripe plums, pitted and sliced
1/2 inch thick

STREUSEL
1 cup all-purpose flour
1/2 Butter Flavor CRISCO® Stick or 1/2 cup Butter
Flavor CRISCO® all-vegetable shortening
1/2 cup firmly packed light brown sugar
1 teaspoon ground cinnamon
1 teaspoon vanilla
1/4 teaspoon salt

1. Heat oven to 350°F. Spray 3-quart shallow baking dish with CRISCO® No-Stick Cooking Spray; set aside.

2. For filling, combine 1/2 cup brown sugar, cornstarch and nutmeg in large bowl; mix well. Add plums and stir gently to coat evenly. Place in prepared pan.

3. For streusel, combine flour, 1/2 cup shortening, 1/2 cup brown sugar, cinnamon, vanilla and salt in large bowl. Mix with fork until mixture is combined and just crumbly. *Do not overmix.* Sprinkle over fruit mixture.

4. Bake at 350°F for 45 minutes or until streusel top is crisp. Cool about 10 minutes; serve warm with whipped cream or ice cream.

Makes 6 to 8 servings

Tip: Streusel is the German word for "sprinkle" and that is exactly how you're going to add the topping. This easy dessert is perfect for summer holiday entertaining.

Helpful Hint

Select plump plums with good color that yield to gentle pressure. Avoid those that are bruised, discolored or have soft spots or shriveled skin. A dull white film, or "bloom" over the skin is harmless and is nature's way of waterproofing the surface.

Crunch Peach Cobbler

(Pictured at right)

1/3 cup plus 1 tablespoon granulated sugar, divided
1 tablespoon cornstarch
1 can (29 ounces) sliced peaches in syrup
1/2 teaspoon vanilla extract
2 cups all-purpose flour, divided
1/2 cup packed brown sugar
1/3 cup uncooked old-fashioned or quick oats
1/4 cup butter or margarine, melted
1/2 teaspoon ground cinnamon
1/2 teaspoon salt
1/2 cup shortening
4 to 5 tablespoons cold water
Whipped cream

1. Combine 1/3 cup granulated sugar and cornstarch in small saucepan. Drain peaches, reserving 3/4 cup syrup. Slowly stir reserved peach syrup into sugar mixture until smooth. Add vanilla. Cook over low heat, stirring constantly, until thickened. Set aside.

2. For crumb topping, combine 1/2 cup flour, brown sugar, oats, butter and cinnamon in small bowl; stir until mixture forms coarse crumbs. Set aside.

3. Preheat oven to 350°F. Combine remaining 1-1/2 cups flour, remaining 1 tablespoon granulated sugar and salt in small bowl. Cut in shortening with pastry blender or 2 knives until mixture forms coarse crumbs. Sprinkle water, 1 tablespoon at a time, over flour mixture. Toss lightly with fork until mixture holds together. Press together to form a ball.

4. Roll out dough into 10-inch square, about 1/8 inch thick. Fold dough in half, then in half again. Carefully place folded dough in center of ungreased 8-inch square baking dish. Unfold and press onto bottom and about 1 inch up sides of dish. Arrange peaches over crust. Pour sauce over peaches. Sprinkle with crumb topping.

5. Bake 45 minutes or until golden brown. Serve warm or at room temperature with whipped cream.

Makes about 6 servings

Double-Decker Confetti Brownies

(Pictured at right)

3/4 cup (1-1/2 sticks) butter or margarine, softened
1 cup granulated sugar
1 cup firmly packed light brown sugar
3 large eggs
1 teaspoon vanilla extract
2-1/2 cups all-purpose flour, divided
2-1/2 teaspoons baking powder
1/2 teaspoon salt
1/3 cup unsweetened cocoa powder
1 tablespoon butter or margarine, melted
1 cup "M&M's"® Semi-Sweet Chocolate Mini Baking Bits, divided

Preheat oven to 350°F. Lightly grease 13×9×2-inch baking pan; set aside. In large bowl cream 3/4 cup butter and sugars until light and fluffy; beat in eggs and vanilla. In medium bowl combine 2-1/4 cups flour, baking powder and salt; blend into creamed mixture. Divide batter in half. Blend together cocoa powder and melted butter; stir into one half of the dough. Spread cocoa dough evenly into prepared baking pan. Stir remaining 1/4 cup flour and 1/2 cup "M&M's"® Semi-Sweet Chocolate Mini Baking Bits into remaining dough; spread evenly over cocoa dough in pan. Sprinkle with remaining 1/2 cup "M&M's"® Semi-Sweet Chocolate Mini Baking Bits. Bake 25 to 30 minutes or until edges start to pull away from sides of pan. Cool completely. Cut into bars. Store in tightly covered container.

Makes 24 brownies

Praline Bars

(Pictured on page 182)

3/4 cup butter or margarine, softened
1 cup sugar, divided
1 teaspoon vanilla, divided
1-1/2 cups flour
2 packages (8 ounces each) PHILADELPHIA® Cream Cheese, softened
2 eggs
1/2 cup almond brickle chips
3 tablespoons caramel ice cream topping

MIX butter, 1/2 cup of the sugar and 1/2 teaspoon of the vanilla with electric mixer on medium speed until light and fluffy. Gradually add flour, mixing on low speed until blended. Press onto bottom of 13×9-inch pan. Bake at 350°F for 20 to 23 minutes or until lightly browned.

MIX cream cheese, remaining 1/2 cup sugar and 1/2 teaspoon vanilla with electric mixer on medium speed until well blended. Add eggs; mix well. Blend in chips. Pour over crust. Dot top of cream cheese mixture with topping. Cut through batter with knife several times for marble effect.

BAKE at 350°F for 30 minutes. Cool in pan on wire rack. Cut into bars. *Makes 2 dozen bars*

White Chocolate Pound Cake

3 cups flour
1 teaspoon CALUMET® Baking Powder
1/2 teaspoon salt
1 container (8 ounces) BREAKSTONE'S® or KNUDSEN® Sour Cream
1 can (8 ounces) crushed pineapple in juice, undrained
1 cup (2 sticks) butter, softened
2 cups sugar
5 eggs
1 package (6 squares) BAKER'S® Premium White Baking Chocolate, melted, cooled slightly
2 teaspoons vanilla
1/2 cup BAKER'S® ANGEL FLAKE® Coconut

HEAT oven to 350°F. Lightly grease and flour 12-cup fluted tube pan or 10-inch tube pan.

MIX flour, baking powder and salt; set aside. Mix sour cream and pineapple; set aside.

BEAT butter and sugar in large bowl with electric mixer on medium speed until light and fluffy. Add eggs, 1 at a time, beating well after each addition. Beat in melted chocolate and vanilla. Add flour mixture alternately with sour cream mixture. Beat in coconut. Pour into prepared pan.

BAKE 70 to 75 minutes or until toothpick inserted near center comes out clean. Cool in pan 10 minutes on wire rack. Loosen cake from side of pan with small knife or spatula. Invert cake onto rack; gently remove pan. Cool completely on wire rack. Sprinkle with powdered sugar, if desired.

Makes 12 to 16 servings

Double-Decker Confetti Brownies

Berry Cobbler Cake

(Pictured at right and on back cover)

2 cups fresh or frozen berries (blueberries, blackberries and/or raspberries)
1 package (9 ounces) yellow cake mix
1 teaspoon ground cinnamon
1 egg
1 cup water, divided
1/4 cup sugar
1 tablespoon cornstarch

1. Preheat oven to 375°F.

2. Place berries in 9-inch square baking dish; set aside.

3. Combine cake mix and cinnamon in large bowl. Add egg and 1/4 cup water; stir to combine. Spoon over berries.

4. Combine sugar and cornstarch in small bowl. Stir in remaining 3/4 cup water until sugar mixture dissolves; pour over top.

5. Bake 40 to 45 minutes or until lightly browned. Serve warm or cool.   *Makes 6 servings*

Peachy Blueberry Crunch

1 package DUNCAN HINES® Bakery-Style Blueberry Streusel Muffin Mix
4 cups sliced peeled peaches (about 4 large)
1/2 cup water
3 tablespoons packed brown sugar
1/2 cup chopped pecans
1/3 cup butter or margarine, melted
   Whipped topping or ice cream (optional)

1. Preheat oven to 350°F.

2. Rinse blueberries from Mix with cold water and drain.

3. Arrange peach slices into *ungreased* 9-inch square pan. Sprinkle blueberries over peaches. Combine water and sugar in small bowl. Pour over fruit.

4. Combine muffin Mix, pecans and melted butter in large bowl. Stir until thoroughly blended (mixture will be crumbly). Sprinkle crumb mixture over fruit. Sprinkle contents of topping packet from Mix over crumb mixture. Bake at 350°F for 50 to 55 minutes or until lightly browned and bubbly. Serve warm with whipped topping, if desired.   *Makes 9 servings*

Chocolate Almond Torte

4 eggs, separated
1/2 cup (1 stick) butter or margarine, softened
1 cup sugar
1 teaspoon almond extract
1 teaspoon vanilla extract
1 cup finely chopped toasted almonds
3/4 cup all-purpose flour
1/2 cup unsweetened cocoa
1/2 teaspoon baking powder
1/2 teaspoon baking soda
2/3 cup milk
   Chocolate Almond Frosting (recipe follows)

1. Line 2 (8- or 9-inch) round cake pans with waxed paper. Preheat oven to 350°F. In small mixing bowl, beat egg whites until soft peaks form; set aside.

2. In large mixing bowl, beat butter and sugar until fluffy. Add egg yolks and extracts; mix well.

3. In medium mixing bowl, combine almonds, flour, cocoa, baking powder and baking soda; add alternately with milk to butter mixture, beating well after each addition.

4. Fold in beaten egg whites. Pour into prepared pans. Bake 18 to 20 minutes or until wooden picks inserted near centers come out clean. Cool 10 minutes; remove from pans. Cool completely.

5. Prepare Chocolate Almond Frosting. Split each cake layer; fill and frost with frosting. Garnish as desired. Store covered in refrigerator.
Makes one 4-layer cake

Chocolate Almond Frosting

2 (1-ounce) squares semi-sweet chocolate, chopped
1 (14-ounce) can EAGLE BRAND® Sweetened Condensed Milk (NOT evaporated milk)
1 teaspoon almond extract

1. In heavy saucepan over medium heat, melt chocolate with Eagle Brand. Cook and stir until mixture thickens, about 10 minutes.

2. Remove from heat; cool 10 minutes. Stir in almond extract; cool.   *Makes about 1-1/2 cups*

Berry Cobbler Cake

Easy Eclair Dessert

(Pictured at right)

27 whole graham crackers, halved
3 cups cold milk
2 packages (4-serving size) JELL-O® Vanilla Flavor Instant Pudding & Pie Filling
1 tub (12 ounces) COOL WHIP® Whipped Topping, thawed
1 container (16 ounces) ready-to-spread chocolate fudge frosting
Strawberries

ARRANGE 1/3 of the crackers on bottom of 13×9-inch baking pan, breaking crackers to fit, if necessary.

POUR milk into large bowl. Add pudding mixes. Beat with wire whisk 2 minutes. Gently stir in whipped topping. Spread 1/2 of the pudding mixture over crackers. Place 1/2 of the remaining crackers over pudding; top with remaining pudding mixture and crackers.

REMOVE top and foil from frosting container. Microwave frosting in container on HIGH 1 minute or until pourable. Spread evenly over crackers.

REFRIGERATE 4 hours or overnight. Cut into squares to serve. Garnish with strawberries.

Makes 18 servings

Cool Tips: You could make pistachio, banana-flavored or even double chocolate eclairs by simply changing the pudding flavors.

Peanut Maple Triangle Puffs

1/2 cup creamy peanut butter
1-1/4 cups confectioners' sugar, divided
1/4 cup maple-flavored syrup
1 package (17-1/2 ounces) frozen puff pastry, thawed
3 tablespoons maple-flavored syrup
1 to 2 tablespoons water

1. Preheat oven to 400°F. Combine peanut butter, 1/4 cup confectioners' sugar and 1/4 cup syrup in small bowl until well blended; set aside.

2. Cut each puff pastry dough sheet into 3-inch squares. Place rounded teaspoon peanut butter mixture in center of each square. Fold squares over to form triangle. Seal edges with fork.

3. Place triangles about 2 inches apart on ungreased baking sheets; spray with cooking spray. Bake 6 to 8 minutes or until golden brown. Remove from baking sheets to wire rack to cool.

4. Combine remaining 1 cup powdered sugar, 3 tablespoons syrup and enough water to reach glaze consistency. Drizzle over puffs just before serving.

Makes 28 puffs

Tip: For longer storage, do not glaze puffs, and store loosely covered so pastry dough remains crisp. Glaze before serving.

Jumbo 3-Chip Cookies

4 cups all-purpose flour
1 teaspoon baking powder
1 teaspoon baking soda
1-1/2 cups (3 sticks) butter, softened
1-1/4 cups granulated sugar
1-1/4 cups packed brown sugar
2 large eggs
1 tablespoon vanilla extract
1 cup (6 ounces) NESTLÉ® TOLL HOUSE® Milk Chocolate Morsels
1 cup (6 ounces) NESTLÉ® TOLL HOUSE® Semi-Sweet Chocolate Morsels
1/2 cup NESTLÉ® TOLL HOUSE® Premier White Morsels
1 cup chopped nuts

PREHEAT oven to 375°F.

COMBINE flour, baking powder and baking soda in medium bowl. Beat butter, granulated sugar and brown sugar in large mixer bowl until creamy. Beat in eggs and vanilla extract. Gradually beat in flour mixture. Stir in morsels and nuts. Drop dough by level 1/4-cup measure 2 inches apart onto ungreased baking sheets.

BAKE for 12 to 14 minutes or until light golden brown. Cool on baking sheets for 2 minutes; remove to wire racks to cool completely.

Makes about 2 dozen cookies

The publisher would like to thank the companies and organizations listed below for the use of their recipes and photographs in this publication.

A.1.® Steak Sauce

American Lamb Council

Arm & Hammer Division, Church & Dwight Co., Inc.

Barilla America, Inc.

Bays English Muffin Corporation

Birds Eye®

Blue Diamond Growers®

Bob Evans®

Butterball® Turkey

Campbell Soup Company

Cherry Marketing Institute

ConAgra Foods®

Delmarva Poultry Industry, Inc.

Del Monte Corporation

Dole Food Company, Inc.

Duncan Hines® and Moist Deluxe® are registered trademarks of Aurora Foods Inc.

Eagle Brand®

Filippo Berio® Olive Oil

Fleischmann's® Yeast

The Golden Grain Company®

Grandma's® is a registered trademark of Mott's, Inc.

Grey Poupon® Dijon Mustard

Heinz North America

Hershey Foods Corporation

The Hidden Valley® Food Products Company

Hillshire Farm®

Hormel Foods, LLC

The Kingsford Products Company

Kraft Foods Holdings

Lawry's® Foods

© Mars, Incorporated 2004

McIlhenny Company (TABASCO® brand Pepper Sauce)

Mrs. Dash®

National Fisheries Institute

National Honey Board

National Pork Board

National Turkey Federation

Nestlé USA

New York Apple Association, Inc.

Newman's Own, Inc.®

North Carolina SweetPotato Commission

Perdue Farms Incorporated

The Quaker® Oatmeal Kitchens

Reckitt Benckiser Inc.

Riviana Foods Inc.

Sargento® Foods Inc.

The J.M. Smucker Company

StarKist® Seafood Company

The Sugar Association, Inc.

Reprinted with permission of Sunkist Growers, Inc.

Sun•Maid® Growers of California

Uncle Ben's Inc.

Unilever Bestfoods North America

USA Rice Federation

Washington Apple Commission

Wisconsin Milk Marketing Board

General Index

Alphabetical Index

METRIC CONVERSION CHART

VOLUME MEASUREMENTS (dry)

1/8 teaspoon = 0.5 mL
1/4 teaspoon = 1 mL
1/2 teaspoon = 2 mL
3/4 teaspoon = 4 mL
1 teaspoon = 5 mL
1 tablespoon = 15 mL
2 tablespoons = 30 mL
1/4 cup = 60 mL
1/3 cup = 75 mL
1/2 cup = 125 mL
2/3 cup = 150 mL
3/4 cup = 175 mL
1 cup = 250 mL
2 cups = 1 pint = 500 mL
3 cups = 750 mL
4 cups = 1 quart = 1 L

VOLUME MEASUREMENTS (fluid)

1 fluid ounce (2 tablespoons) = 30 mL
4 fluid ounces (1/2 cup) = 125 mL
8 fluid ounces (1 cup) = 250 mL
12 fluid ounces (1 1/2 cups) = 375 mL
16 fluid ounces (2 cups) = 500 mL

WEIGHTS (mass)

1/2 ounce = 15 g
1 ounce = 30 g
3 ounces = 90 g
4 ounces = 120 g
8 ounces = 225 g
10 ounces = 285 g
12 ounces = 360 g
16 ounces = 1 pound = 450 g

DIMENSIONS

1/16 inch = 2 mm
1/8 inch = 3 mm
1/4 inch = 6 mm
1/2 inch = 1.5 cm
3/4 inch = 2 cm
1 inch = 2.5 cm

OVEN TEMPERATURES

250°F = 120°C
275°F = 140°C
300°F = 150°C
325°F = 160°C
350°F = 180°C
375°F = 190°C
400°F = 200°C
425°F = 220°C
450°F = 230°C

BAKING PAN SIZES

Utensil	Size in Inches/Quarts	Metric Volume	Size in Centimeters
Baking or Cake Pan (square or rectangular)	8×8×2	2 L	20×20×5
	9×9×2	2.5 L	23×23×5
	12×8×2	3 L	30×20×5
	13×9×2	3.5 L	33×23×5
Loaf Pan	8×4×3	1.5 L	20×10×7
	9×5×3	2 L	23×13×7
Round Layer Cake Pan	8×1½	1.2 L	20×4
	9×1½	1.5 L	23×4
Pie Plate	8×1¼	750 mL	20×3
	9×1¼	1 L	23×3
Baking Dish or Casserole	1 quart	1 L	—
	1½ quart	1.5 L	—
	2 quart	2 L	—